THE CHOSEN PLACE

*Growing Up on a 1940s Homestead
in Old Chugiak, Alaska*

The Chosen Place

*Growing Up on a 1940s Homestead
in Old Chugiak, Alaska*

Darlene Halverson

Eagle River, Alaska

Copyright © 2010 by Darlene Halverson
All rights reserved. No part of this book may be reproduced in any form without permission except by a reviewer who may quote brief passages in a media review.

Photo Credits: Personal collection of author
John and Bernice Stockhausen
Nancy Stockhausen Hart
Kenny and Mary Pilgrim
Bernadine Statz
Carol Statz McCann
Cheryl Stockhausen Horst
Lenore DeLoughery Mickelson
H.M. Kurriger, 1948
Virginia Kirk
Chugiak-Eagle River Historical Society
Marjorie Cochrane, *Between Two Rivers*

Cover Design: Nancy Stockhausen Hart

Newspaper credits:
Milwaukee Journal article (p. xxxi)
Anchorage Times article (p. 39)

Published by:

Northbooks

17050 N. Eagle River Loop Road, # 3
Eagle River, Alaska 99577
www.northbooks.com

Printed in the United States of America

ISBN 978-0-9815193-5-7

Library of Congress Control Number: 2010933339

Dedication

I dedicate this book to my parents, John and Bernice Stockhausen, who spent countless hours retelling their stories of the resilience it took to face an undeveloped piece of land that dared them to tame it.

To my sister, Nancy Hart, for sharing our childhood memories together.

To my brother, John (1952–1971), who was born five months before we moved from the homestead cabin. Even though he didn't get to experience the five years we lived there, he heard the stories many times over the years.

To Mary and Kenny Pilgrim for their encouragement and assistance and for Mary's diary of daily events on our journey to Alaska.

*How dear to this heart are the
scenes of my childhood,
When fond recollections presents
them to view.*
—Samuel Woodworth

Contents

Foreword	ix
Acknowledgments	xi
Preface	xiii
Introduction—Let's Go To Alaska	xvii
On to Alaska—Alcan Diary	1
Claiming the Land	40
A Dump of Treasures	54
Orphan Bear	64
Springy Branches	75
Christmas Brew	83
The Agreement	90
Mama's Apron	97
Giant George's Bus	102
Ice for Mama	114
Waiting for Santa	122
Raising Chickens	145
Rooster's Domain	155
Keepers	164
Garden Under the Ground	170
Runaway Dough	178
Wishing for Water	190
Family Comes to Chugiak	196
School Days	204
Perfect Shot	214
Changes	224
Cabin of Memories	247
Epilogue	255
Appendix I — Mary Pilgrim's Diary	257
Appendix II — BLM Land Patent	266
Sources	268

Foreword

There was a time in Alaska, only a few decades ago, when there was no TV, no GPS, no cell-phone satellite communications, no search and rescue units on call, no roadside assistance in case of emergency, very few medical services, and lots of gravel roads We had neighbors who knew your name and were ready to help you out when needed. Those days were called the "homestead years" that extended from the 1940s through the 1960s.

I've had fun and lots of good memories discussing the publishing of this book with other old-timers. I'd ask them, "Do you remember the Army dump on Fort Richardson where we could pick up lots of stuff we needed to make life a little more comfortable? And free, too!" They'd nod and then go on to describe some of the "dump" treasures they still have in their garage, like a barracks wall locker in which they keep emergency food in case of another earthquake. Or a pair of (now very outdated) Army wooden cross-country skis that gather dust in the storage shed—just for emergencies, of course.

Darlene has stories of this "dump of treasures" and other tales of homestead life through the eyes of a young girl, growing up and sharing the dream of her father and mother to pioneer a new land. The American Legion post in the Peters Creek area of Chugiak is located on a piece of their original homestead filing.

This book is an enjoyable read for both the old and new Alaskans, and especially youngsters to realize what it was really like to grow up on an Alaska homestead.

Ray Holmsen
Northbooks

Acknowledgments

To my parents John and Bernice Stockhausen for the hours they spent with me at the kitchen table reminiscing about our life on the homestead in Chugiak, Alaska. I thank them for their confidence in me to write our memoirs for future generations of family and friends.

My sister, Nancy, gets special hugs for sharing all our unforgettable childhood experiences and reminding me of those that I'd forgotten, and for cheering me on in my endeavor to write about them. She helped by gathering information and sharing her pictures. She let me see our homestead years from her perspective also.

A special thank you to my husband, Peter, who supported my efforts from the first chapter to the final sentence, always motivating me to one day publish and congratulating me on a job well done. He helped me understand and write about the construction of the cabin and all the outer buildings and answered the multitude of other questions I needed information about.

Without Mary Pilgrim's diary of our trip to Alaska, we would have no recollections of that event in our lives. Kenny Pilgrim's decision to travel with us made it possible for Mom and Dad to achieve their dream of a life in Alaska. Without his assistance during the times when Dad's truck wouldn't start in the morning or broke down along the highway, we would have turned around and gone back to Wisconsin never having fulfilled our dream. Their companionship over miles of isolated roads gave us treasured memories never to be forgotten.

Many thanks to Janet Holmsen, my copyeditor, for all the suggestion on rewriting sentences for better clarification and accuracy, for correcting the manuscript several times, for carefully checking through the text for grammar and spelling errors, and for cleaning up my punctuation.

I am grateful to have chosen Ray Holmsen to publish my memoir. We spent hours discussing the layout of the book, the book cover, placing pictures and captions, and many thanks for being flexible in setting priorities and deadlines.

Thank you to Michael Burwell, my writing instructor at the University of Alaska, who recognized the value of my book and encouraged me to publish the story of my family's life on a homestead in Alaska. He motivated me, and I thank him for suggesting I write from the child's perspective.

Thank you to all the friends and family who donated pictures and for your interest in my book.

Preface

I am writing to the future generations of young people who will never know a world without digital conveniences. You won't ever experience the hand-cranked telephone and probably wouldn't want to, after holding the iPhone in the palm of your hand, looking at every conceivable subject on the Internet using the tiny touch keys. You can order the latest version of any computer on the Internet and pay for it with your own debit card and have FedEx deliver it overnight or in two days up here in Alaska. It's hard to imagine life being any other way. You live in a fast-paced world with new gadgets advertised every day.

Life once moved at a snail's pace, and I invite you to travel with me through my early life on a homestead in Alaska and meet my parents, who strived to occupy and develop a piece of land and live the life they chose without being subject to many restrictions.

I rediscovered my childhood when I began writing my family's homestead history from 1947 to 1952. Whenever Mom, Dad, my sister, Nancy, and I got together, we would talk for hours about our homestead years. We had lively discussions of "Do you remember when," and we ended by saying, "We should write about those days. They were the best years."

After one of our discussions, Mom said, "Darlene, why don't you write about the five years we homesteaded."

All conversation ceased, and all eyes were on me, waiting for the answer. I said, "Mom, I don't know anything about writing. I don't think I can do it."

She said, "Yes, you can."

Wow, moms sure have confidence in their kids.

I began the process with sparse notes and ended by flooding the pages with information I was acquiring as they decribed what those years meant to them. There was delightful enthusiasm in their voices as they spoke fondly of their time on the homestead, and I listened with eagerness for more recollections.

Suddenly and intensely, particular emotions arose from my memories of childhood days. I began to see our life coming alive on the pages of a book, and there was no stopping me as I filled them with a history that very few people ever have the chance to experience.

It was during these stimulating remembrances that I discovered the creative writing class at the University of Alaska. I was mostly taking notes and wasn't sure how to put it into a memoir. Suddenly, I knew that all the memories I wanted to pass on to future generations of our family and those still living might be realized. I spent four years in the class, writing of my family's remarkable homesteading experience in the Territory of Alaska in a small area twenty-two miles north of Anchorage that had been named Chugiak by the recently formed community club. With each chapter that I wrote, I'd remember bits and pieces of our bold undertaking, and slowly I was able to see the whole picture and bring it to life on the pages of a book.

While writing my memoirs, I had the chance to become aware of my childhood, realizing few children had the opportunity to live such an extraordinary adventure. Committing my life to paper brought new insights and an awareness of how advantaged my childhood turned out to be.

My mother showed me how to cast aside frivolous things in life and look at the things that really matter. She allowed me to see visually the spirit it takes to envision a new and better life. I've learned to do for myself and not to count on others to do it for me and to respect myself and always be proud of who I am. She taught me about strength and endurance in difficult situations and to persist calmly when faced with something requiring a lot of planning or effort to do.

I learned from my father to follow my dreams, to persevere and never give up. He taught me to make decisions early in my childhood by asking my opinion even though it was only to agree with his decisions. He'd say, "What do you think?" From an early age I was gaining the ability to decide about things in a clear way without too much reluctance.

Through my parents' example, I learned to set goals and accomplish them. Their goal was to plan, prepare, and follow through. It was applied to every project they set about doing to make our life more comfortable. I learned because they let me know what it meant to have a purpose, and that I could reach any goal I set my mind to achieve.

They had an ethic of working hard that I learned through being involved in everything from building the cabin to helping in the garden. Even though I whined a lot about chores, I felt satisfaction and pride in a job well done.

My immediate and extended family will be interested in my parents' life in Alaska, in part, because Dad had a brother and sister and their families living in Alaska also. It's an intriguing place, and many want to know what it offers that keep people from moving elsewhere. I can tell you that my father had a dream like no other he had ever longed for. He and Mom thought long and hard about their decision. It was a strong desire for something not within immediate reach, and there was a continual ache within him to see Alaska and be a part of its ruggedness.

My memoir describes my childhood the way I perceived it from my parents' memories and from the highlights I can recall, especially those that provide useful information as well as being out-of-the-ordinary as life was in Alaska during 1947 to 1952.

The experience of writing *The Chosen Place* provided so much pleasure each time I put pen to paper and began to remember all the cherished memories told to me while sitting around the kitchen table. I hope you find as much enjoyment reading it and begin to understand what it was that kept pulling my Dad toward the unknown. He had a powerful bond connecting him to a whole new way of life for himself and his family in Alaska.

INTRODUCTION

LET'S GO TO ALASKA!

"Hey, Kenny, do you remember the great adventures we had riding the rails when we were care-free kids?" Dad asked his best friend, while sitting on a stump and casting his fishing line out over the lake.

"Yeah, those were the days."

"I'd like to do it again," Dad said, reeling in the line.

"You mean relive the old days? Those days are long gone. It's not going to happen. You got a wife and two daughters up at the tent getting our lunch ready," Kenny said, pointing his thumb toward the slight incline where the camp tent stood, sheltered by tall pines.

"Nope, I'm not interested in reliving the past. My mind is on the future. I've been seriously planning to move to Alaska and homestead up there. Actually, I've made up my mind to do it. You know I've been talking about it a lot over the past few years."

Kenny stared at Dad in disbelief. "Jumping trains and riding the rails is one thing, but when you talk about moving your family to some place beyond the realm of conventional living, that's something else all together."

Dad laughed, propped the pole against a scrawny pine, leaned forward, supporting his elbows on his knees, and looked straight into Kenny's eyes. "I've been thinking long and hard about it, and I'd like you to come along. Now, that would be the adventure of a lifetime."

"Hold on for just one minute. We're not as young as we were when we leaped onto boxcars. Heck, we're not even young any more. I have a wife I need to think about and a good paying job.

We both have steady jobs bringing in a good income. Do you really want to give that up, not knowing what the future holds for you in a harsh, frozen land four or five thousand miles from the rest of your family?"

"Wouldn't you like to start all over again?" Dad asked. "I don't want to spend the rest of my life in Wauwatosa, Wisconsin, working in a factory and bartending at night. There has to be something more to life than living from day to day in a crowded city with neighboring houses on each side of my pa's house, where I rent the upper flat and there is just a small back yard for the kids to play in. I want more than that for my family and me. I want land and my own house in the wilderness. I don't want to look out at my neighbor's house."

"Wilderness is right. You're talking wilderness you can get lost in. Have you talked to Bernie about your plan to move her to some uninhabited far-away part of the world?"

"I'm going to make it happen, and yes, Bernie and I have talked about it. The more I talk to her, the more interested she becomes. As a matter of fact, she mentioned it the other day. I was reading the newspaper, and right out of the blue, she said something about Alaska. That caught me by surprise since its never happened before. It's usually me bringing up the subject."

"Well, I'll have to say that you caught me by surprise. I remember how we spent all our free time planning places to go during our teenage years. Well, times have changed since growing up. I would like to see time stand still sometimes. I guess I have dreams, too, about what life might have in store for me, but then that's the dream of boys, not grown men with responsibilities."

"Do you remember the day we watched the train move slowly from the railroad station, speculating where it might take us that day?" Dad asked, watching a smile move across Kenny's face. "Then, with very little deliberation, we made the decision to hop aboard and explore one of those mysterious places that always seemed out of our reach, yet held the promise of something new. It took a lot of courage to jump aboard one of the box cars with no destination in mind. Then we'd leap off and explore a neighboring town and hop on the next train going back. Each trip found us venturing a bit farther away to cities that took a couple of days to explore."

"Yeah," Kenny said, beginning to reminisce.

"That's what I'm talking about. One of those unknown places that seems out of our reach, yet it holds the promise of something new. For me, that's Alaska."

"Most of the time the boxcar was empty, but once in a while there would be a tramp sound asleep in the corner," Kenny said, continuing to recall their boyhood years. "Then one day, we came face to face with three scruffy-looking men who were also looking for a free ride and willing to take our money in a game of poker to pass the time. We'd watch them throw money into the center of the circle, shuffle cards, pass them out, and the victor scooped up the winnings."

"Oh, yeah," Dad said, immersed in the retelling of years gone by. "I still don't know how I got duped. I come from a family of card players. Games are played with passionate enthusiasm, slapping each card energetically on the table and giving a rowdy shout when the cards are in our favor. Poker is a game of great fun and enjoyment, and I'm good at it. So, when the man sitting across from me said, 'Hey, kid. That's a nice looking leather jacket. Want to bet it on a game of cards?' I just couldn't resist the challenge."

Kenny laughed and continued the story. "You thought you were dealt a great hand and bet your leather jacket and lost. I remember you weren't sure how you were going to explain to your folks how you lost the jacket you worked so hard to earn. Your ma was hopping mad when she learned about the rail jaunts. Man oh man, did she ever bring our carefree days to a halt."

"And if you recall, we went back to daydreaming of all the places we wanted to see. I have one more place I want to set eyes on, and that's Alaska, and I want you with me when I get there. How about one last time to experience what it's like to travel to a place in order to discover what it's like or what is there."

"You know what? You've almost convinced me. Not quite, but almost," Kenny responded, "because now you have to convince Mary that venturing off to some far-off land will be something she would rather do than live in the comforts she is used to right now. After you do that, maybe we can make some plans for your long-awaited trip to Alaska."

My father, John Stockhausen, found distant places far more appealing than life in Wauwatosa, Wisconsin. There was a whole world out there that he wanted to travel through. The less civilized the better, but Alaska pulled him like no other place on earth. The following is his story of preparations to leave Wisconsin, travel the road through Canada, and the life he lived on his homestead in Alaska. One of the noteworthy parts of the story is that his best friend, Kenny, had the same unwavering desire to occasionally step outside of his comfortable life, and decided that this might be the last chance to explore the unfamiliar.

My mother, Bernice, always looked forward to Uncle Bruno's visits to the home of her parents, Harry and Emma Dobbratz, in Wauwatosa. Uncle Bruno was going to the Village Bar to change the records in the juke box, and she asked to tag along.

My dad was the bartender at the Village Bar in Wauwatosa and glanced up when Bruno pushed the door open with his shoulder; one hand carried the tool box and the other held the door for Mom. He always came by himself, so Dad was surprised to see a young woman with him and took a second glance. Bruno set his tools by the jukebox and they sat down at a nearby table. Dad brought a bowl of popcorn to them, and Bruno introduced his niece. Mom liked Dad right away, and they learned more about each other throughout the evening. He told her about his day job in an upholstery shop. He was surprised to learn that they lived so near to each other and had never met. They made plans for Dad to come by her home for a first date. The song "Josephine" was playing on the juke box, and from that moment it was always their song.

What she remembered most about their first introduction was his likeable, easy-going personality. Dad remembers the dimples in her cheeks when she smiled. He began calling her Bernie soon after they met. He thought Bernice was too formal.

People sat at the bar, mesmerizing Dad with tales of Alaska. Most of them had never lived there, but had heard stories about climbers conquering Mt. McKinley for the prestige and to view the magnificent mountains and valleys from the summit. Then there were stories of men who walked glaciers and lived to recount their extraordinary experiences. They discussed hearing about adventurous travelers stopping to fish for salmon in icy-cold rivers, bragging about their catch. He longed to have that life and call Alaska his home.

Mom and Dad dated for two years and married in 1939. Mom wore a light blue street-length dress, and Dad wore his dark navy suit. He was hired on at Falk's Foundry making molds to pour molten cast iron into during World War II. He made good wages and was able to put money in a savings account each week. He continued working weekends at the Village Bar, where they had first met. It wasn't long after they married when I came along. Fifteen months later Nancy joined us.

Our small family was happy and life treated us well. We lived comfortably in a large upper flat above Dad's parents on 69th Street in Wauwatosa. Nancy and I had cousins next door to play with and other kids on both sides of the street. The street had a long sloping hill that was perfect for roller skating. I'd carry my skates up the sidewalk and put them on at the top. I was fascinated with the tiny key that tightened the skates to my shoes. Then down the hill I'd go, trying to beat my cousins to the bottom. I kept the key on a bracelet and carefully tied it to my skates when I put them away.

The iceman came by selling his huge chunks of ice several times a week. We always knew the time he'd be arriving and ran to the curb to meet him, along with all the kids we played with, trying to be the first in line and hoping for the biggest pieces of ice to lick on during the hot summer afternoons. We watched as he grabbed a large square of ice with ice tongs that he clamped tightly around it and pulled it from the back of the truck. He'd carry it upstairs and put it in the ice box. On rainy days when we couldn't meet him outside, he always had a couple of loose chunks with him when he brought the ice upstairs.

Mom slowly softened to Dad's desire to leave Wauwatosa and chase after those tales of Alaska that resulted from men swapping captivating accounts and raising their beer bottles to the man with the most outlandish story. He wanted to find out if Alaska was everything he had read and heard about it. His older brother, Edward, was in the military stationed in Anchorage, and he sent home detailed letters about living in Fairbanks, Hope, and visiting other areas. Dad's sister, Eleanor, was now living in Alaska with her husband, Frank DeLoughery. He was editor of the Seward newspaper. Dad's mother shared the letters with him, and he devoured every word eagerly.

In the meantime, Kenny began dating Mary, and eventually they married. They lived close by, so it was easy to visit them and swap tales of riding the rails. Dad asked Kenny to go with us to Alaska, and now it was time for him to persuade Mary. He counted on a good outcome when he asked her the all-important question: "Would you be willing to travel with Bernie, me, and the kids to Alaska? I don't want to make the trip alone over such a desolate road. I want you and Kenny to accompany us on the long journey." He told her he had been thinking about going to Alaska for the past two years, and his goal was to have all the arrangements in place and be on the road within a few months.

Kenny and Mary took a few days to absorb what life would be like, making such a drastic change in their lifestyle. Mary, not wanting to be too hasty in her decision, took more time to contemplate. After a bit more persuasion, they settled in to prepare for this unexpected turn of events. Kenny was a veteran of World War II, having served in the United States military and honorably discharged; therefore, he could fill out a homestead application. The plan was to file on 160 acres and build two homes and work the land together.

The first thing on the list of preparations was transportation. After World War II, Kenny and Dad heard about trucks that had been designed for the Army and were being sold to independent contractors at surplus sales. Dad purchased a 1941 Chevrolet one and a half-ton 4 x 4 truck with a fourteen-foot flatbed. It was equipped with a winch he knew would come in handy on the trip through Canada. Kenny bought a smaller truck with a white hood, gray fenders, and slightly smaller flatbed.

The owner of a filling station on North Avenue told Dad and Kenny they could park the trucks for an indeterminate amount of time while they made repairs. The station was just a few blocks from our home, so it was easy for them to spend their free evenings and weekends working on the trucks. A thirty-gallon gas tank was added, and two additional fifty-five-gallon drums were mounted behind the rear wheels under the bed of Dad's truck for storing gas.

Dad had a homemade trailer that he built a year or two earlier for camping at the lake. He removed the axle and wheels from the trailer and mounted the trailer on the bed of the truck. He helped Kenny build a box-like structure with small windows on three sides and a door in the back. It would be used only for sleeping accommodations and personal possessions. The bed was built about three feet from the floor with storage room underneath. Cooking would be done in our living area.

Dad had mentioned his desire to go to Alaska many times as he visited with his parents, Nicholaus and Anna Stockhausen, but when he actually told them he had purchased a four-wheel-drive Army truck from a military auction and was making plans to leave, they realized how serious his intentions had been.

"Why would you want to go to Alaska where you have no assurance of finding work?" his dad asked. "You have a good job and a nice place to live. Why leave that behind when you have no idea what type of work you'll find in Alaska? The sensible thing would be to stay here where you have everything you need. Why risk your family and everything you've worked so hard for?"

Over the years, Dad had spent hours talking to his mother about someday when he would be living in Alaska, and she would say, "Yes, John. Maybe, someday." But after hearing he bought a truck, she was a bit hesitant about the reality of how soon he would be moving away.

"Think about your family, John. I worry about you taking them so far away. How in the world can you think it would be a suitable place to raise your two daughters?"

"I want my own piece of land, Ma, a place I can call home. I want to homestead in Alaska. I want to build my own house and have plenty of land for a garden, and lots of open space for the girls to run around. I've been talking about Alaska for years. It's my dream, Ma, and I want to live it."

Dad's parents were reluctant because of the distance that would be between them. His mother worried about Dad finding a job, building a home, and caring for his family. Once the shock was over, his parents adjusted slowly to Dad's decision. Grandpa was a carpenter and started collecting tools that he no longer needed, telling Dad he would need them to build the cabin. They spent time sketching out and making changes to the cabin on paper.

One afternoon, Dad and Grandpa went down to the basement where Grandpa kept his home brew. He poured them both a glass and removed the bottle capper from the tool bench, turning it slowly, and rubbing the dust from it. "Here," he said, passing the capper to Dad and gently laying it in his hands. "I want you to take this with you. When you are finally settled in your cabin, you might want to make some home brew, and you'll need a really good bottle capper. You might not find one in Alaska."

Mom was eager to try something new, and her mother, Emma Hixson, encouraged her. "Bernice, if you and John have decided that Alaska is where you want to be, then by all means, do what makes you happy." Grandma had a bit of an adventurous spirit herself, so it seemed right that she would be optimistic. She enjoyed traveling with her husband, Floyd, on their motorcycle. Of course, she had concerns, and she discussed them with Mom over coffee. "What do you think life will be like for you in Alaska?"

"I think it will be hard," Mom said, "with no electricity or running water. I have no idea where we'll finally settle, and that's stressful to think about. We'll have two months to build a home before the first winter snow, or else we'll be living in the trailer

John is putting on the back of the truck. There might not be a school for the girls to attend, and we'd have to find a correspondence program for them. John might not find work right away, so we'd have to live on the money we've been saving to get us through the first few months."

Grandma Hixson slowly sipped her coffee nodding her head in agreement. "Tell me about something good that will come from the move."

"John has been longing to see Alaska. He talks about it, reads about it, and has asked me to be a part of his ambition to achieve his dream. I think I might have just a little bit of the wanderlust that's driving him," Mom said, smiling at Grandma. "I think this is our moment in time, and why not wrap our dreams around that moment and let it take us home to Alaska where we want to be. It's something we can do together. I guess what I'm trying to say is that I want the same thing that John wants. A place that we can call our own."

Dad continued working on the interior of the trailer that he designed so that everything inside would remain stabilized as the truck shifted on rough roads. The table was hinged to the wall and could be lowered and made into a bed that rested on the two benches used for seating at meal time and opened to accommodate blankets and other bedding items. The bunk beds were secured to the wall, one above the other, giving Nancy and me ample space for sleeping. The kitchen had everything the modern woman could wish for to prepare meals to feed six hungry travelers. The cupboards were mounted to the wall beside a sink that drained outside. Next to the cupboard was a kerosene cookstove with an oven, and the ice box sat beside it and served no purpose on the trip, so it was loaded with two cases of canned chocolate milk. Dad would figure out where to find ice to fill it after land was cleared, the cabin built, and we were settled, and he had secured a job. Dad spent time contemplating how to store Mom's bulky Singer sewing machine, her sewing basket, and all the colorful material. After careful consideration, he decided he would take it apart and store it wherever the pieces would fit.

Projects were slowly crossed off the list of jobs to be accomplished. It seemed that new things were always being added to the list as quickly as they were crossed off. When they were finalizing the plans, buying the food and other necessities, Mom took Nancy and me shopping so we could buy stuff to keep ourselves entertained through the long days of driving and during the evenings. Paper dolls were at the top of our list, then paper and crayons, and lots of books. Because popcorn was always a part of our evening before leaving 69th Street, Mom said we would continue to have popcorn on our trip. She let Nancy and me put bag after bag of popcorn into the grocery cart.

Mary bought a notebook prior to leaving to keep a record of gas, food prices, breakdowns along the road, flat tires, daily mileage, and where we stopped each evening. Over the years, when there was a question about the trip, Mary's diary would remind us of the determination it took to make the journey to Alaska.

We left Wauwatosa, Wisconsin, on Monday, June 9, 1947, two days after Dad's birthday. He felt the trip was the best birthday present of his entire life. The trucks were still parked on North Avenue. They had been there since the day they were purchased. The gas station owner said they brought business and curious spectators.

Mom called her dad, Harry, the evening before the trip to tell him all the last details of getting ready and to let him know that mail could be sent general delivery to the post office in Anchorage. Even though we said good-bye to family the night before, they were all there in the morning for more hugs and to wish us a safe journey. The *Milwaukee Journal* was aware of our trip months before and sent a reporter and cameraman to inform its readers about the families that were "Alaska bound." The reporter posed us for the pictures while the family waited on the sideline to give last minute advice, make sure we had everyone's address, and plenty of snacks.

Grandpa handed Dad a new deck of cards for the game Sheep's Head, the family's favorite German card game. Grandma gave Mom a box of her homemade cookies and pieces of colorful material to make clothes for Nancy and me. Grandma Hixson managed the restaurant in the bar that her second husband, Floyd, owned next to the gas station. She put together a tasty picnic lunch so we wouldn't have to take time for lunch preparations the first day. After lots of tears, hugs, and advice, we were ready to leave.

Life can sometimes take a turn that is just the way a person wants it to be. The longing to move North was finally becoming a reality, and Mom and Dad expected it to be the dream they visualized for themselves. They were twenty-eight and thirty years old, both with a positive outlook of what they could achieve through their willingness to work hard in a new land. They looked forward to a life unlike anything they'd ever known. Their new life was even better than they hoped for. The following is the story of their trip to Alaska, their family, and the life they made for themselves living their Alaskan adventure.

Bernice Dobbratz, age 18, finished high school and entered a trade school in Milwaukee, Wisconsin, learning sewing and cooking skills. She never dreamed that one day these skills would be vital to life on an Alaskan homestead. She canned fish and moose meat, preserved meat through the warm summer months, and could spice up a moose roast to give it lots of flavor. She made all the clothes that Nancy and I wore, including the snow pants made from brown wool Army blankets.

John Stockhausen, age 18, is wearing his second leather jacket after losing the first one in a game of poker a couple years earlier. He was born into a family of nine children and grew up on a farm. He learned carpentry from his father and painting from his brothers. He looked forward to deer hunting season when all his brothers and father spent several days in northern Wisconsin. From an early age he always wanted to see the world.

Mom and Dad married on April 15, 1939, in Wauwatosa, Wisconsin. They had a small reception of close friends and relatives at the home of Dad's parents. His father played the concertina and entertained everyone with waltz and polka music. Mom enjoyed the outdoors as much as Dad. They'd pack a picnic lunch and invite friends to go with them to the country. Many weekends were spent with friends camping at their favorite lake on the outskirts of Milwaukee.

The Stockhausen family after church in their front yard in Wauwatosa, Wisconsin circa 1930s.
Back row-standing left to right: Gerhardt, Anthony, Bernadine, father Nicholaus, mother Anna, John, Edward
Front row, kneeling: Christine, Genevieve, Ervin, Eleanor

Darlene, Mom, and Nancy in our back yard on 69th Street in Wauwatosa, Wisconsin. We went from Sunday dress up to country casual after moving. Mom and Dad were comfortable with the down-to-earth folksy attire worn in Alaska.

Edward Stockhausen enjoyed traveling. He was in San Francisco in 1939, hoping for passage on a ship to the Orient. Due to WWII he was unsuccessful, so he traveled up the west coast to Alaska and enlisted in the Army, eventually earning the rank of Master Sergeant. He returned to Wisconsin to marry Kathleen Stieber on October 8, 1947. She accompanied him back to Alaska where they raised their family. They returned to Wisconsin after spending several years in Fairbanks.

Photo courtesy of Cheryl Stockhausen Horst

It was June 8, 1947, the day before leaving for Alaska. Dad's sister, Genevieve, wanted to take a picture of us by the Army truck with the trailer on it. She knew where we'd be on Sunday afternoon, because Mom often helped in the kitchen of the restaurant her mother and Floyd owned. We hurried across the street to the gas station where the truck had been parked for several months while Dad readied it for our trip, and Mom forgot to take her apron off.

The only picture we have of the doorway into the trailer. Darlene standing just below Nancy on the ladder.

MONDAY, JUNE 9, 1947 THE MILW

An 'On to Alaska Pilgrimage Due to Start Here Today

Two families and two young men "took off" from Milwaukee over the week end. For the youths, it was an adventure. For the families, it was the beginning of a new life. For both of them it was "Alaska bound."

Johnny Stockhausen, his wife and their two children made a final inspection of the former army truck on which he had built a house-trailer-like living quarters. Ken Pilgrim and his wife, Mary, did the same to their truck.

Don Nelson, 20, of 2855 N. 33rd st., and Harold Brown, 22, of 2611 N. 36th st., packed the last of their "duffle" into their small panel truck, and headed out of town. The youths plan on "taking it easy" hunting and fishing along the Alaskan highway. They plan to return in three and one-half months.

For the Pilgrims and the Stockhausens, it was a little different kind of a trip. The Stockhausens lived at 2139 N. 58th st. The Pilgrims had a house trailer in the camp at 7417 W. Blue Mound rd.

The Stockhausens decided to go to Alaska three years ago, but they didn't like the idea of doing it alone. "They finally talked my wife into it," said Pilgrim.

Alaska is the destination of the folks shown in these pictures. The group includes Mrs. Bernice Stockhausen, in the doorway with Nancy, 6, and Darlene, 7; John Stockhausen (left), 2139 N. 58th st.; Kenneth Pilgrim and his wife, Mary, who live in a trailer camp at 7417 W. Blue Mound rd. The families have been planning the trip for three years and each has a trailer body on a truck. The youths are Don Nelson (left), 20, of 2855 N. 33rd st., and Harold Brown, 22, of 2611 N. 36th st., who will travel in a panel truck. —Journal Staff

This article appeared in the Milwaukee Journal *announcing our trip to Alaska. The bottom photo of two young men who were also beginning their journey to Alaska were not a part of our family travel group.*

Courtesy of The Milwaukee Journal

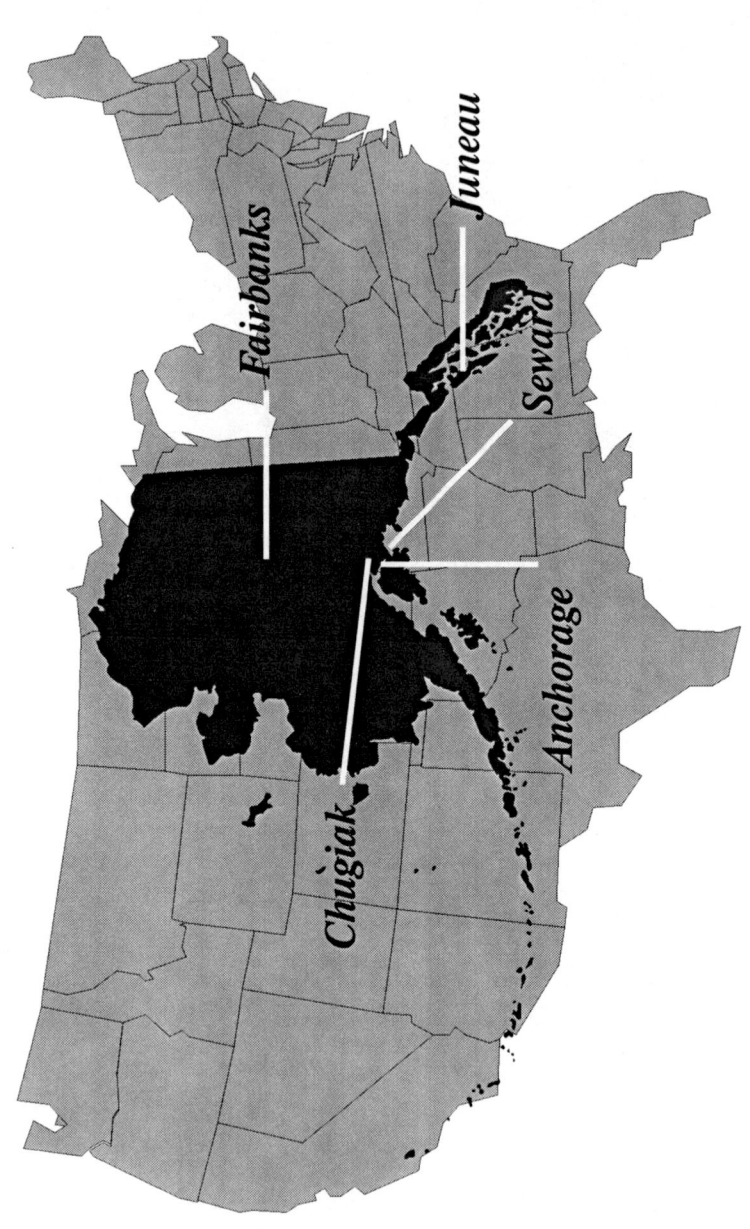

How Big is Alaska?

ON TO ALASKA

A 1947 JOURNAL OF TRAVELING THE ALASKA HIGHWAY

We all have dreams. But in order to make dreams come into reality, it takes an awful lot of determination, dedication, self-discipline, and effort.

—Jesse Owens

MONDAY, JUNE 9, 1947

Dad helped Nancy up and into the truck where she could safely cuddle between him and Mom. He gently took my hand and, with a hug, he delivered me into Kenny and Mary's capable hands, where I would spend many days in their watchful care. We were ready to set out on the great adventure of a lifetime. We had just said good-bye to family and friends, having no idea when we would see them again. Soon Milwaukee, Wisconsin, would be just a part of our past, a place only to return to for an occasional visit.

It was a warm day on the ninth of June. A perfect sort of day for beginning a long trip. The windows were down in the Army truck that had been purchased specifically for the difficult trip ahead of us. The breeze felt cool as it swirled around the interior of the truck. The mood was cheerful, yet melancholy. Dad was finally attaining his long yearned-for trip to Alaska, but a heavy-hearted feeling ached deep inside. It was hard to leave family behind. He was venturing out on a trip with an outcome that could not be envisioned; it had to be lived each day.

Mom also wondered what was ahead of them. She was leaving friends and family behind; she had been content with the comforts of the life they had lived in the upper flat owned by Dad's parents, and she had two daughters to think about. Was it the right decision? Hopefully, it was. . .only time would tell. Nancy settled between the two of them, quite content, reading her comic book. I was very happy resting my head against Mary's arm.

Mary and Kenny let Dad take the lead traveling toward Portage, which would be our first stop. I was looking forward to it, because I'd get to visit with cousins I hadn't seen in a long time.

After a lengthy discussion about leaving family behind, silence overtook us. It was during this time, when each was deep in personal thoughts, that the oil line in Dad's truck broke. How could there be problems this soon. After all, we were less than one hundred miles into our journey and still in Wisconsin. While the line was being repaired, we decided it would be a good time to have the lunch Grandma Hixson had prepared for us. Everyone joked about how they had thought Dad's truck was the one in better condition.

Dad's oldest sister, Bernadine, and her husband, Leonard Statz, lived on a farm in Portage. Arrival there was at three o'clock with only one hundred miles accomplished the first day. We spent our first night on the farm. The evening was spent discussing the happenings of the day and the events prior to our departure that morning. We talked about the *Milwaukee Journal* making a visit to 68th and North Avenue to do a story and take pictures of us. It was a very newsworthy event to have two families pack up all their worldly possessions and embark on a trip to Alaska. The Alaska Highway had just recently opened to civilian traffic, and we read about conditions of the highway and knew it would be a harrowing motor trip.

The farm was a peaceful, quiet place to spend the rest of the day and evening. Nancy and I played with our cousins. The

Baraboo River was a few yards from the house and was lots of fun to throw rocks into. It was also time for the cows to return to the barn and the milking process to begin. The evening meal was a banquet laid out for all to enjoy. Everyone retired in a state of exhaustion, letting the crickets lull us to sleep.

TUESDAY, JUNE 10

On the farm everyone rises early, and today was going to be the day to make up the miles lost yesterday, due to the inconvenience of the broken oil line. Breakfast was delicious and served in the farmhouse kitchen. Bernadine helped Mary and Mom pack a lunch, and everyone went outside for picture taking. Gathering everyone together was quite an accomplishment, what with kids wanting to play and adults in their many conversations, it seemed to take forever. It was nine twenty-five and time to leave. With lots of hugs and tearful good-byes we were ready to start the day's drive. Dad gave Bernadine one last hug and she gave him words of advice. It was hard for family to understand the lure of the great land, and they couldn't fathom the pull it had on Dad.

Dad and Mom again discussed family and wondered what was ahead of them. It was another warm, sunny morning, and they wanted to make better mileage today. The truck was in good working condition now that the oil line was fixed. It had been forty minutes since waving good-bye to everyone at the farm when the truck motor quit running again. Dad brought the truck to a quick halt. He eased himself out of the truck, stating that the timing gear broke. Mom could sense some frustration in his voice and began to wonder if this second day with problems was going to set the tone for what else lay ahead of them.

In the meantime, Kenny pulled his truck to a stop behind them, hoping there wasn't a problem. After observing the situation, Dad's truck was parked and both men drove to Wisconsin Dells for the parts they needed. Kenny decided it might be a good plan to purchase an extra timing gear for his truck on the off chance that he could find himself in this situation farther along the highway. After the parts were purchased and the men returned, it was time again for a little teasing about who had the better truck now.

After the departure of the men there was lots of extra unexpected time, so Mary, Mom, Nancy, and I ventured out on foot. The walk took us through many intriguing shops, some with handmade items created by the Indians from the local area. Nancy and I were especially intrigued with the bright beadwork. After a long walk back, Mom and Mary settled themselves to wait for the installation of the timing gear. The motor shutdown halted the trip at ten in the morning and it was now five thirty in the afternoon and time to make up some of the lost hours. We pushed forward on Highway 12 out of Tomah and finally stopped for the night near Camp McCoy. The mileage for the day calculated out at eighty miles. Everyone retired that evening feeling some emotional overtones and glad the day was finally over. We hoped that tomorrow would be more gratifying and yet felt very fortunate that it was only a timing gear that delayed the trip.

WEDNESDAY, JUNE 11

Yesterday seemed to drag with little accomplished, so it felt energizing to begin a new day. The morning was uneventful, the mileage was noted, and the mood was very cheerful. During lunch, everyone joked about traveling all the way to Menominee without any mishaps. Dad has always been a man with a happy-go-lucky type of personality. A little harassing never ruffled him, and he always had a humorous comeback that got everyone laughing. They chuckled again as they put liquid solder in the radiator of Dad's truck.

After lunch we waved good-bye to Wisconsin and entered Minnesota at the St. Croix River, paying a toll of five cents which was garnered from each vehicle passing over the bridge. There seemed to be a problem with Dad's truck after crossing the bridge.

Kenny towed the truck for a short distance until it could be determined what new development was ailing the engine this time. The day ended with our arrival at the home of Mary's brother, Meredith. It was three o'clock, and we had driven one hundred seventy-five miles, which was great cause for celebration. Meredith invited us to stay for dinner and spend the night. Kenny's cousin and his friend came to visit with him.

Observing both trucks being parked in the backyard stimulated conversation about how Kenny and Dad came to purchase them. They talked about the work that went into getting the trucks ready for the trip and how they spent all their spare time at the gas station working on them.

Dad showed the men the inside and talked about all the things we brought with us that needed to be stored in every available space. The icebox was in the back corner. The oval mirror and the framed canvas picture, portraying a tent campsite beside a river, were stored under the bunk beds along with the card table, four folding chairs, tools, crosscut- and rip saws were stored under the bunk beds. The guns were placed behind all of that. The sewing machine was taken apart and put in several places for safekeeping. The battery-operated radio was kept on the floor while traveling and used in the evening to listen to the news. Mom's flat irons and kerosene irons were stored in the back of the cupboards. Mom wrapped all the special Christmas ornaments and heavy tinsel, putting them in a box along with strings of tiny colored bulbs. She didn't want to take the chance of not finding decorations at Christmastime in Alaska. They marveled at the compact space with plenty of room to move around.

Dad bought two kerosene lanterns that would be used in our cabin. He felt we needed to be prepared in case there was no electricity in the area where we chose to homestead. We would use them in the trailer during the evenings when everyone had the opportunity to relax after a long day's journey. Even though there were windows to let in the evening light farther into Canada, we needed light at night until reaching the place where the midnight sun shone most of the night. We were looking forward to the evenings of popcorn and card games. Kenny and Mary had less room in the home they had built on the bed of their truck. It was used only for sleeping accommodations with just enough room for their personal possessions.

THURSDAY, JUNE 12

In the morning, it was difficult to say good-bye to family again. It always brought nostalgia and quiet time for reflection. During the morning break at Waverly, the first traveler's check was cashed. Mom and Mary headed for the coffee shop and unwound. Lunch was at Murdock. Entry into South Dakota was at a quarter past three. We drove until exhaustion overtook us and ended the day early after the late-night card playing the evening before.

The perfect location came into view just ahead. Dad was in the lead truck that day with Nancy positioned between him and Mom. Nancy noticed the white school house ahead and asked to stop and play on the swings and slide. The trucks were parked alongside the building, and Nancy and I were ecstatic to have the playground all to ourselves. We played for an hour until supper was ready and never seemed to become weary. Everyone retired early, after convincing Nancy and me that we would have time to play the next morning. The mileage for the day was 179, making it the best travel time to date.

FRIDAY, JUNE 13

As promised, Nancy and I had time to play in the school yard the next morning. It was fun looking through the windows of the building and envisioning what it would be like to go to school in a small building in the country. We were finally coaxed into the trucks at eight thirty and we settled in for another day of driving.

There seemed to be a greater distance from one town to the next. South Dakota had an arid climate, and trees were sparse. The drive was hot and stifling, even with the breeze from the open windows. There was a stop in Milbank and another in Aberdeen, taking time to buy groceries and a coil for Dad's truck. The day went by slower than usual. Maybe it had to do with the stuffy heat.

Everyone breathed a sigh of relief when the trucks were parked beside a cool lake just before nightfall. It was another fun evening for Nancy and me, frolicking in the calm, chilly water. Chairs were grouped close to the lake after the evening meal. With coffee in hand, it was time to relax and talk over the events of the last five days of travel. Mary got paper and pencil and calculated the mileage for the day at 185. They were satisfied with the mileage they had accumulated the last three days.

SATURDAY, JUNE 14

Travel began around nine o'clock, with some conversation about the pleasurable evening we had spent by the lake. The Missouri River was crossed, and the surroundings were somewhat the same as the day before: no trees and hilly. There were white-faced steers grazing on endless grassland.

Everyone must have been deep in thought, because both drivers turned onto the wrong highway with neither being the wiser. It wasn't until they had traveled five miles that they noticed the town they were entering was not the one listed on their map. The mistake was laughed at as they reversed their direction, and it felt good to be back on the main highway leading north.

McLaughlin was a very dirty, rough, western town and there were no toilets available for weary travelers, so we continued north to McIntosh where flashlight batteries and candy were purchased. We spotted the local hamburger restaurant and couldn't resist the temptation to devour a big, juicy hamburger with all the trimmings.

The weekend break was at Petrified Wood Park in Lemmon, South Dakota. The distance for the day was 135 and we gained an hour due to the time zone change.

It was still early in the day, so Mom and Mary washed clothes and hung them to dry among the petrified wood in the park. Nancy and I scouted the area close to camp with the promise that everyone would venture out farther later in the day.

Meanwhile, Kenny wanted to get his haircut and a battery cable for his truck. Mary went with him and bought drinks and groceries and stopped at the post office to buy stamps to mail letters home to relatives.

SUNDAY, JUNE 15

Sunday morning was occupied with ironing and fussing with odds and ends that needed tending. Letters were written to everyone back home informing them that we had traveled 854 miles during the first week and enlightening them about some of the more interesting circumstances encountered so far.

Mary, Nancy, and I went into town to a movie. Upon our return to camp, Mary found out that Kenny, Mom, and Dad went out and "did the town" without her. She was somewhat miffed at them for not waiting and including her.

MONDAY, JUNE 16

The leisurely weekend and respite from driving was rejuvenating, and we got on the road at eight thirty. After entering North Dakota, there was a stop in Hettinger for gas. The roads were under repair and the terrible conditions made traveling slow and tedious. A warm wind was blowing, and tumbleweeds drifted aimlessly as far as the eye could see.

Entry into Montana found the countryside more appealing. The hills were greater and there was an abundance of trees. Time was taken to relax and have lunch near a grove of trees, then we continued on to Miles City, where Dad had his truck's radiator flushed out. The Big Sheep Mountains held our interest for most of the afternoon until Dad's truck crested the top of a hill and was beginning its descent, when five of the six lug nuts sheared off one of the back tires. It was a harrowing experience to go through, and it took several minutes to regain composure.

Some time was spent working on the tire, the sun was setting, and it was time to locate a place to spend the night. A field came into view and the trucks were steered into it. Dad's task was the tire and Kenny changed the oil in his truck. Nancy and I seemed to dissolve into the high grassy field to run and play and appear again when Mary summoned everyone for supper.

An entry was inscribed in the travel log: 207 miles today. Many miles had been driven despite the road repairs, the scary tire incident on the hill, and the repair time.

During the night it stormed. There were tremendous bursts of thunder and luminous lightning striating across the sky, resulting in a sleepless night.

TUESDAY, JUNE 17

The next morning Dad and Kenny drove back to Miles City to have five lug nuts made for the wheel. It developed into a day of waiting, with part of the time spent unwinding at the local gambling establishment playing with $2.45.

Returning to camp, they informed Mom and Mary that they learned that rattlesnakes inhabit the grassy areas. Nancy and I had spent most of the day in the high grass and everyone was thankful that we were unharmed.

The tire was finally put back on the truck, and we left the field at four. A stop was made in Forsyth for food and film, and to give Mom and Mary an opportunity to try their luck gambling. It was terrific entertainment and made great conversation that evening.

The mileage was ninety-seven including the thirty miles they had backtracked to Miles City.

WEDNESDAY, JUNE 18

Traveling began at around nine. We took a break in Custer, by-passed Billings, took Highway 87 and saw Bull Mountains. Coal mines were scattered throughout the region. A few food items were purchased at Klien and lunch was in Roundup. Stopped in Lewistown and noted that the water was extra good compared to what it had been.

There was a remote location on a hill with a river flowing down into the valley just out of Stanford that was selected for the campsite. The mileage was 343, making it a record-breaking day.

After supper Dad and Kenny spied a skunk in the underbrush and, without much contemplation, shot it. It wasn't until a brief time later that they realized the error they had made. The skunk haunted us, making it a thoroughly miserable night tolerating the wretched odor. We woke feeling groggy.

Breakfast was prepared, served, and cleaned up quickly. We all pitched in and picked up the campsite. We were on our way within forty-five minutes, thankful to leave the foul scent of the skunk behind us. We breathed the fresh smell of air into the sensitive nerves of our noses.

THURSDAY, JUNE 19

The day began shortly after eight o'clock, noting the snow-capped Little Belt Mountains in the distance while passing through Louis and Clark National Park.

A few afternoon hours were spent in Great Falls. The city grew along the Missouri River, with the business district on the river's east bank. Prairie land covers the area as far as the eye can see giving a sense of wide open spaces. At one time, the region was inhabited by the Blackfoot Indian Nation.

The first stop was the post office. Mary got a letter from her mother and one from Augusta. Nancy and I got haircuts for one dollar each, while Mom and Mary bought groceries, and Kenny bought a grease retainer and rear axle. Hamburgers at the local restaurant were a treat.

We left Great Falls at quarter past three on Highway 91 out of Vaughn, driving for a few hours and found a place to spend the night. We accumulated another 127 miles.

FRIDAY, JUNE 20

The morning began at nine with a stop at Sunburst and Sweetgrass before arriving at the border crossing and customs at Coutts, Alberta. It took twenty minutes to clear through customs. We had to show the officer all the money we possessed to prove that we could finance our trip through Canada without assistance from their government.

After clearing customs, we took Highway 4 toward the wheat farming community of Milk River. The gophers seemed to be everywhere and became the center of concentration and conversation on a monotonous drive.

Farther along the road, the detour signs were the main focus of attention. The alternative route was a horrendous mess of muddy potholes. It weaved through an undulating makeshift path along the periphery of the main road. It was extremely treacherous driving, and we felt relieved when the end of the detour was finally in sight.

Having conquered the alternate route and coming through it feeling victorious, a stop was made in Lethbridge to relax. The town was known as "the place of black rocks." In 1872, coal mining sprang up throughout the area and the town developed adjacent to the mines. An irrigation project began in 1899, bringing agriculture to the region.

After exiting Lethbridge, the road continued west on Highway 3 toward Fort Macleod. The day seemed extra long after the grueling trip through the muddy area. The odometer read 150 miles. We spent the night beside Oldman River.

Dad placed four bottles of Pabst beer in an onion sack and walked to the river bank and laid them on the river bottom. In the cold water, it would take approximately ten minutes for the beer to chill. He chuckled softly to himself as he thought about the evening his father-in-law, Floyd, came to the house to say good-bye and presented him with ten cases of beer from his bar to take along on the trip to Alaska. The only place to store it was under Kenny and Mary's bed, which had been installed about three feet from the floor. The evening was spent playing Sheep's Head and eating popcorn.

SATURDAY, JUNE 21

Traveling commenced at twenty past nine on Highway 2 out of Fort Macloed. The town grew when the Northwest Mounted Police established a post there. A brief stop was made in Nanton for gas and lunch. Exhaustion brought the day's journey to an end just before entering Calgary. Camp was set up at Fox Creek for the weekend. The camping spot cost one dollar per night, and the mileage for the day was 110.

The rest of the afternoon was spent exploring Calgary and viewing the overwhelming Tamerack Forest. Calgary began when the Northwest Mounted Police arrived and set up a post in 1875. In the 1890s cattle ranching evolved, and in 1914 oil was discovered.

We toured the area and found it pleasant to have the time to look in on an artist who painted exceptional copper kettles that hung on the walls of his log cabin.

SUNDAY, JUNE 22

In the morning, two live chickens were purchased for one dollar. They would make a delicious Sunday dinner but first would have to be slain and chopped up. In preparation to doing "the deed," both chickens slid out of confinement just short of being grabbed, causing terrible mayhem. Kenny was washing his hair and didn't have his glasses on. He took off in pursuit of a chicken and stumbled just before grasping it. At last, they were in the clutches of both men and were wrestled all the way to the chopping block. The dinner was delicious and everyone laughed in reminiscence of the earlier chase.

Kenny and Dad worked on the trucks after hauling water from the creek for washing clothes, resulting in a busy afternoon. Later in the evening Mom made popcorn, Nancy and I read comic books, and a couple of rounds of Sheep's Head were played. We were beginning to notice how light it was at night. The curtains were closed, but that didn't help much to darken the sleeping area.

Mary calculated the mileage for the second week at 954.

MONDAY, JUNE 23

We left Calgary at ten o'clock after purchasing gas, oil, and snacks, and took Highway 2 out of Carstairs and headed in the direction of Edmonton. We noticed English army trucks with right-hand steering wheels. Lunch was eaten at Olds and the night was spent on the outskirts of Edmonton. The mileage was 178.

TUESDAY, JUNE 24

It was half past nine and a trip to the post office was first on the schedule at designated cities. Mary got letters from Augusta, Ethel, and her mother. Time was spent exploring the town.

The capital of the Province of Alberta is Edmonton and is located on the North Saskatchewan River. The Northwest Company and Hudson's Bay Company were competing fur companies that built a large number of forts around the area.

It was mandatory that a visit be made to the office of the Royal Canadian Mounted Police for all travelers venturing out on the Alaska Highway. The Canadian government required a permit to use the highway and each individual driver needed to apply in person for the permit.

To get a permit, the traveler must have the following: one spare tire for every two on the road, tube repair kit, shovel, ax, tools, 15 gallons of gas, spare generator, points, coil, condenser, fan belt, light bulbs, four quarts of oil, set of spark plugs, chains, and tow chain.

We didn't want to find ourselves stranded on a wilderness road having no garage service for repairs. It was isolated and remote, a place none of us wanted to find ourselves waiting for a passerby's help. Having the list of things available for repairs would make travel less worrisome.

A safe trip would be top priority on our minds. We felt that the trucks were in good operating condition except for a few minor repairs and the occasional dead battery. We had more than enough funds, and we were in no rush to drive the highway.

The trucks were taken to the local garage and greased before setting out on the unknown road ahead. During the wait, everyone settled back with a Coke, reflecting on what they had been told of the road conditions ahead. The evening was spent on the outskirts of Edmonton. All the supplies listed in the permit were stored and ready to be used if the need should occur. It was a short day with an accumulation of eighty miles.

WEDNESDAY, JUNE 25

The oil was changed after breakfast, and everyone was settled in the trucks at nine thirty, hoping to triple yesterday's mileage. There was a speedy stop for supplies at Tawatinaw and then a brief lunch at Smith. The afternoon dragged on as the trucks slowly traversed the seventy miles along Slave Lake and on into Enilda.

In High Prairie, there was time to stretch while Dad and Kenny purchased a grease gun, and then it was back to traveling.

The night was spent at Triangle with everyone very weary and glad to have the day end. There was a light meal served and bed was most inviting. We had traveled 221 miles.

THURSDAY, JUNE 26

The morning started at a quarter to nine on Highway 34 to Valleyview for drinking water and then on to the Smoky River, where the trucks were driven onto a ferryboat and carried across the river. Kenny took pictures to remember the experience.

After a long day, the arrival at Grand Prairie was much anticipated. Mary was surprised when a reporter asked to interview her regarding her trip to Alaska. She also got to meet the founder of the town. It made for interesting conversation over drinks before continuing along the highway.

Agriculture, lumber, and mining surrounds Grand Prairie, and it is the major trading center of the Peace River region in northern Alberta.

While traveling Highway 2 out of Grand Prairie, Dad and Kenny found the road in disrepair and observed the muddy conditions just ahead of them. They approached, very cautiously, what looked like a gigantic mud hole. The mud proved to be unduly slippery with deep holes that rolled the trucks from side to side as they skidded through it. Just when they thought they made it through without mishap, both trucks slithered deep into the mud. Dad knew the winch would come in handy at some point on the trip and stepped out of the truck and into the mud that sucked him in almost to his knees to secure the winch to a tree. Once attached to the tree, he was able to pull his truck loose from the slick goo. He was then able to fasten the winch onto the front of Kenny's truck and pull it free from the treacherous mud. The mud dried like a coat of plaster on the trucks, causing huge chunks of dirt to fall off every time the doors were slammed shut. We were all grateful to have survived the mud and thankful for the winch that gave us the extra hoist out of the brown sludge. Dad spent time before supper sweeping out the dried chunks of mud from the interior driver's side of the truck, hoping he'd never experience mud like that again. He cleaned his boots and hoped they would dry by morning. The day ended 159 miles closer to our destination.

FRIDAY, JUNE 27

Left at eight o'clock and crossed into British Columbia at Brainard. At Pouce Coupe, a fire permit was secured.

Milepost 0 dominates the main street in Dawson Creek, signifying the beginning of the Alaska Highway. When the highway was punched through Canada to Alaska, it was known as the ALCAN (Alaska-Canadian Highway). The military men on the construction crews thought it was an unappealing name for a project of such magnitude. In 1943 Canada agreed with the suggestion that the official name would be the Alaska Highway.

Dad and Kenny had their guns sealed at Dawson Creek Police Department.

The road led north out of Dawson Creek, and the few settlements were many miles apart. Dad and Kenny were apprehensive about the condition of the road. The repairs were minimal but passable for those travelers who were patient enough to slow down, making it easier on vehicles and passengers. It was a rocky, rough road to Alaska. The road was constructed on muskeg and permafrost, which produced jarring potholes and jolting bumps.

The Peace River country around Dawson Creek is an area of rich farmland. Wheat grows well during the long days of summer. We took our time crossing the scenic Peace River and then stopped to take pictures high on a hill overlooking the beautiful river and bridge. It was decided that this would be the perfect place to have lunch with a view.

Dad's oil line broke, and late in the day there was a flat tire on one of the trucks. We were tired upon our arrival in Fort St.

John that evening. The gravel seemed to nibble away at the tires. Making a stop at the coffee shop, we were told that during the smoothing of the road, steel off the grader blades caused many tires to go flat.

Fort St. John originated in 1806 along the Peace River as a trading post for the Sikanni and Beaver Indians.

It was a productive day, having driven 209 miles. Time was spent making repairs to the oil line in Dad's truck and fixing the flat tire. Mom made popcorn later in the evening, but a rousing game of Sheep's Head would have to wait until tomorrow night.

SATURDAY, JUNE 28

The next morning Kenny had to pull Dad's truck to get the engine to turn over and start. The actual starting time was clocked at a quarter past ten. After being on the road for a short time, the generator on Dad's truck began acting up. Some time was spent at Sikanni River trying to make it functional again. Lunch time was approaching but we pushed forward, trying to make up some of the time lost. Ultimately, hunger overtook us, and the trucks pulled off the road on Pink Mountain. The mountain was very impressive with its elevation of 3,600 feet, and Mary wanted a picture of the scenery before moving on. The clouds moved in while she ate lunch and she wasn't able to photograph the valley and distant mountains. Instead, she decided to snap a picture of the cloud that obscured the view.

The road seemed to take its toll on the trucks and wore out the tires. Numerous potholes comprised the complete surface of the road. There was no place a person could drive and avoid them, and there was no getting away from the dusty road. The dust was in the trucks and lay thick on the windows.

Beaver Creek came into view in the late afternoon. It had been a laborious day spread over a scant forty-eight miles. Spending the weekend here was discussed and agreed upon.

After relaxing for awhile and talking over the results of the day, everyone felt grateful that the mechanical problems were easy to remedy. Mom and Mary chose to get started on washing clothes after noting the clouds moving in their direction.

After dinner water was hauled in, heated on the stove, and dishes were washed and placed in the cupboard. It was time to unwind. This required a deck of cards and four people who always looked forward to this time of day with enthusiasm. Cards were their passion and they played with great fervor.

SUNDAY JUNE 29

It was Sunday and there would be no traveling today. Even though it was considered a day of rest from the hot, dusty highway, there was plenty of work to do on the trucks. It was dreary and rained on and off all day. Mom washed the rest of the clothes and hoped they would dry on the makeshift clothesline that Dad had assembled. Washing clothes was a real feat. All the water was heated on an open fire outside, poured into the large galvanized tub, and the clothes were scrubbed clean on a washboard. The water had to be hot enough to get the clothes clean, yet cool enough to be able to put hands into it. Wringing the clothes was like wrestling a snake: it took great strength. The clothes were hung dripping wet, taking most of the day to dry. If there was a wind they dried faster.

Mary was the historian and kept a record of the events of each day. We just finished the third week and had driven 895 miles that week.

Nancy and I enjoyed each stop that brought with it the occasion to run, explore, and play. There were always different flowers to smell and pick, trees to climb, dirt and water to make mud pies, and tall grass to hide in. We shared a bowl of popcorn and played with paper dolls while Mom, Dad, Mary, and Kenny played Sheep's Head.

MONDAY, JUNE 30

It was almost ten, and everyone was eager to get moving again. The day of rest was nice, but we always reminded ourselves that every minute on the road brought us closer to Alaska. After several attempts to get Dad's truck started, Kenny hooked the tow rope onto the truck to pull it until the engine sputtered and began to run. The road was usually dusty, but due to the rain the trucks traveled closer together. Driving became hazardous, and the road built up a slippery coat that spattered the vehicles.

The mid-morning rest stop was at Lum 'N Abner's Cafe and Trading Post for groceries and candy to snack on. It was intriguing to browse through an authentic trading post of early pioneer days.

It was lunch time when the trucks finally pulled into Fort Nelson. Dad purchased a battery for his truck and Kenny repaired his flat tire. The lunch conversation was about the mother moose and her calf that had ambled up onto the roadway and surveyed the travelers for, what seemed, a considerably long time. Nancy and I found the huge lumbering animals entrancing. We were caught up in the memory, and we hoped to see more moose on the road. It absolutely was one the highlights of the trip for us.

Fort Nelson began to thrive with the construction of the Alaska Highway passing though the vicinity. The town was named for the fort and trading post built during the 1800s, and remains of the fort can be observed across the Fort Nelson River.

With the new battery in Dad's truck, we left Fort Nelson behind, winding through some of the most stunning scenery imaginable. The north Canadian Rockies were craggy, and in some places the road pushed against the rocky edges of sheer cliffs. It was areas like this that were extremely dangerous. Landslides were likely because of the construction of a road that was carved out of unstable hillsides. We were traveling up one such mountain, shifting gears and continually slowing down. Dad's truck had almost crested the top, when it lurched to a stop and began rolling backward. Mom perceived the danger of the situation they were in and hastened to remove herself and Nancy from Dad's truck and told Mary and me to get out of Kenny's truck. She concluded that walking the rest of the way up the hill and down the other side would be less worrisome. She urged Dad to apply utmost caution in manipulating the truck. With much maneuvering, the truck finally reached the peak and began its descent.

Launching out on a summer walk on top of a Canadian mountain meant being overtaken by mosquitoes and gnats. Mary, Mom, Nancy, and I picked up our pace, and with swiftness descended the hill, beating off the relentless bugs as the distance between them and the truck dwindled. Such relief to climb into the truck only to find that the mosquitoes were now inside, since windows had been left open. We again embarked on another swatting spree as the trucks began to journey along the dusty, ever-winding, crooked road.

Dad and Kenny fought the road for 158 miles and decided to set up camp at Mill Creek. During the evening everyone nursed their mosquito bites and talked about the road conditions. We knew there would be a multitude of potholes and many more miles of crooked road stretching ahead of us. The challenges of the day called for change and relief with an enjoyable activity such as Sheep's Head and popcorn.

TUESDAY, JULY 1

The day commenced at ten o'clock, traveling through the magnificent beauty of the wide valleys and mountain passes. The clear lakes and roaring rivers made rest stops a pleasure. Summit Lake is the highest summit on the highway with an elevation of 4,250 feet. It was an area too beautiful to just drive past and was definitely picture-taking scenery.

While occupied with taking pictures, it began to snow. How could there be snow on the first day of July? It was a sight to behold. Nancy and I laughed and frolicked, trying to capture several big flakes in our hands. The respite from driving lingered somewhat longer than usual to let us enjoy the experience of observing snow in July. It certainly would be something to write home about. Lunch was beside the beautiful Racing River and more pictures were taken. The rest of the day was spent viewing the ever-present magnificent scenery. There were no breakdowns or flat tires during the day.

The mileage was 186, and changing oil was on the evening schedule.

WEDNESDAY, JULY 2

It was Mary's birthday. At breakfast everyone wished her a happy day and knew she would always remember where she was on this very special day.

Traveling began at half past nine with everyone hoping it would be another perfect day. The road took us a short distance through the Yukon Territory and then back again into British Columbia. At Lower Post, British Columbia's most northern town, groceries were on top of the list of errands that needed to be done. Hudson's Bay Company Trading Post was part of the historic town and also the location of an Indian village.

A short time later we arrived at Watson Lake, Yukon, a few miles from the border of British Columbia. The elevation is 4,212 feet making it one of the highest places on the highway. It grew into a thriving city since it was close to the border. Also when the engineers designed the route, they made the decision to put the highway down the main street of Watson Lake, thus boosting the economy.

When passing through Watson Lake, travelers want to stop and view the famous assortment of signs that started in 1942 when a soldier posted a sign along the highway with the name of his home town and the miles from home. Additional signs were displayed by other workers, and after the opening of the highway, tourists also left the names of their cities, making the collection of signs a sight to behold. It is a place to stop and chat with other curious onlookers and take pictures.

It was late afternoon when Dad's fuel pump broke. The trucks were parked, and it was unanimously decided that supper would be prepared early while the men mended the fuel pump. It was a clear, sunny evening with lots of daylight left. After washing the dishes, we drove late into the night accruing 186 miles.

THURSDAY, JULY 3

It was a quarter to nine and the weather was breezy and cool. The morning drive was uneventful as we traveled along Teslin Lake. In the Indian language, Teslin means "long waters." Teslin was thriving before the Alaska Highway was built. The village had what was known as the mythical Crow Rock. According to the legend, rain will ensue if a white man places his feet in the crowfoot marks on the age-old rock. There was a trading post in the village, so we stopped for provisions.

We passed through Johnson Crossing at the junction of the Alaska Highway and the Canol Road. The roadway was built during the Second World War, linking the Norman Wells oil fields on the MacKenzie River with the industrial site in Whitehorse.

Arrival at Whitehorse brought with it great rejoicing, and everyone welcomed the chance to get out of the trucks and stretch tired muscles. It had been a long, grueling, dusty trip through desolate country, and the Alaska border was just over three hundred miles away.

First thing on the agenda was a stop at the post office to check the mail. There was a letter from Mary's mother, Kenny's dad, and one from Bernadine Statz. There was jubilation and great excitement as letters were opened and read immediately. It was comforting to hear from family, and it left us feeling a little homesick, yet feeling close and in touch with family.

With spirits lifted, everyone relaxed and had ice cream. It was time to get the essentials taken care of so that the rest of the day could be spent touring the town.

When people travel through the Yukon, they remember books they've read about the Klondike Gold Rush and the droves of gold seekers on their journey north through Whitehorse. Visiting museums and viewing artifacts remind them of the gold rush era. The barracks that the Army and civilian contractors occupied during the construction of the highway still remain.

The business section of Whitehorse is located on the banks of the Yukon River. People inbound from Alaska had to stop in Whitehorse for a travel permit, granting them approximately seven or eight days to reach Dawson Creek. Miles Canyon, located seven miles south of Whitehorse, was a sight to behold with its high rock walls.

After spending several hours in Whitehorse, we found a place to pull off the road for the night. The recorded miles were 203 for the day.

FRIDAY, JULY 4

Travel began at eight thirty. The road passed a small Indian village named Champagne. It was a trading post on the famed Dalton Trail in 1902. At Cracker Creek, we watched for Old Man Mountain. In the rocky crags of the mountain, a face seemed to materialize.

The morning had begun with excitement abounding for Nancy and me. It was the Fourth of July and no place to buy fireworks. Even so, Mom and Dad were going to make sure we would still have a special holiday. We stopped at the Macintosh Trading Post and bought candy and popcorn.

There was a brief stop at Soldier's Summit, where ceremonies had taken place on November 20, 1942, marking the official opening of the Alaska Highway.

Kluane Lake is 2,525 feet above sea level. By mid-June, the ice on the lake usually breaks up. As we passed by, there were still chunks of ice floating on the largest lake in the Yukon.

Destruction Bay got its name during the construction of the Alaska Highway when the Army camp located there had an unexpected wind storm that blew down the tents.

At Burwash Landing Dad got the generator fixed. Mary took a bath and washed her hair, in a public bath, for the first time since leaving Minneapolis, Minnesota.

That evening we finally came to rest by Glacier Creek. After dinner the holiday was celebrated with popcorn and candy bought earlier. Nancy and I had fun throwing rocks into the creek, pretending they were firecrackers. We laughed, flinging them with great force, causing loud splashes that produced explosive sounds. It had been a festive evening, but it was late and the next day would begin early.

There was a time change during the day and the clock was set back two hours. The mileage was 197.

In June and July there are twenty hours of daylight during a twenty-four hour time period. It never gets dark. At midnight, the sun is still shining and it is troublesome at times to sleep. The quietness and the miles of isolation along the road generated the feeling of being alone in the world.

SATURDAY, JULY 5

Traveling began at eight o'clock. Everyone was excited, because today we would reach our goal. In just a few scant hours we would be in Alaska. It was dusty and hot, and the miles seemed to pass slowly. We stopped after crossing the White River Bridge. The color of the water gives the river its name. It is caused from glacial silt and volcanic ash. It is one of the Yukon's most perilous rivers.

The miles brought us to Canadian Customs. Travelers on their way to Alaska don't have to stop unless they had their weapons sealed at Dawson Creek. Dad and Kenny had their guns unsealed, and we began the final twenty-mile journey to the border.

There were smiles on the faces of everyone as we approached the sign marking the border. Just over the border, the trucks were brought to a halt and we bounded out, and with great rejoicing yelled, "We made it!"

Excitement mounted as we continued our drive farther along the Alaska Highway. The mood was jubilant until the truck hit a pothole and a flat tire was the result. Nancy and I explored the area while the tire was changed.

A trading post came into view and, because of the festive mood, candy and Cokes were purchased to eat and drink as we drove slowly over the dusty road. Gardiner Creek had a large pull-off area, so the decision to discontinue the day's drive was quickly met with everyone's approval. It was the first day in Alaska and all of us wanted to savor the feeling of finally accomplishing a goal that began a year ago. It seemed the perfect place to set up camp for the weekend.

There were very few clouds drifting across the sky and the sun would shine late into the night, making it a good time to get a head start on the washing. While the water was heating, chairs were set out and everyone relaxed and discussed how they came to be here in Alaska on July 5, 1947.

Memories were abounding, and we began sharing thoughts at the same time. While reminiscing, we realized it didn't take much deliberation to make the decision to come to Alaska. It was something Dad had wanted to do for a long time. Mom liked the idea more each time Dad mentioned moving to Alaska. Mary and Kenny were glad for the invitation to join us in the journey. They had listened many times as Dad spoke of his desire to see Alaska, and now they were also a part of the adventure. They said yes, and were happy with the decision to explore a wilderness territory so far from home.

The Alaska trip took one year of planning. Lots of short-term goals needed to be met. With each preparation, their objective came closer to being realized. Parents were encouraging, yet worried about the distance and remoteness of Alaska. They thought that leaving home, extended family, and a job might be overwhelming.

So here we were with our feet planted firmly on Alaskan soil. It took determination to make the dream a reality, and we had not been threatened by stories of hazardous road conditions, dangerous hills, or undependable bridges that wash out during the spring flooding. We knew there would be miles of solitude with no other travelers on the road. Nothing deterred us from our goal. Mom, Dad, Mary, and Kenny raised their glasses and offered a toast to fortitude. Nancy and I had fun listening to the ping of our glasses of Coke clinking together. We finished the evening with popcorn and comic books and listened to the laughter of an enthusiastic game of Sheep's Head. We had traveled 137 miles.

SUNDAY, JULY 6

We woke to the sound of the rippling waters of Gardiner Creek. It was our second day in Alaska. Lots of work needed tending to. Mom got an early morning start washing clothes, and both she and Mary cleaned house. Kenny and Dad spent time working on the trucks, while Nancy and I picked beautiful delicate flowers with the hope that they would adorn the table that evening. We explored, climbed trees, chased the large ravens, and spied on the squirrel that was feasting on the bread crumbs we snatched from the bread basket.

That evening Nancy and I lay on our bellies on the bed, playing Old Maid and waiting patiently while Mom made popcorn in her cast-iron roasting pot. Mary totaled the mileage for the fourth week at 1066.

MONDAY, JULY 7

Everyone was energized and eager to see what Alaska had to offer us. We pulled away from Gardiner Creek at eight o'clock with a twelve-mile trip off the main highway to Northway Army Fort to get a generator for Dad's truck. The Army had no generators available, so we backtracked and continued on to the U.S. Customs at Tok Junction.

Tok is located at the junction of the Alaska and Glenn Highways. Souvenirs, food, and a map were bought at the local store.

The map was studied, and the trucks turned south onto the Glenn Highway toward Anchorage. The wildlife was plentiful and gave cause to pull to the edge of the road to observe the black bears or moose that came into view.

The day drew to a close with a feeling of relief, knowing that Anchorage was a two-day drive. We had passed through another time zone, making the day seem endless. The mileage for the day was 186.

TUESDAY, JULY 8

The day's journey began at eight o'clock, crossing the Tok River, passing through Mentasta Pass, over the Chistochina River, and on to Gakona where the Glenn Highway from Tok meets the Richardson Highway.

Continuing along the Glenn Highway, we passed Glennallen, named after both Capt. Glenn and Lt. Allen who had explored the Copper River region.

We were weary travelers by the time we reached Sheep Mountain at lunch time. The mountain is 6,300 feet high and can be seen for eleven miles along the north side of the highway between the Tahneta Pass and Caribou Creek. The road travels along the edge of the mountainside with numerous curves all the way down and a sharp hairpin turn at the bottom before crossing the bridge.

The trucks were parked at the base of the mountain in a pull-off area. After the mid-day meal, some time was spent walking on the bridge and inching our way down the steep bank to the edge of the river. The hike along the river was enjoyed by all of us. It was time to continue our journey to Palmer, so we scrambled up the bank and readied the trucks to vacate the pleasant spot we had chosen for our lunch stop. Dad and I were in the trailer making sure everything was secured and the others were outside. Attention was focused on a Model A Ford traveling at breakneck speed down the mountain road. The car lost its brakes coming down the mountain, and the occupants inside could not maneuver the dangerous curve that stretched to the bridge. Their car struck the steel bridge and careened twenty-five feet into the creek. Inside the car were four young men from Minnesota. One man was seriously injured and the others had minor injuries.

After rendering assistance, Dad and Kenny drove to the communication center a few miles away to inform them of the accident. Fort Richardson was notified, and a helicopter and doctor were sent to the accident site. The man with the chest injuries was secured to the outside of the helicopter to be airlifted to Anchorage but an air pocket prevented it from lifting off the ground. An ambulance was summoned from Anchorage and arrived four hours later. We did our best to comfort and assist the young men while they waited.

The doctor rode back to Anchorage in the ambulance, and the helicopter was finally able to lift off. After their departure, the stretchers were loaded on the top of Kenny's truck to be returned to Anchorage.

It had been an afternoon that left us feeling tense and anxious. The day ended early, so there would be time to unwind.

The entry into the travel log was 144 miles.

WEDNESDAY, JULY 9

It was one month since leaving Wisconsin. Travel began at eight o'clock with everyone eagerly anticipating their arrival in Anchorage today. The Matanuska Glacier was magnificent to view and the many lakes and rivers glistened in the morning sunlight, and the riverbanks were made for rock collectors. Nancy and I were fascinated with the size and colors of boulders, rocks, and pebbles we happened on at rest stops.

Palmer finally came into view. It is located approximately fifty miles northwest of Anchorage. In 1916 it began as an Alaska Railroad station. It became the administrative center for a farmers' cooperative, and it was a community solely centered on an agricultural economy. In 1935 government-financed colonists arrived and set up permanent dwellings and farms in the Matanuska Valley.

The spare tire was fixed in Palmer, and Dad put a charge in the truck battery. Food was purchased for the evening meal and everyone was excited, knowing that the end of the journey was just a few miles away.

When we were about twenty-two miles north of Anchorage, we saw an incredibly beautiful lake reflecting the mountain that almost touched the edge of the water. A man was in a field next to his home. We decided to stop and inquire about the area we were traveling through.

Mary and Kenny parked their truck alongside ours. Nancy was riding with them, and she was already out and heading for the lake. I slid from the seat of Dad's truck and started down the path following her. Nancy was yelling at me to hurry up. Suddenly, she stopped, let out an ear-piercing scream and started running toward me. I saw about twenty white geese squawking, their heads stretched forward and running toward us.

I turned and ran to the truck where Dad was standing, and only then did I turn to see if Nancy was behind me. I grabbed

Dad's arm and kept screaming as the geese came closer. I was terrified, watching them close in around me. I could see they were almost as tall as me when they stretched their necks. They pecked at my feet while I jumped around screaming and trying to escape them. Dad scooped Nancy and me up in his arms and put us in the truck.

The man walked toward us saying, "They thought you were going to feed them." It didn't make me feel any better as I wiped the tears streaming down my cheeks. When I felt better, I noticed Nancy had already recovered from the shock of being chased.

The man introduced himself as Reese Tatro and said he owned half the Mirror Lake acreage. The other side of the lake that bordered Bear Mountain was not available for homesteading. His wife, Gracie, came from the house when she heard all the commotion in the driveway.

Reese told Dad about an area located one mile south on the right side of the highway where a road had been built by the Army. The military used the area for cutting wood. They had surveyed and sectioned off 320 acres per section. There were metal section posts set in concrete on all four corners and one in the middle. The area was open for homesteading.

Reese and Gracie became our first neighbors. Dad was glad he stopped to talk to them. They gave us lots of information about the area and mentioned the neighbors living close by. There were a couple of roadhouses about three miles away. Everyone got their water from Peters Creek.

Turning on to the rough side road, branches scraped the sides of the trucks as we moved through the small growth of trees beginning to heighten since the last cutting. Dad and Kenny parked the trucks after driving a couple hundred yards down the bumpy road. We got out of the trucks and stood quietly looking over the land that would soon belong to us.

The land was flat and dry with Bear Mountain to the east. The trees were enormous with thick trunks. Dad said they were just the right size for building a cabin.

Dad knew he wanted to homestead the land. He knew this was the place that would make his dream a reality and expressed his thoughts to Mom. "I've always wanted to live in Alaska, and this piece of land is the opportunity I've been waiting for. I like the layout of the land, and I can visualize what it can become. What do you think about this area?"

Mom smiled at Dad and said, "I like it, too."

Dad gazed at the surrounding area. He turned to Nancy and me saying, "What do you think about it?"

We were always excited when he asked us what we thought, and Nancy and I always agreed with whatever he was asking us about. "Yes, let's get the land. Let's get the land," we chanted, jumping up and down with enthusiasm.

Mary and Kenny agreed that the land was suitable for the two cabins that had been planned for the property.

We ate the lunch that was packed at breakfast and began the drive to Anchorage. Only a few families lived in the area.

Fort Richardson is located north of Anchorage. The stretchers were returned before continuing into Anchorage.

In 1913 Anchorage came into its own as a tent city when work on the Alaska Railroad began. Anchorage got its name in 1914 due to its location on Cook Inlet, making it the perfect anchorage for incoming ships. A post office was built for the fast-growing town. The settlement grew and prospered in 1915 when land was surveyed and developed south of Ship Creek, and 887 lots were sold by the General Land Office to the highest bidders.

We arrived in Anchorage at three in the afternoon on July 9, 1947. Excitement was high as the trucks moved through the downtown area. It was the place Dad had envisioned for many years, and now it was a reality. It also was the end of a long journey; a journey finally fulfilled. As we drove down 4th Avenue, Mom and Dad smiled at each other, knowing what the other was thinking. They knew this "great land" would be their home for many years to come. The first stop was the post office for long-awaited letters from back home, and then to the land office to check on property for homesteads. The inquiry began with much frustration. The clerk said, "There is no land open for homesteads on that side of the road."

When Dad and Kenny got back into the trucks, they told us about their discussion with the clerk. "We didn't let that stop us from inquiring further. We asked to see the map of the area. The clerk brought it out and laid it on the counter and watched while Kenny and I studied it. The land is available for homesteading."

The final stop was the hospital to see the young men from Minnesota and get a report on their progress. On the next trip to Anchorage, there was another visit with the injured men at the hospital, and Mary had the occasion to see General Eisenhower, who happened to be visiting troops.

Time was also spent visiting with Dad's brother-in-law, Frank DeLoughery, who was in Anchorage. What a surprise that he happened to be in town on this particular day. He was getting supplies to take back to Seward, where he and his family lived.

It was a busy afternoon, and the evening visit with Frank was the highlight of the day. It was time to consider a place to spend the night, and it seemed to take forever to find a suitable location where the trucks could be parked. Everyone was exhausted, yet exhilarated, savoring the feelings that come at the end of a journey that took us 4,200 miles into the wilderness.

Drifting off to sleep, Dad thought about the trip over the highway. He had attained his long sought-after goal, and knew this was just the beginning of many more objectives that needed to be met. Finding land, building a home for his family, and becoming employed were foremost on his mind.

Mom knew she would be challenged every day. It would take fortitude, resilience, and persistence. She knew she possessed all of these qualities. She also had worked hard to make the trip to Alaska a reality and was glad to be here.

Because there were so many problems with the truck, Mom said that she and Dad would probably have given up and returned to Wisconsin without finishing the trip to Alaska if Mary and Kenny hadn't been with us.

Leonard and Bernadine Statz, Dad's sister and brother-in-law, standing by the barn. The first night of our trip was spent at their dairy farm. Aunt Bernadine insisted we sleep in the house because we had many nights ahead of us to sleep in the trailer Dad had bolted to the bed of the truck. She made a delicious breakfast in the morning and packed a lunch for us. I'm sure the lunch included her tasty poppy seed cake.

Photo courtesy of Bernadine Statz

The trucks parked in the yard. Leonard Statz holding Marjorie, Dad, and Kenny.
Photo courtesy of Mary Pilgrim

Mary, Mom, Darlene, Nancy, Kenny, and Dad having their picture taken at the farm before beginning the journey to Alaska.

Photo courtesy of Mary Pilgrim

Everyone gets their picture taken by Bernadine. (left to right: Dad, Nancy, Carol, Julie, Barbara (hidden), Bernie, Darlene, Leonard holding Marjorie, Henry (on the hood), Mary, and Kenny.

Photo courtesy of Mary Pilgrim

A bridge of this magnitude probably wasn't in Canada. We must have stopped while traveling through one of the states on the trip North.

The weekend break was at Petrified Wood Park in Lemmon, South Dakota, arriving early Saturday and staying through Sunday, washing clothes, cleaning, and organizing for the following week. There was always maintenance to be done on the trucks. Left to right Darlene, Mom, and Nancy.

Mary and Kenny Pilgrim beside one of the buildings in Petrified Wood Park, dressed to go to town for groceries and to the post office for stamps. Anxious relatives back home insisted they keep in touch with them while traveling the road through Canada that had just recently opened to civilian travelers.

Photo courtesy of Mary Pilgrim

Washing clothes was waiting for Mary on weekends. A small stool and blocks of wood brought the tubs to a manageable level, but still made it back-breaking work. A make-shift clothesline was attached to the travel home and tied to bushes, using poles to hold the line up. There was always the hope that the weekend would bring lots of sun and light breezes. In the lower right corner is the winch that was installed on Dad's truck. He was grateful for it when pulling the trucks out of mud holes along the unpaved road. The picture was taken at Beaver Creek, British Columbia, Canada.

Photo courtesy of Mary Pilgrim

In celebration of being in Alaska, we took time to fish near Tok. It was a short walk through the swamp to the wooden dock on a placid lake in the woods. An hour was spent relaxing with fishing line in the water, waiting for the bite that would signal fish for supper. Back on the road, we took off shoes and wrung out socks. Mom had the rifle to save us from bears.

The road over Sheep Mountain was narrow and treacherous, built against the mountainside and along the steep embankment with dangerous, sharp curves leading to the bottom. There is a hairpin curve leading to the bridge over Caribou Creek. Our trucks are barely visible in the pull-off area at the bottom of the hill.

Our midday meal was in the pull-off area at the bottom of Sheep Mountain. Our attention was focused on a Model A Ford traveling at breakneck speed down the mountain road. The car had lost its brakes, and the occupants inside could not maneuver the dangerous curve that stretched to the bridge. The truck struck the bridge and careened twenty-five feet into Caribou Creek. Inside the car were four young men from Minnesota. One man was seriously injured and the others had minor injuries. Mary had nursing experience, and with Mom's help they tended to the young men. Dad and Kenny drove to the communication center a few miles away to inform them of the accident. A helicopter was dispatched and later an ambulance arrived. The men spent several days at Providence Hospital in Anchorage.

3 Minnesota Youths Injured

Fourth Unhurt As Car Plunges Off Bridge

Three Minnesota youths were receiving treatment for injuries today in Providence hospital after their car crashed through a railing at Caribou creek bridge at Mile 106 on the Glenn highway yesterday.

The injured are: Kenneth Gaddis, 21, Fort Ripley, Minn.; Louie E. Hanson, 20, and Gerald R. Huff, 20, both of Staples, Minn. A fourth, Martin Kowalski, 19, also of Staples, was uninjured.

Gaddis received severe chest and knee injuries; Hanson is suffering from an injured head and hip; and Huff is receiving treatment for injuries to his back. Hospital attendants today said the three were "doing as well as could be expected."

Their Model A Ford had been driven all the way from Minnesota without trouble when the accident occurred just a little more than a 100 miles from their destination, Anchorage.

Crashing through the railing of the steel bridge, the car landed on its roof about 50 feet below the bridge in the creek. The impact was so terrific that the motor of the car was found about 40 feet away from the car.

Word was dispatched to the army at Fort Richardson and a helicopter, piloted by Lt. C. O. Weir, accompanied by Medical Officer Capt. William Northern arrived at the scene of the accident about an hour and a half later. The helicopter was able to land about 50 feet away from the crash.

First aid was given the men. Meanwhile an AT-7 had also been sent to check the progress and arrangements had been made to fly the injured men one at a time to Palmer where the AT-7 was to bring them to Anchorage. However, an ambulance, driven by Jim Phillips of Anchorage, arrived on the scene and the men were brought to Providence hospital.

Anchorage Times, July 9, 1947, courtesy Times Publishing Company, Inc.

Claiming the Land

Chugiak, 1947

Dad and Kenny were relieved that they had already filed on the land, and they felt positive that it would be approved. Kenny was a veteran of World War II and had special rights in connection with the public lands. He had given the land office a certified copy of his discharge papers, showing when he entered the service and when he was discharged. He filed on 160 acres for the sum of sixteen dollars. The description was S.W. 1/4 sec. 3, township 15, range 1W. Veterans applying for public land to be used for homesteading must live on the land for a period of seven months the first and also the second year and farm one-sixteenth of the land each year.

While waiting for the application to be approved, we took possession of the land through squatter's rights. Dad said, "We need to make the land a permanent residence."

"What does that mean?" Nancy asked.

"That means I'm going to unbolt the trailer from the bed of the truck and place it on wooden blocks on the ground."

"Can I help?" I asked.

"Sure. You and Nancy can watch the trailer and make sure it settles safe and sound on the blocks," he said, showing us where to stand so we wouldn't be in the way and could watch the trailer come down safely.

The application was approved several days later. Dad and Kenny were ready to begin clearing land. A decision had to be made quickly about the placement of the cabin. It was the middle of July and winter snow would be piling up in late September

UNITED STATES
DEPARTMENT OF THE INTERIOR
GENERAL LAND OFFICE
4—181
Form approved by Comptroller General, U. S.
November 22, 1939

RECEIPT N⁰ 3554459

DISTRICT LAND OFFICE, Anchorage, Alaska, July 11, 1947
(Date)

Received of Kenneth M. Pilgrim Gen. Del. Anchorage, Alaska
(Name) (Address)

in connection with Hd. oris. Sec. 2289 R. S. U. S. 011543
(Kind of application and act under which made; number and date of lease, etc.) (Serial number)

THE SUM OF Sixteen . . . . .00/100 DOLLARS
in cash or by U. S. Postal Money Order

and/or

THE SUM OF _____ DOLLARS

by _____, SUBJECT TO COLLECTION.*
(Indicate form of remittance—check, draft, etc.)

Filing fees on 160 acres	$10	00
Commissions at .0375 per acre	6	00
S.W. ¼ Sec. 3 Township 15 Range 1 W.		
Total,	$16	00

*When tender is by check, draft, or form other than cash or U. S. Postal Money Order, this receipt will not become an acquittance until collection is made.

This Receipt is evidence only of the receipt of the amount indicated, and must be issued at the time the remittance is received, without regard to the subsequent allowance or rejection of the application, entry, etc., due notice of which will be given.
In case of error in this Receipt, notify the Register where issued, and the Commissioner of the General Land Office, Washington, D. C.
In writing to the local land office or the General Land Office concerning the application or entry in connection with which this Receipt issued, always give the above Serial Number and the Receipt Number.

16—15013   U. S. GOVERNMENT PRINTING OFFICE

Circular No. 1588

UNITED STATES
DEPARTMENT OF THE INTERIOR
General Land Office
Washington

CODE OF FEDERAL REGULATIONS
TITLE 43 - PUBLIC LANDS: INTERIOR

PART 181 - PUBLIC LAND RIGHTS OF SOLDIERS AND SAILORS

SPECIAL RIGHTS OF VETERANS OF WORLD WAR II IN CONNECTION WITH THE PUBLIC LANDS

Sec.
181.36 Statutory authority.
181.37 Homestead entry by veteran; credit for military or naval service; computation of service
181.38 Homestead entry by widow, or minor orphan children, of veteran
181.39 Patent to minor orphan child, or children, on entry made by veteran or his widow
181.40 Preference right of application to veterans

AUTHORITY: Secs. 181.36 to 181.40, inclusive, issued under Act of September 27, 1944 (Public Law 434 - 78th Congress).

SPECIAL RIGHTS OF VETERANS OF WORLD WAR II IN CONNECTION WITH THE PUBLIC LANDS

Section 181.36 - Statutory authority. The Act of September 27, 1944 (Public Law 434 - 78th Congress), grants to veterans of World War II, certain benefits in connection with the public lands, in addition to those conferred by the Soldiers' and Sailors' Civil Relief Act of 1940, as amended (54 Stat. 1178, or early October. Plans started coming together in the evenings when there was time to relax.

Kenny and Dad would fell the large spruce on the property, hauling them the short distance to the cabin site. Within a few days construction on the log cabin began. The first cabin would be the home of Kenny and Mary. Mom, Dad, Nancy, and I would continue living in the trailer that was home for us traveling to Alaska.

The cabin would be approximately one hundred yards from the main road. A quarter mile of road was built farther into the property where a growth of larger spruce trees could be cut, limbed, and hauled to the building site. Dad and Kenny used a two-man cross-cut saw to drop the trees. The front of Dad's 4 x 4 truck had a winch that was used to haul the logs from the woods. They were pulled with a tow rope and stacked near the site chosen for the cabin. Dad built a boom on the truck to lift the logs into place.

A fire had passed through the area many years ago, and what was being cut were second-growth spruce trees. The winch could drag one or two logs at a time; it would take forty-five minutes. Since the logs were twenty-four feet long, Dad and Kenny decided the cabin would be twenty by twenty feet.

There would be two windows in the cabin. One window would give a view of Bear Mountain and the other a woodland scene. Most of the birch trees were left standing when space was cleared for the cabin. They would give protection from the elements of nature. The land was flat and drainage was not a problem. The cabin was away from the small hill that would later be chosen for the root cellar.

In the early morning or during the evening, Dad and Kenny hauled water from Peters Creek, located almost two miles from the homestead. Fifty-five-gallon drums with tops removed were filled almost daily. Most of the time filling water barrels was very tedious, but on one particular day all of that changed. They just happened to spot a large salmon swimming upstream. With a glint in their eyes and a smile on their faces, they dashed into the creek and grabbed the slippery fish with their bare hands, threw it up onto the rocks, and finished it off with a baseball bat. It weighed about thirty-two pounds and provided a tasty dinner. It also made for great supper conversation that evening.

A hole was dug in all four corners of the foundation and one at the intermediate point of each line. Cement was poured into each of them. A steel rod was placed into the middle of the hardening concrete. It extended two feet above the ground. An auger was used to bore a hole through the log. Then the first row of logs was pounded down onto the cement footing. All additional logs were notched and then spiked into place.

After working on the cabin for one week, Kenny and Mary decided that Alaska was not the place for them. They began making plans to leave on the first of August, but they would help with the hardest part of building the cabin. Now everyone worked diligently to get the logs hauled in, bark removed, and placed on the foundation.

We weren't going fishing as often, and I asked Dad why. He said, "We have to make hay while the sun shines." It seemed like the sun shone all the time. The daylight never ended during July. Mom covered the windows with blankets to keep the light from shining in at one o'clock in the morning. Dad worked until half past ten at night. He wanted to put the logs in place before Kenny and Mary left.

A decision had to be made about the acreage they were giving up. At the land office, Dad filed on eighty of the one hundred sixty acres. We would have to live on the property for fourteen months. Land would have to be cleared and five acres planted. Then the land could be purchased for $1.25 an acre. A man from the land office occasionally stopped by to check on our progress, and he was always very friendly and impressed with the changes on each visit.

August came quickly, and soon it was time to say good-bye. During the next few days, Dad helped Kenny get the camper on to the back of his truck and bolted down. There was a day in Anchorage to get all the supplies needed for the trip. The evening before their departure was spent reminiscing about the time Dad and Kenny hopped a train early in their teen years and spent a few months riding the rails. Nancy and I listened and laughed at their stories while eating popcorn.

Mom and Dad told them how much they had enjoyed their companionship as we drove from Wisconsin together and thanked them for all the help they had given us when our truck kept breaking down along the way. Since Nancy and I had taken turns riding with them on the trip, we thought of them as family. It was difficult to say good-bye. We cherished their friendship and appreciated all the help they had given us.

After Mary and Kenny left, we sat together for our evening meal and talked about our friendship with them and how they had helped us through the most difficult job of getting most of the logs into place. Mom spoke about how thankful she was that they shared those first two weeks with us. The log cabin was now our home, and it would take a lot of hard work to complete it.

Later that evening Mom talked about finishing the cabin before the first snowfall. "We will all have to work together to get the job done. You girls are very hard workers and can be very helpful."

Dad smiled at Nancy asking, "What do you think about that?"

"I can pound nails," Nancy said gleefully.

"What will you do, Darlene?" Dad asked, turning his attention to me.

"I don't know," I said, trying to think of something that would make them proud of me.

"Maybe you can collect the moss. That's a very important job," Mom suggested, smiling warmly at me.

Nancy and I did our share by gathering moss and stuffing it between the logs. We were always praised for our hard work. Mom looked pleased and regarded our loads of moss with lots of enthusiasm and big smiles. "Oh, girls! What a great job you're doing. Each box of moss is larger than the last." That made a big impression on us, and the box seemed to become heavier each time we returned with our load.

When we wore ourselves out, we spent time crawling up the logs and walking carefully across the last log put into place. Our antics always brought a concerned look from Mom.

When Mary and Kenny left, the logs were six high on the cabin. Mom helped Dad get the last rows of logs onto the cabin. She moved them into place as Dad lifted them with the boom and winch. We all helped peel the logs and gave a sigh of relief when it was finished.

The Athabascan village of Eklutna was located three miles north of our homestead. The Eklutna Industrial School was being torn down, and the contractor was selling wood and also giving some of the wood scraps to anyone who was willing to haul it from the property. Dad wanted the lumber for the roof. The windows had been removed and put up for sale. We had bought two of them earlier so the logs could be cut to the window size.

It was always fun to go to the village; sometimes we spent an hour there. Several of the buildings hadn't been torn down yet, and Nancy and I hurried from one building to the next, having great fun running up and down the stairs and exploring the empty rooms. We had the most fun when the kids from the village came out to play and explored the buildings with us.

When the cabin was ready for the roof boards, Mom joined Dad, pounding nails for hours. Dad let Nancy help, and she loved every minute, kneeling beside him gripping the hammer. Nancy and I helped by placing the boards against the cabin walls so that Dad could pull them up onto the roof. After the boards were nailed down, they were covered with rolled roofing that came in 100-square-foot rolls. The only time Mom and Dad came off the roof was to prepare meals. Nancy and I usually set the table and washed the dishes. We always got a big hug from Mom for our effort to help out.

It took six weeks to finish the cabin, and we were looking forward to moving in. There was one door, and it was always called "the front door." Dad said we would have a back door when he put an addition on to the cabin in a couple of years. The door was made with log slabs on the outside and plywood on the inside and a window. The doorknob was made from a crooked limb that Dad had found. After peeling and smoothing it, we all felt it had the perfect grip.

The porch ran the length of the cabin. It was used to stack wood for the barrel stove and the cookstove.

The floor was finished with what Dad called "V siding," a tongue and groove siding with a V notch used to finish the outside of houses. We learned very quickly that we could only sweep the floor in one direction. The dirt collected in the V of each board. On "deep cleaning" days, Nancy and I took turns sweeping each board individually, which was time consuming. The lumber came from the Army dump, and we made use of everything we found.

The first thing we bought was a wood-burning cookstove from Northern Commercial Company. We had been using the propane camp stove from the trailer. Now we were ready for a brand new large stove with an oven and a reservoir.

Cupboards were built on the wall next to the front door. On one of our many visits to the Fort Richardson dump, Dad found our heating stove. It was a fifty-five-gallon drum. He also found a metal furnace door. He cut out one end of the drum to fit the door. He bolted angle irons onto the barrel for the legs. A piece of flat metal was fastened to the top, and kettles used for heating water were placed on it. Sand was put into the bottom of the barrel to keep the heat from burning a hole through it. Sand was also used on the floor in case sparks escaped from the fire when the door was opened. Six-inch stove pipe was used for the chimney. Sometimes the barrel stove would get so hot, the stove pipe would turn bright red from the heat passing through it.

The wood box was built under the living room window. It had a cover on it with a twofold purpose: to hide the wood and double as a seating area. It was positioned between the barrel stove and the cookstove.

We moved in with several pieces of furniture that came to Alaska with us. The card table and four folding chairs were placed in the middle of the room. The singer sewing machine stood against the bedroom wall. Dad hung the framed, hand-painted velvet picture on the back wall. It depicted a peaceful scene of a campfire and tent beside a river. The oval mirror hung on the bedroom wall. Both the picture and the mirror were family heirlooms given to Mom. She remembered to bring everything needed to be comfortable in our new home: bedding, towels, cookware, and flat irons.

The battery-operated radio kept us up-to-date on world news. There were radio programs to listen to in the evening and music and fifteen-minute soap operas during the day.

The ice box was stored on the porch. The crosscut saw and ripsaw hung on the porch wall. The small tools found a place on the floor beneath the saws. My grandfather was a carpenter, and Dad had learned building skills from him. They had gathered up all the tools needed to get the job done.

Dad built a four-poster wooden bed frame for the bedroom. The mattress had been used in the trailer, and the wire mattress springs came from the dump. When Mom draped the spread over the bed, it became a warm and cozy room.

A small area was left in the corner of the back wall for the room Nancy and I shared. It was large enough to fit a dresser and the bunk beds from the dump. I slept on the top bunk because I was the oldest and Mom didn't have to worry about me falling. Some nights the cabin got extremely hot, making it difficult to sleep in the suffocating heat. Dad would get up and try to cool the glowing embers just enough so there would still be sparks in the morning to restart the fire.

We realized very quickly that there was no comfortable seating for relaxation. The folding chairs didn't relieve the stress or tension of the day. When Dad had some extra time, he built a double chair from lumber and birch poles. Mom said it was the most comfortable love seat she ever sat on, especially after making the throw pillows. She could ease into it and curl up with a good book. Mom read by the light from the kerosene lanterns on cold winter nights. There was no electricity in our area. Now she had all the comforts of home.

After we were settled in, Dad spread a foot of sawdust along the foundation of the house to keep the floor warm.

We woke every morning hearing Dad whistling happily. He was always excited to start the day. Mom hummed along with the music on the radio. They were content with life on the homestead. They claimed their land and, together, they built a home. They were ready to fulfill their Alaska dream.

Reese Tatro told Dad about the area that was open for homesteading, where the Army cut wood and had built a usable road. When Dad parked the truck and saw the land, it was the place he wanted to homestead. Mom snapped a picture of the driveway before we headed for Anchorage to file on the land.

After filing on the land and waiting for it to be approved, Dad and Kenny took possession of the land through squatter's rights. Kenny's camper was the first to be placed on wooden blocks on the ground.

The cabin was twenty by twenty feet and finished in six weeks. Darlene and Nancy log walking; Mary and Mom peeling the logs.

Nancy and Darlene standing on the front porch. We were given the job of collecting moss and tucking it snuggly between the large spaces of each log.

The winch on Dad's truck was used to pull logs from the growth of large spruce about a quarter of a mile farther into the property. The driveway was overtaken with tangled shrubs, giving the appearance that the Army hadn't cut trees in this area for many years.

We wanted our picture taken in the front yard during our first winter. Kindling stacked from the floor to the roof on the porch was ready for the cold winter days and nights ahead. The barrel that was used to catch rain water from the gutter can be seen between the two birch trees. The pile of wood on the snow was waiting for someone to store it on the porch.

Dad built the kitchen cupboards and painted them white. Mom purchased the white enamel wood-burning cook stove from Northern Commercial Company in Anchorage. Most of the dishes and cookware were packed and brought with us from Wisconsin. The fat lamb cookie jar on the top shelf was also from Northern Commercial, and it was continually filled with chocolate chip and oatmeal cookies.

Darlene, Nancy, and Mom sitting on the foot of sawdust along the foundation of the house. It was used as insulation to keep the floor warm.

Anchorage 011576

4—1043

Vol 77 Au 299

The United States of America,

To all to whom these presents shall come, Greeting:

JUN 12 1950

WHEREAS, a Certificate of the Land Office at Anchorage, Alaska, is now deposited in the Bureau of Land Management, whereby it appears that full payment has been made by John J. Stockhausen, according to the provisions of the Act of Congress of April 24, 1820, entitled "An Act making further provision for the sale of the Public Lands," and the acts supplemental thereto, for the following described land:

Seward Meridian, Alaska.

T. 15 N., R. 1 W.,

sec. 3, SE¼SW¼.

THE WELCOME

White birch trees guard
the forest, beckon him
with quivering limbs.

Green, slender ferns extend
and wave spidery wings
in delicate anticipation.

Black soil greets an open
hand, then spills quietly
in the bouyant wind.

He aspires,
reflects,
yearns.

In the forest, he finds his land.

A Dump of Treasures

1947

I like sitting beside Dad at the coffee shop watching him sip steamy coffee. His forehead wrinkles, and his eyes squint while it works its way down his throat. He always buys me a Coke, and I feel so grown up sitting beside him. Between swallows, he enjoys visiting with others who stop in for a neighborly chat.

Today they're talking about the Army dump. A neighbor is telling Dad about some of the things he finds there. "Last week I brought home brand new Army blankets, enough to keep my family warm through the winter. You ought to take some time and go look it over. The military discards lots of lumber every day that you can use to build your cabin."

Gosh, what fun to have all those blankets, I thought. I'd have a tent for myself and my doll, Molly. Nancy's tent could be close to mine, and we'd be neighbors and enjoy coffee together. I'd say, "Hi, Miss Nancy. Have you been to the dump today?" And she'd say, "Yes, my dear. I got these teacups there."

Through foggy thoughts of blankets and teacups, I hear Dad calling me. I turn to see him beckon me to join him at the door. I jump from the chair and run to him. "Can we go to the dump, Daddy?" I ask, while walking to the truck.

"The next time we're in Anchorage we'll stop by the dump and see if we can find something useful," he says, helping me into the truck.

The days pass slowly, and on Saturday Mom, Dad, Nancy, and I are finally on our way to Anchorage. During the first half hour of the trip, the conversation was about all the stuff we could find at the dump. "Can we go there first?" I beg, tapping on Dad's arm.

"Let's get our errands done first, and then we'll have lots of time to spend there on our way home."

Arriving at the dump, I'm excited. I waited so long to see what it looks like. Staring out the truck window at all the boxes and dirt and mess everywhere, I didn't see the teacups or the blankets for the tents. "What's here, Mama? Is this the dump?" I ask, surveying the long, low sloping mounds of boxes.

"Yes, sweetie, this is the dump everyone has been telling us about, and it's chock-full of unbelievable treasures. It's a stockpile of thrown-away clothes, food items, and lumber no longer needed by the military. It's a matter of looking through all this stuff that's thrown away to find what we can use. Look around and see if you can find a treasure that might be hiding in one of the boxes. Let's stay close together. Don't wander too far from me."

"How will we know when we find a treasure?" Nancy asks, looking at Mama for the answer.

She looks at us and smiles. "You'll know you found a treasure when you discover something of value hidden inside a box, something we can take home with us and use." Mama always made everything exciting.

I am ready to follow Nancy as we begin our journey over and between the heaping boxes that never seem to end, snooping inside some of them, hoping to find treasures. "This is a dump?" I ask, remembering what Mama said about this place. "Where's the blanket for my tent?"

"Maybe, it's in one of these boxes," she tells me, waving her hand wide over all the boxes.

I look over the length of the dump, thinking it went on forever and believing I'd never be able to walk from one end to the other. What if the blanket is at the other end or over the top and on the other side? The very thought of climbing the long slope to the top seems like a never-ending hike, staggering between the boxes. Stumbling over my feet several times makes me think it might be a good idea to just turn around and head back to the truck. Nancy was several steps ahead of me, trying to sweet-talk me to keep on going with the promise we'd reach the other end if we kept moving.

"Look! I made it," she yells, waving her arms from the top of the mound of dirt and boxes. She is six years old and a year younger than me, yet she moves lickety-split up the mountain of boxes while I groan and slowly worm my way along a narrow path. Nancy yells and waves to Mama, and just as I reach the top of the mountain I turn and, with great exhaustion, wave too.

"Be careful, girls. Don't go down the other side. Stay where I can see you," she hollers.

At the top, I can see for a thousand miles. I turn a full circle, flabbergasted to see boxes, lumber, chairs, and stuff everywhere. "I wonder which box my blanket is in. I'll never be able to make a tent if I can't find it. Will you help me look through the boxes?" I stare at Nancy while she takes her time deciding if she'll help or not.

"We'll start looking for it. Most of the boxes are open, so we won't have to stop while we look for other stuff," she says, gazing at the boxes around our feet.

From the top of the mound, we see soldiers pushing boxes from the back of trucks. Some leave while others take their place emptying another load of treasures. Soldiers yell to one another as trucks pass. They leave a trail of dust that fills the air. Several people move into the areas after the trucks pull away. The dust cloud doesn't seem to bother them.

"I hope I find the blanket for my tent before they do. Let's see if Mama will go with us to look at the stuff the soldiers just left."

Nancy glances up at me from the boxes she is walking around. "Just start looking. We'll work our way back to Mama."

There is no stopping us once we begin digging through everything within our grasp. Stumbling upon some paperback books, Nancy bends over for a closer look. "Wow! Look what I found. Daddy really likes cowboy books," Nancy calls out, grabbing an armful and heading back to Mama. "We found a treasure."

I had just reached the bottom of the mountain of boxes when my foot brushes against something soft, tripping me. I fall against Nancy, and the books fly from her arms. Even though I wasn't hurt, I cry out in pain while Nancy gathers the books into her arms and turns to leave. "Don't tell Mama about the books without me being there."

"You're not hurt. Get up or you won't be there when Mama sees the books," she says, moving toward the truck.

What I see, as I get up, sends screams into the air that could burst eardrums. Nancy turns, heading back toward me. "My tent! I found my tent," I scream, jumping up and down. "Oh, my gosh! There are three blankets for tents." I grab the unfolded blanket on the top, holding it up with both hands.

Mom turns toward us when she hears the scream, drops her armful of stuff, and begins running in our direction. "Are you okay?" she calls anxiously, looking for cuts and bruises.

"We're okay," Nancy yells. "Darlene found some blankets for her tent and I found these books. Did we find treasures, Mama?"

"You certainly did. Your father will be very pleased with the books, and I'm glad you girls found blankets for your tents."

"I found the tent, Mama," I tell her proudly, reminding both of them that I tripped over this marvelous find.

"Can I make a tent, too?" Nancy asks Mom.

"Yes, you can, and I know what I'll do with the third. I decided that if we ever found warm wool blankets, I would make snow pants for both of you. The wool will keep your legs extra warm while playing in the cold snow when winter comes. You both discovered wonderful treasures today."

When we get home we find the perfect place for the tents on the grassy area beside the clothesline. Dad cuts a branch from a scrawny tree and nails it between two birch trees. Nancy and I drape the blanket over the pole, and Dad finds spikes to anchor the corners as we quickly crawl inside with our dolls. We decide that one tent will be big enough for both of us and then scramble out to hug and thank Dad, and Nancy runs to get Mom so she can see the beautiful Army blanket tent.

On one of our many visits to the land of treasures, Mom meets another lady scrounging the dump. They visit and walk together, and soon Mom discovers the lady is a nonstop talker. Mom finds several boxes of long john underwear. The lady stops and begins rummaging in one of the boxes. Her face lights up, and she shouts, "Oh! Look! Do you know what you can do with these?"

Mom opens her mouth to speak, but the lady is already telling Mom what she can do with the underwear besides wear it. She picks up an undershirt in one hand and the long john bottoms in the other. And then she starts to rattle on, "You can dye them, cut them up, and make a rag rug. It will be beautiful when you dye them all different colors and crochet them into a colorful round rag rug. The one I made was huge and filled the whole living room. Yours can be that big, too." Then she went into great detail explaining how to make the rug.

I wonder what a rag rug might look like, but I don't care enough to stick around and find out. I see Nancy leaning over something several feet ahead of me and curiously charge forward to see what she's staring at. It's another book. "There's never any books for me to read. Why are they all for grown ups?"

"What's dye?" I ask Mom, while she's opening the package.

"It's stuff used to give color to this fabric. When we are all done mixing the fabric with the dye, we will have beautiful colored underwear. What color would you like to pour into the pot?" she asks, smiling at me.

I choose red and delight in watching the material change to red before my eyes.

It's Nancy's turn next to choose a color. Mom was right. When we had finished dyeing all the material, we had the most beautiful red, yellow, green and blue underwear hanging on the clothesline. Nancy and I sit on the step watching them blowing in the wind.

"Look! A rainbow on our clothesline," Nancy says.

In the evening while we listen to the radio, Mom begins cutting the material into long strips. She sews the pieces together and lets us help roll them into big balls of material. Feeling silly, Nancy and I have fun throwing them back and forth as we laugh and tumble around on the floor.

Finally, the day arrives when Mom takes her crochet hook from the sewing machine drawer. After we decide which color to begin with, she puts a red ball of fabric on her lap. She twirls the strip of cloth around her finger and the hook does something magical each time it sinks into the fabric.

One afternoon, Nancy and I ramble all over the dump trying to find something for ourselves. We stop to watch Army trucks roar along the outer skirts of the dump coming to an abrupt stop below us. Sitting down on a box, we watch soldiers pitch boxes from the truck, patiently hoping we would find a discovery worth waiting for.

"Maybe they're dumping gold, and we can buy new dresses for our dolls. I want the pink dress we saw at the store," Nancy says.

"No, it's going to be boxes of jewels, so we can decorate the tent," I tell her.

After what seems to be a very long time, the soldiers get into the truck and drive away. We wait until the truck is out of sight and spring into action, leaping forward with long strides to what we imagine will be gold and jewels.

What we see turns out to be the best find ever, even better than the three Army blankets I found, and lots better than the barrel Dad found to make the heating stove. It was even better than the long johns and western books.

"Oh my gosh! Berries! Millions of berries," Nancy shouts and covers her mouth with both hands while moving in for a closer look. Suddenly she is yelling and waving her arms above her head. "Mama. Come see what I found."

"I found them, too," I tell her. "Remember that when you tell Mama about the berries."

"Okay, okay," she answers, running toward Mom and Dad. "Hurry. Come see what we found."

They seem to be taking their sweet time examining all the boxes as they move along. Surely, they would move faster if they had an idea of the wonderful surprise we have for them. Nancy hurries over and squeezes between them, hanging on to both their jackets pulling them forward. When they are close, she runs ahead and points to the boxes. "Look, Mama. We found a treasure. We found berries."

"Oh, my goodness. You girls have definitely found a treasure. What beautiful strawberries."

Some of the boxes broke apart when they were flung from the Army truck. Other boxes are still in one piece. Dad inspects them, telling us we have eagle eyes to spot such a find. He picks up a couple of boxes and heads in the direction of the truck, wanting to move it closer so we won't have so far to carry the berries. When he returns, there are other people with him.

Everyone seems as excited as we are with the discovery. Walking beside Dad in the direction of the truck, I point at the others who are gathering by the berries, "Why do we have to share with them?"

"Because they share with us. Remember when Mr. Tatro gave us the bag of potatoes from his garden? And how about the time the lady, we didn't even know, told us where to find the crates of canned food. It makes sense to return an act of kindness. Neighbors always help each other. We live way out in the country, and we depend on the few neighbors we have near us to help in times of need, and they depend on our help when they need it."

On our arrival home, we busily stack boxes of berries on the porch. Mom put lots of berries into a big bowl, sprinkling sugar over them and dividing them up into individual bowls. Dad finds the canned milk, and we take turns pouring it over the ripe, red berries.

The next morning Nancy and I wake to the smell of strawberries cooking on the wood stove. Hurrying out of bed, we find Mom's first batch of jam is already cooling on the table. She spreads warm jam on homemade bread for us to enjoy.

Nancy and I help make a berry pie. I press the dough in the pan, and Nancy spoons the berries into it. Mom puts another crust over the top, and we take turns pressing the edges together. After the pie is in the oven, we clean more berries, and by the end of the day, the table is covered with jars of jam that we will enjoy throughout the winter. Mom wraps ribbons around several jars and gives them to a neighbor who wasn't at the dump when we discovered the mouth-watering berries.

Mom works on her rug whenever she has time, and it finally grows so big that she has to spread it on the floor under the table and chairs. We all help straighten it and stand back staring at the beauty of it. From then on, Mom sits on the floor using the crochet hook to make the rug grow. One evening she asks, "Do you think the rug is large enough?"

Reading the book he found during our first trip to the dump, Dad looks up and leans forward to take a quick look at the circular rag rug that has been growing with each passing day. "It looks finished. What do you think, girls?"

"Let's make it as big as the whole room," Nancy stretches her arms to help us see how big that might be.

"It sure grew big," I run my hand over the bumpy texture of the rug. "Now the rainbow is on the floor, and it looks beautiful."

After much discussion, we all agree the beautiful rag rug is done, and it brightens up the whole cabin.

"Let's sit on it and have a tea party," Nancy suggests.

"I'll get the strawberry muffins," Mom says.

"Will you make a rug for my tent?" I ask her.

The military's waste provides us with lumber, food, clothing, and lots of odds-and-ends making our life on the homestead comfortable. We return to the dump many times over the next few years until it closes to the public in the early 1950s. Dad often chuckles saying, "Thank you, U. S. Army." We didn't know how great we had it.

Nancy and Darlene put up their Army blanket tent every summer and played inside with their paper dolls. They told each other stories about an imagined beautiful young girl who lived a fantasy life beyond belief.

Mom made beautiful rag rugs from new long johns found at the Army dump. She cut them into strips and dyed them. When she finished crocheting the small rug, it turned out to be as huge as the larger one.

Orphan Bear
1947

Standing motionless, my hands slowly moved upward to cover the whispering gleefulness that had begun to escape my lips. I gazed in delight at the two cuddly black bears nestled together under a huge birch tree. There was an instantaneous meeting of our eyes. One of the bears sprang forward, surprising me. My hand flew from my mouth and my screams pierced the air as I jumped backward. Suddenly, the bear was toppling to the ground, rolling and twisting to recover its footing, gasping and coughing from the tightened rope knotted securely around its neck.

Stumbling backwards, I fell against Nancy and we both tumbled to the ground. The bears pulled hard on the ropes, trying to reach us. "Oh!" I shrieked, untangling myself from Nancy and pulling on her sweater, tugging us farther from the bears.

Dad ran up and lifted both of us to a standing position. "You girls are lucky that the bears are tied up," he said. "Otherwise, they would've been on top of you."

"Daddy, they tried to eat me," I blurted out, shaking as I clung to him.

"Is that true, Daddy? Do they want to eat us?" Nancy asked.

"No, I think because they're cubs, they would rather play with you. Now, if they were grown-up bears, then you would have a reason to be scared."

"What are cubs?" Nancy asked, staring at the two bears.

"They're baby bears. These two look like they were born only a couple of months ago, but it won't take long for them to grow up," he said, walking toward the bears.

Nancy and I clung to each other as Dad moved toward the black, furry bears. They continued to pull against the ropes, and they made growling sounds as he moved into their territory. They jumped on him and sniffed his clothing, finally settling down to let Dad touch them. He turned toward us and asked, "Do you want to pet them?"

With a bit of coaxing from Dad, Nancy was finally convinced the bears wanted to be friends. Even though she was six, and a year younger than me, I always felt she was the stronger. She was always willing to be the first to try something new, while I tended to hold back.

Dad held the bears as Nancy inched toward them, her hands behind her back. They were making strange grunting sounds as she moved closer. I was afraid they might leap on her. When she felt brave enough, she lowered her hand so it was just touching the black fur of the bear closest to her. It rolled over onto its back to have its stomach rubbed. Nancy giggled as she bent over to touch one of the paws. "Come on, Darlene. They want to play. They won't hurt you."

I eyed the scene with uncertainty and then moved forward. The bears were rolling around in the dry dirt, and they sprang up as I shuffled towards them. Dad grabbed the rope as one of the bears jumped forward. I backed up, letting out an earsplitting scream, startling the bears and causing them to stiffen like statues.

"Don't scare the bears. They just want to play with us," Nancy scolded. "Come on, they won't hurt you. See, they let me touch them."

I moved forward again as one of the bears came up to me. Dad held the rope tight, not letting the cub leap and frighten me again. I found myself between the two bears, and all the dust being kicked up caused uncontrollable sneezing. When I felt safe with the bears and knew they wouldn't hurt me, I asked, "Where did they come from?"

Dad told us the bears were captured by a man who lived a mile from our home. He said the mother bear wandered into his yard, tipping the garbage barrel and rummaging through the trash. He shot it, and a short time later the two cubs came out of the woods. He coaxed them near and tied them to a tree in the yard. Dad had seen them earlier when he stopped to visit. Later in the day, he took us to see the cuddly baby bears.

The next day, Nancy and I walked the mile to visit the bears. Whenever we were out walking, we always sang one of our favorite songs or took turns telling an imaginary story to one another. On this day, we talked about seeing the bears again and picked berries for them to eat. We decided to name them Moe and Blackie.

I remembered the day before and all the dust they kicked up. I had given my clothes a good hand-brushing afterwards and could still smell the dust and feel it in my hair after I got home. Dad told us not to go near the bears when we visited them by ourselves, so we watched them come toward us until their ropes were stretched. We threw the berries at their bowls and laughed as they scrambled for the tasty treats. Not wanting to get dirty and be sprinkled with powdery dust again, I moved backward several steps to watch them play with each other.

Just about every day we visited the bears. They seemed to enjoy us as much as we did them. The one thing they wouldn't put up with was being petted on the top of the head. They would snap at us. We learned quickly to let them take the lead and tumble, roll, and leap at each other. It was fun watching them stand on their hind legs and snort like pigs. I always came away sneezing and full of dust. Nancy never seemed to worry about being dusty and never took time to brush herself off.

One afternoon we hurried to see our new friends. When we arrived to play, the bears were nowhere in sight—only the ropes. The man who had captured the bears told us that one of them climbed the tree and somehow hung itself, and the other one gained its freedom when it slipped its head from the rope. We lost our friends!

Tears formed in Nancy's eyes. She turned and started for home. "Wait for me. Wait for me," I called, catching up to her.

My heart broke. No more bears to play with. Mom held us, and Dad tried cheering us up, but nothing seemed to help. The bears were gone forever. "I want my bears back," I sobbed. That night I dreamt about them, and I told Nancy about it when I woke. I spent the morning telling my doll Molly what had happened and somehow it made me feel a little better.

After lunch Nancy and I were playing tag, running wildly around the yard. Suddenly, we stopped as we came face to face with a cub bear. We were startled at first, and so was the bear. We stared at it, and the bear peered back. There was total silence for a few seconds until Nancy clutched my arm. "Our bear," she gasped, running toward it.

Such joy! Such a reunion! We played for awhile then coaxed the bear toward the trailer. "Come on, Moe," Nancy called out, as the bear followed along behind her.

"How do you know it's Moe?" I asked. "It might be Blackie."

"No, it's Moe. He has the brownest nose."

"Yeah, it is him," I agreed. "Let's tell Mama."

"Mama! Mama!" Nancy shouted, frolicking with Moe.

Mom was terrified at seeing Nancy romping around with a bear. "Girls! Girls!" she screamed, "Get away from that bear!"

"But, its our bear, Mama. It's Moe. Don't you recognize him?" Nancy asked, running around Moe.

Suddenly, Mom was yelling for Dad. He ran from the cabin he was building a short distance from the trailer. He stopped short as he came face to face with Nancy hugging the bear.

Look, Daddy, it's Moe!" I shouted, pointing in the direction of the bear, the dust, and Nancy, giggling and romping around in the midst of it all.

"You're right. It sure is." The bear recognized Dad's voice and ambled toward him.

"Can we keep Moe, please, please?" Nancy begged.

"We need to think about what is best for the bear. If we keep it, we ruin its chance of living on its own in the wild," Dad explained. "It will grow to trust people, and one day it will walk toward someone who doesn't know it's a tame bear. No, girls, we can't keep it. It's the only choice we have."

We continued to beg, but our begging fell on deaf ears. When Dad's answer was always no, we pleaded with Mom to let us keep Moe for our very own. "You heard what your father told you about the bear, and he's right. It's a wild animal and needs to learn to take care of itself in the wilderness, away from people."

Moe came to play almost every day. We ran to meet him with open arms, petting his wiry, black fur. He was welcomed with open arms. We loved him more than all our dolls and teddy bears. At night, he went to a secret place we never knew about.

There were days when we caught sight of Mom and Dad watching from the cabin they were building, probably not sure what to do about the friendship that was growing between two girls and a bear named Moe.

As summer days slipped by, Moe grew more cautious. He didn't wander into the yard every day, and when he did, he'd back away as we moved toward him. I didn't understand why he didn't want to be near us anymore. He seemed to be afraid of us. "Come on, Moe," I'd beckon. "We won't hurt you." No amount of coaxing could bring him close enough to touch. I just wanted Moe to play with me. But he never played again. Now, when Moe came into the yard, he immediately climbed a tree and stayed at a distance.

Dad tried again to explain about the wildness within the bear that kept him at arm's length, but I didn't want to understand. "Bears are normally afraid of people unless they are around them as young cubs. As the bear grows, there's a frightening side to it. There's the danger of a deadly encounter. You never know if the bear will attack or walk away. Moe is old enough now to feel that wildness within himself."

Dad would always try to make Moe's visits enjoyable for us. He cut a skinny birch tree and trimmed the branches from it. Mom would put honey on a piece of bread, attach it to the scrawny, limbless tree, and the treat was lifted into the branches where Moe situated himself. It was such fun to watch him grab the honey bread with his paw and mouth at the same time. He had the longest tongue, making us laugh as we watched him wash his face. Then he would wait for us to move away from the tree before climbing down and slowly walking away. He would turn back to look from the edge of the woods. I wondered if Moe knew he was a mean, vicious bear. Maybe that's why he didn't want to play anymore. I wanted to run to him and wrap my arms around his big neck.

Toward the end of summer, we only saw Moe occasionally. Usually, we would see him watching us from far across the yard. When Moe visited in the morning, we'd yell, "Hi, Moe!" He'd gaze at us almost as if he were longing for those fun days when he'd stroll from the woods to meet us. Instead, he'd amble back into the dense underbrush turning one last time to look back.

One day in September I was by myself in the log cabin. It was almost finished. The roof was on and the windows and door would be in place soon. It was fun to play and pretend that my dolls and I lived there. I would make believe there was a door by putting a box in the doorway. Seated on the floor with my back to the doorway, I talked to my doll Molly. "Your yellow braids are a mess," I told her, loosening the blue ribbons around them. I heard the noise of the box being pushed from the door and was glad that Nancy had changed her mind and decided to come and play.

"Did you bring your doll?" I asked, turning toward the door. Moe loomed in the doorway, his massive body filling the lower half of it. Neither of us moved or seemed to know what to do. I hadn't seen him for awhile. He was huge. He barely fit through the opening. His wiry, black hair brushed the sides of the door. I didn't remember him being so big. Frozen on the floor, I stared into his black marble eyes and hugged Molly against my chest. It scared me to see him so close. I stood up, my doll fell from my grasp and tumbled by my feet. I inched toward the cupboards, eyeing Moe with each tiny step. He stopped just inside the doorway, his head turning slowly studying me. I climbed onto the counter. Sitting on my knees, I was higher than Moe. I was terrified and too afraid to talk to him like I would have done earlier in the summer. We continued to stare at one another. Moe's head turned upward, sniffing the air. He looked at me again, then managed to turn his massive body around and walk out the door as quietly as he had come in. Jumping from the counter, I ran to the doorway, watching him disappear into the woods.

Moe's visits finally stopped. Mom said it was time for Moe to go into hibernation. We thought about the fun we would have with him next summer. What a grand reunion it would be. We learned several weeks later that our reunion was a dream that would never come true. A friend of Dad's stopped by and told him that a neighbor, who lived a few miles from us, had shot a black bear that wandered into his yard. "It was the darnedest thing," the man said. "The bear didn't seem to be the least bit afraid of people. Came right up on the front porch looking for a handout."

"It can't be true. I won't believe it," I sobbed.

"I'm so sorry about Moe," Mom said, holding me tight.

"He's my Moe."

"I know he was, and he'll always be your pet bear."

"I took care of him all summer."

"And you did a very good job of caring for him."

"I want him back. I don't want him to be dead. I already made plans for next summer when we'll play together again."

"I know you did," she said, using her finger to wipe the tear rolling down my cheek.

"Why did he have to die?"

"You knew Moe as a friendly bear that liked to visit. Our neighbors couldn't tell Moe from other wild bears. It was a terrible mistake."

"Is Moe in heaven?" Nancy asked, looking into Mom's teary blue eyes.

"Yes, I suppose he is," she said holding her tight in her arms.

"Is Blackie there with him?"

"Yes."

"Are they happy to see each other?" she asked, tears flooding her eyes.

"Yes, they're happy."

Mom held Nancy and me in her arms saying, "You will always have memories of an orphaned bear who found two little girls who loved him very much."

Our family mourned Moe's death. I never felt such sadness. For a long time, I would glance toward the woods with the hope of catching a glimpse of Moe looking for me. I didn't want to believe it was Moe that had been shot. Maybe it had been another bear, but somehow I knew I would never see him again.

Dad feeding berries to our soon-to-be pet bear. Moe and his twin were orphaned when a neighbor shot the sow, not realizing there were cubs close-by.

Quiet Encounter

Seated on the floor
of the almost finished cabin,
I visit with my doll, Molly.
"Your braids are a mess," I tell her,
loosening blue ribbons, combing
fingers through yellow yarn.

Hearing a noise from the doorway,
I'm glad Nancy has come to play.
"Did you bring your doll?"
There's no response.
"Don't try to sneak up.
I know it's you."

Turning, I see the massive
awkward body of wiry, black hair
brush the doorway, pushing through it.
Grating claws announce his arrival.
He's bigger—no longer the cub
I played with.

Frozen on the floor, I stare
into black marble eyes, Molly falls
from my grasp tumbling at my feet.
Inching toward the cupboards eyeing
him with each quivering step,
I climb upward.

He stops once inside, head
turning slowly, studying me.
Sitting on bended knees, I'm too
terrified to speak as I might have
earlier, while frolicking on
a cool sunlit afternoon.

Staring at one another, his neck
strains upward sniffing the air,
glancing at me for one final moment.
Turning the giant bristly body, he
slowly lumbers out the door
as quietly as he came in.

Jumping from the counter,
slowly tiptoeing to the doorway,
I watch him disappear into the woods.
Snatching Molly's pale, faint body,
I hurry, eager to tell of my bravery
in the face of danger.

A quiet visit with Moe,
the bear I frolicked with through
an amazing Alaska summer.

Springy Branches

1947

It snowed all night and let up late in the morning. The sky was completely covered with gray clouds that looked like they could dump another wet mess on us. It was just as dark in the morning as it was the day before when it started snowing late in the afternoon. Even the snow took on a gray tinge.

It was nine o'clock in the morning, and the kerosene lamps were casting shadows throughout the cabin. One lamp hung from a beam over the area where Mom cooked, and the other was always on or hung above the kitchen table. The coals in the barrel stove were bright red when Dad threw two more birch logs on the fire just before breakfast. I always woke to the sound of wood crackling, popping, and hissing and Dad whistling.

I ate breakfast in a hurry. Mom liked it when we all sat down together and enjoyed the food she set in front of us, but I wasn't in the mood this morning to talk. I excused myself, moved toward the door, tugged my snow pants from one of the hooks nailed to the wall, pulling them on and buttoning the waistband. Mom made my snow pants from an Army blanket I found when we visited the Army dump for the first time last summer. They were actually warmer than the store-bought pants I had outgrown. She said they were made from wool, and that's why I stayed so warm on a cold day.

"What's your hurry, Darlene? Come back and finish your toast," Mom said, sipping coffee.

"We don't have time. Come on, Daddy. Let's go."

Nancy and I had spent several mornings tromping through the woods looking for a Christmas tree. We had found one near the path that led to the rabbit snares Dad had set. This was the morning we were going to take him to the spot where we'd discovered the perfect tree.

Nancy was still chewing her toast as she put on her snow pants. I finished buttoning my coat and went over to the table for my toast. "Can I take it outside with me?"

"Yes, but don't run while you're eating."

Once outside, I turned in the direction of the fifty-five-gallon steel rain barrel to see how much snow had collected in it. It was already half full of frozen water. Last night's snowfall added several inches, filling it almost to the top. Stuffing the toast into my mouth, I reached into the barrel, grabbed a handful of wet snow, and shaped it into a ball of ice.

Dad found the barrel on one of our many trips to the dump. It seemed like just about everything we had was from there. At the time, I had asked him what he wanted it for, and he said, "I'm sure we'll find a use for it." He was right. When we got home, he pulled it from the bed of the truck and set it a few feet from the front step.

When I questioned why he put it there, he pointed to the roof and said, "See that rain gutter I put along the edge? The rain from the roof will flow along it and spill into the barrel. We won't have to make so many trips to Peters Creek for our water."

I bit into the frosty ball. It was icy cold and nearly froze my teeth. Jumping around and shaking my hands frantically, I could finally swallow the cold slush as it dissolved into warm liquid. I dropped the ice ball and kicked it hard with my foot. It rolled over several times collecting more snow. I bent, pushing it with my hands until it was just about the right size for the bottom of a snowman.

I heard the door open and close behind me. I turned just in time to jump out of the way as Nancy leaped over the stairs like a torpedo and landed on top of the snowball, smashing it. She fell sideways, toppling into the snow. "That's what you get for smashing it," I snapped.

"Wow! This is perfect for a snowman!" Nancy lifted herself to her knees, scooping snow with both hands. We rolled two huge balls and placed one on top of the other.

While rolling the head of our snowman, Dad came from the cabin. "Are you girls ready to get the tree?" he asked, putting on his hat. He paused for a moment before he walked down the two steps and grabbed the shovel to clear a path.

"My mittens are wet," Nancy grumbled, heading for the door.

Mom brought out a pair of red mittens for Nancy and blue ones for me, and we traded our wet ones for the dry. She kissed us both on the cheek saying, "You be careful, both of you. Stay close to your father." With a wave and a promise to do as she said, we were off in the direction of the beautiful tree.

We seldom walked the trap line with Dad. Nancy and I were scared of the moose that sometimes wandered across the path. We always saw tracks, but only once did we see a moose nearby nibbling at a tree branch. I remember startling it, and I almost knocked Nancy down while moving backward and bumping her. The moose took off in the other direction. Dad said the moose was more afraid of us than we were of it. After that we did a lot of talking as we walked and rarely ventured onto the path without Dad.

The spruce trees had a heavy layer of wet snow weighing down their branches. It was hard to find the one Nancy and I had picked out. Every now and again a chunk of snow would fall from one of the branches, and it would spring upward, relieved of its load. It always fascinated me to watch as the rest of the branches tried to dump their heavy loads from the vibration of just one branch.

About four inches of soggy snow covered the path. Nancy was ahead of Dad, and I was last in line. The path she was breaking was narrow, and I was getting tired as I pushed through the heavy snow cover. I kept stepping in the deeper snow along the edge of the trail.

I tried hard to keep my balance and walk in their footprints. My boots filled with snow, and I stopped to scoop it from the tops of them. "Stop! Wait for me," I yelled, while Dad and Nancy continued walking, but at a slower pace. "Didn't you hear me? I need to stop!"

They came to a standstill and waited impatiently, eager to be on the move again. The snow wasn't too deep, so there was no need for snowshoes. Dad wouldn't take us with him when he had to break a trail. The snowshoes were too big for us, and we'd continually pitch sideways and sink.

Just ahead of us, Nancy saw the spruce tree we had picked out the day before. "There it is, Daddy," she shouted, pointing at the tall spruce surrounded by smaller ones just off the path.

"That's a mighty big tree. That one won't fit in our cabin, but I bet the one right next to it would fit just fine."

"It's really small," Nancy concluded.

"It's actually about six feet tall. It just looks small next to the other trees."

"It doesn't have very nice branches. I don't think that's the one I want. Our tree has to be perfect. Don't you think so?"

"I guess you're right. We'll keep looking."

We moved slowly along the path, eyeing all the spruce trees. There seemed to be something wrong with each one: too tall, too small, not enough branches, a broken top. The perfect tree was nowhere to be found, especially with all the mounds of snow covering them.

Dad checked each rabbit snare as we passed it. He'd stop and make sure it was set properly, and we'd continue on to the next. When we reached the end of the snare line, not a single rabbit was caught in the shiny pieces of wire. "The rabbits are sure smart today, aren't they?" I said, turning toward Dad to see his reaction concerning the empty snares.

"They sure are. Unlike us, they stayed in their burrows today," he remarked, kneeling to observe the area around the snare.

I was glad. I secretly hoped the rabbits would find another place to run. I remember being quite interested in the whole process of capturing rabbits. It brought back to mind the evening Dad was seated at the table, tinkering with a spool of wire, shaping pieces of it into circles. Leaving my paper dolls spread out on the floor where Nancy and I were playing, I walked to the table, put my knees on the chair, and leaned my elbows on the table intent on seeing what Dad was doing. "What are you making?" I inquired, resting my chin in the palm of my hand.

"A snare."

"What's a snare?"

"It's used to trap rabbits."

Now I was really interested. I lay across the table to get a closer look. "Can we bring the rabbits home and play with them?"

Dad didn't answer right away. He moved the kerosene lantern closer to add more light to his work. He looked up at me and said, "Remember when we talked about living off the land? We hunt and trap for our food."

"Can I make a snare? Where are you going to put them?" I asked, not wanting to hear any more about eating rabbits.

"Come on over here, and I'll show you how to make one. What's nice about this kind of snare is that it doesn't need to be concealed."

"What does conceal mean?" I asked, pushing myself from the table and scooting around it.

"It means to hide. I don't have to hide the snares. All I need is a springy branch to hang the wire from. I set them along the rabbit runs."

That night I learned about rabbit runs, made a snare, and went with Dad the next day to set it. The first time I saw a dead rabbit caught in one of the snares, I was glad it wasn't the one I made and helped to fasten to a springy branch along the path. "Daddy, can I take the snare I made off the branch and throw it away? I don't want to catch rabbits anymore."

"You can do whatever you want with your snare," he said, gently putting his hand on my shoulder.

When he cut my snare from the tree, I was relieved to see the branch spring upward, released from its burden. When we got home that day, I threw it in the garbage barrel, glad to be rid of it, knowing I had saved hundreds of rabbits.

I was in the lead as we turned and began walking back along the path. Nancy pushed in front of me. I glared at her, but let her go first. I usually got to be first in line on the way back. I acted like I cared, but I didn't want to be first today. It was easier walking in the back and letting her continue to break trail.

We concentrated on the task of finding a tree, stopping several times to inspect those that looked like they might be the one we were in search of.

Dad pointed toward a clump of trees about fifty feet off the path. "I see the tree we're looking for. It's right over there. It's the small tree between the two larger ones."

We stepped from the lightly packed snow on the path into deeper, wet snow that led to the trees. Dad broke a trail, and

Nancy and I tracked along behind him. I didn't let the cold snow that was melting in my boots bother me. I was too excited about the possibility of actually finding our special tree.

Walking around the tree, we were surprised and happy to find it had lots of branches. "What do you think, girls? Can you picture this tree all decorated? There's a small spot right there that looks pretty bare. I can drill some holes, add some extra branches, and fix that."

"Is it too tall?" Nancy asked, staring at Dad.

"Nope, it's just about the right size."

"Then let's cut it down and take it home," I added. The snow was beginning to burn my ankles. I was anxious to get home and empty my boots.

"Step back, girls," Dad warned, lifting the ax and hitting it against the tree trunk to release the huge mounds of snow. As the branches sprang upwards, he turned to avoid the plunging snow, but not before some of it collected on his collar and worked its way around his neck before it slid down his back. He let out a holler that would scare away any moose in the area and pulled off his coat to wipe away the snow around his neck.

Nancy and I laughed so hard that we ended up sprawled in the snow. It worked its way up my jacket sleeves. It felt like fire scorching my wrists. I wasn't laughing anymore. Now I was frantically attempting to remove mittens so I could wipe away the snow.

There were several black ravens perched in the trees near us. Suddenly, there was a tremendous uproar of flapping wings and strange cawing noises when Dad took the ax and chopped at the tree until it fell. He grabbed it by the trunk, pulled it to the path where he dropped it, and tied a rope around the trunk of the tree to make it easier to pull.

Dad held my arm while I stood, removed my boots, and shook the snow from them. With boots cleaned out and a few minutes to rest, we were ready to take our tree home. We took turns pulling it. When we finally got home, Dad stood the tree up, shook the snow from it, and leaned it against the house.

"Mama, come see our tree," Nancy yelled, stepping onto the porch.

Mom opened the door and stepped out wiping her hands on her apron.

"Hurry, Mama, hurry," Nancy urged, jumping off the porch. "Do you like it?"

"You picked out a beautiful tree," Mom said, giving her approval. "Hold the tree up, John, so I can get a better look at it."

Dad grabbed the tree from its spot against the house, stood it up, and shook it. The branches moved as if they were shivering.

Nancy, Mom, and Queenie posing by our first Christmas tree from the nearby woods. Dad drilled holes into the trunk and added extra branches, giving it a full and springy bounce when the tree was lifted for a final approval before taking it into the cabin.

CHRISTMAS BREW

1947

Dad opened the door, pushing it inward as he backed into the cabin with his arms wrapped around a five-gallon oak barrel. He set it down and closed the door.

"Is that the barrel you got at the dump? Is that the one we're going to make the home brew in?" I asked, pointing at the barrel he brought in the house.

"That's the one," he told me, taking his boots off by the door and hanging his coat on the hook.

"Can we make root beer first?" I asked, sitting on the barrel, letting my feet roll it back and forth over the floor boards.

"Let's do that first. We all like root beer," he answered.

"Yeah," Nancy said, running to the cupboard and pulling the root beer extract from inside. "Let's make it now," she begged, handing it to Mom.

"The bottles need to be sterilized," Mom told her. "Remember when we found them at the dump during the summer? They weren't clean then, and they gathered more dust in the box outside."

Making the root beer was exciting, and it didn't take very long. Mom used water, the wonderful smelling root beer extract, and some yeast.

Nancy breathed in the mouth-watering aroma. "It smells so good. I can't wait to taste it. When will it be ready?"

"It has to set for a couple of hours," Mom said, covering it with a cloth. "We'll try some of it when it cools."

After it cooled, we all had a glass of the delicious drink before Dad placed the caps on the bottles. I helped Mom wipe them off, and Nancy placed the bottles on their sides on the shelf. They stayed that way for five days, and then they were set upright for another five days.

Dad said, "Making beer is more complicated than making root beer. It takes planning to produce a brew that knocks the socks off of those who drink it." He made the yeast starter several days earlier, saying he wanted a strong fermentation. I didn't know what he was talking about, but I listened anyway, because he enjoyed telling me about his beer. I decided that words like "fining" and "clarify" made the beer better tasting.

He put the biggest pot we owned on the wood stove and said, "Beer needs to boil to be successful. I need to get rid of the germs in the pot before I put in the yeast."

Dad added the malt extract and let me pour the sugar. At first it smelled rather nice, but later Mom had to open the door when the horrible smell of yeast filled the cabin.

Once the beer went from the pot to the barrel, it was left to ferment for a few days. Each day Dad would check the beer. "Why are you always, looking at the beer?" I asked.

"I check to see if it's still foamy. When all I see is beer and no more bubbly foam, I can bottle it."

He had a small record book that he kept notes in about his beer. Every time he looked at the beer, he would take a hydrometer reading and write something important about it in his notebook. I liked looking at the scribbles on the pages. I knew they were important, so after I sneaked a look without him knowing about it, I always made sure to put the notebook back in the same place I found it.

I learned a lot about making beer. Dad told me there were some important things to remember: "I need to have patience," he said, "because I want this to be a tasty batch of home brew. The bubbles mix all the ingredients into a tasty flavor. I can't bottle it just when I want to. The beer lets me in on the secret of when it's full of flavor and ready to be bottled."

"How does the beer do that?" I asked, snooping further into the secrecy of making beer.

Dad lifted the cover from the beer barrel. "See all the bubbles? Listen, and you'll hear them making all sorts of different sounds. The larger bubbles make a louder popping sound than the smaller ones. They seem to have their own secret code to tell me when the mixture is done. The beer says things that only the experienced beer maker can understand."

"What kind of things? Does it really tell you stuff?"

"All the bubbling sounds let me know that the beer needs more time to develop a strong zesty flavor. When it's done and I take the first swallow, I want to say, 'Ahhh, now that's a great tasting beer.' The next time I take the cover off there will be fewer sudsy bubbles. Then one day, I'll look into the barrel and won't see anymore bubbles making noise on top of the beer. Then I'll know it's time to take that first sip, and then I can bottle and cap it."

Finally, when the time came to bottle the beer, Mom helped Dad set the barrel on the table. He took two chairs and placed them a few feet apart and put a board across them to set his quart bottles on. He placed the lantern next to the barrel for better lighting and took one last reading.

Dad took a hose and put one end into the barrel and grabbed the other end with his right hand, bending the hose tight between his fingers. I watched as he lowered to his knees and put the hose into his mouth. I leaned closer, not wanting to miss whatever it was he was about to do. I watched as he sucked beer into his

85

mouth. Suddenly his cheeks looked like they might explode. He pulled the hose from his mouth and bent it to keep the beer from pouring out. His big cheeks melted as he gulped down a mouthful of beer. He squeezed his eyes shut, then opened them wide, raising his eyebrows. "Wow!" he choked. "That's some mighty powerful beer!" He cleaned the end of the hose and put it into the first bottle.

Mom put a sterilized cap on the mouth of the bottles, and Dad capped them using the bottle capper he brought with him from Wisconsin. He said, "Grandpa made a lot of home brew in his day, and he wanted to make sure I had this handy gadget when I found time to make some beer."

While Dad wiped the bottles, Mom cleared a spot on the shelf behind the barrel stove to set them for the weeks it would take to age the beer. "Why do you have to wait so long before you can drink the beer?" I asked, watching him wipe the bottles and hand them to Mom.

"It takes a few weeks for the carbonation to dissolve into the beer," he said. "It'll be ready by Christmas."

As the weeks went by, we were always reminded that the beer was aging on the shelf next to the hot stove. Once in awhile, we were startled awake in the middle of the night by a large explosion. I listened to the beer splash on the floor until only drips could be heard. Sometimes, it was hard to tell the difference from the dripping sound and the crackling embers in the hot barrel stove.

I listened as Dad moaned each time a bottle exploded. I'd hear him say, "Another lost bottle of beer." Then he'd roll over in bed and go back to sleep. Cleaning up the sticky mess was the first job Mom and Dad would tackle in the morning.

A week before Christmas a large box arrived from my grandmother in Wisconsin. Dad brought it home from the post office and set it on the table. He walked cautiously back to the door, brushing snow from his coat and removing his boots. Nancy and I pushed in close, tugging at the twine that wrapped around the box and begging to open it.

Mom brushed the snow from the box into the palm of her hand, walked to the cupboard to let it fall wet and heavy into the dish pan. She wiped her hands on her apron saying, "Wouldn't it be fun to open it on Christmas Eve? It's only a few days away."

Our begging finally paid off. "Okay," Mom said, smiling. "I'm just as excited as you are to see what's inside." She got the scissors and snipped the twine from the box. We stood on the chairs and ripped the paper from the box and pulled open the top. Nancy reached in quickly and pulled out a handful of gifts. I shoved my hands deep into the box, grabbing more presents when Dad said, "Slow down. Let's have fun opening them. These might be all the presents we'll get."

I pulled my hands from the box and stared at him. "Daddy, we're getting lots of presents from Santa. If we don't open Grandma's presents, there'll be too many gifts under the tree when Santa gets here."

"It looks like there are several gifts addressed to all of us. Let's open them and put the rest back in the box to put under the tree after we decorate it," Mom said. "Give this one to your father to open."

Dad reached out, and I handed it to him. It was heavy and round with a strong smell filling the air. He put the wrapped gift to his nose, took a deep breath, and grinned. "That's the smell of stinky, aged Wisconsin cheese."

Mom, Nancy, and I moved closer to Dad. He opened the gift, and sure enough, it was stinky cheese. He got up and walked to the cupboard for a knife, came back to the table and cut several slices of the cheese. He handed each of us a piece, then took one for himself, smelling it again. I stood next to him, holding the cheese away from my mouth and nose. I wasn't sure I wanted to eat something that smelled so terrible. I felt sick, watching with horrifying disbelief as Dad bit into it. "Ahhh," he sighed. I took another look at the awful cheese I was holding and handed it back to him. He was just as pleased with the next gift of stinky sausage, and just like the cheese, he knew what it was before Mom unwrapped it.

Nancy unwrapped the next present. My grandmother's tasty, homemade butter cookies were inside the tin. She made beautiful cookies using a cookie press. Some were decorated with colored frosting, and others were garnished with red and green sprinkles. The cookies were something I was going to fully enjoy. I held the tin close to my nose to savor the fragrance of vanilla. Mom put some of them on a plate and set them on the table. So far, this was the best part of the Christmas box.

I watched Dad get up from his chair and walk to the cupboard to check his homebrew. "I think it's ready," he announced, reaching for a quart bottle, opener, and two glasses. Carrying them to the table, he sat down, opened the bottle, and poured half into Mom's glass and the rest into his, being very careful not to disturb the yeast at the bottom. "The cheese and sausage will taste mighty good with the beer," he said, smiling.

He got up, walked to the davenport, sat down, and held the glass toward the light of the kerosene lantern to check the color. I hurried over and sat down on the armrest, tucking my bare feet under him and resting my elbows on my knees. This was the day he'd been waiting for. He brought the glass almost to his lips breathing in the aroma. I leaned closer watching him sip and swallow the beer.

"Now that's some flavorful beer," he grinned and added, "drink up, Bernie. You're not going to find a better-tasting beer anywhere else."

"Can I have a taste?" I asked, reaching for the glass.

"Just a little sip. It's a powerful concoction."

That one little sip caused a prickly sensation in my throat. I didn't want any more. I wrinkled up my nose and mouth and handed the glass back to Dad. I thought it was going to be sweet, because I was the one who poured all the sugar into the mixture when he made it.

Dad wrapped his large hand around the glass and said, "This tastes like it was made by the brew master himself. Don't you think so, Bernie?"

"Yes, of course it does, John. The aroma is wonderful, and the beer seems aged to perfection."

When Dad looked up at me, wiggling his eyebrows, I asked, "Why doesn't it taste like the root beer we made?"

'Well, it's a completely different formula."

I pulled my feet from underneath him, swung my legs to the floor, saying, "I think the cookies will taste real good with the root beer."

Our first Christmas in Alaska, Mom made rag dolls, and Grandma Hixson sent us baby dolls.

The Agreement

1948

Dad talked about having a garden that would produce enough vegetables to last throughout the winter. He said it would probably be at least next year and a lot of hard work to get to that point in time. There were five acres of trees to cut and burn. Then he had to get rid of all the stumps. His plan was to plant the entire area with oats.

The Bureau of Land Management said homesteaders had to build a house, clear five acres of land, and cultivate it within fourteen months. They would send an authorized person to make an inspection during and after the designated time frame. According to the Homestead Act, it was imperative that those who applied for acreage were accomplishing the homestead requirements they had agreed to. The inspector's visit was to see that residence and cultivation requirements had been met.

It was spring of our second year, and we had four months left to fulfill the homestead agreement.

Dad had a job with the military, trucking supplies from the dock in Anchorage to Fort Richardson. He didn't have time during the week to work the land.

He had been thinking that the decision to take half of the one hundred and sixty acres might prove to be a difficult task, clearing the acreage required by the Alaska Homestead Act. After discussing it with Mom, they made the choice to return half of the eighty acres.

He rose early on the weekends, whistling while he stoked the fire. The whistling worked like an alarm clock. The only difference was I couldn't turn it off.

Dad began cultivating the land in early May. He cut down the trees; Mom, Nancy, and I piled them to be burned. Borrowing a bulldozer from our neighbor, Dad cleared the stumps from the five acres, pushing them into long rows to be burned.

We burned on a day when the wind was calm and we kept an eye on the fire all day to make sure it didn't get out of control. Even with keeping a watchful eye, sparks drifted into the underbrush, and we frantically beat at the low green bushes that were beginning to smolder. There was no water except what drained from the roof into a barrel on a rainy day. Mom beat the grass and shrubs with the broom. Nancy and I helped Dad fill buckets with dirt, and he scattered it on the small brush fires that seemed to be spreading. I worked quickly, shoveling the dirt into the bucket, half crying and half terrified that the fire would get out control. It took about an hour before we could finally take a deep breath and sigh in relief. Dad spent the next half hour scattering more dirt over several areas to make sure there were no stray embers left. The rest of the day was spent walking along the row of burning trees and stumps to make sure the fire was kept in check.

After we all calmed down, Dad pointed and told Nancy, "Go lickety-split that way, and yell if you see stray sparks."

"Can I take the broom with me, just in case?"

Dad nodded and watched her start down the row with the broom over her shoulder. He turned to me, pointing in the other direction, "I want you to go fast like a rabbit in that direction and patrol that area along the trees. Watch the sparks as they fly off the trees. You know how to put them out if they land on the grass."

I grabbed the bucket half full of dirt and started my patrol, guarding the ground from any spark that might touch it.

The logs finally burned themselves out. Mom decided it was a good time to go inside and start frying the chicken dinner. Dad took off his hat, wiped his forehead with his sleeve, and called

Nancy and me to come walk with him. He said, "I'm proud of all the hard work you did today. It wasn't an easy job to do, walking around in the sparks. You were very careful while doing so. We made a great team today. Now I know I can count on your help when I need two strong girls with lots of energy to get a job done."

Mr. Tatro offered his Allis Chalmer tractor and disk harrow to break up the soil and get it ready for the oat planting. Preparing the land took two months. Nancy spent many days riding on the tractor with Dad. He would occasionally jump off and remove brush still lying in the field. She always enjoyed helping him with the outside chores.

Clearing the land and tilling the soil moved more quickly than Dad anticipated, giving Mom the opportunity to put in a garden sooner than expected. She sectioned off a small area to plant some vegetables. Early June was the best time to begin planting seeds. Mom, Nancy, and I worked in the garden during the week while Dad was at work. The soil was loose from tilling and raking, so we let it settle a couple of days. The time was spent tossing the huge rocks off to the sides.

The day finally came when we carefully opened the seed packets. The rows were spaced to give the seeds growing room. We had packages of radishes, beans, peas, and carrots. They were carefully planted about three-inches apart. We stood back and looked at our plot of black dirt and buried seeds. The rows were straight, and there weren't any weeds. Mom said, "The chickweed will grow faster than the vegetables. We'll want to pull it out before the garden starts growing, or it will deprive our vegetables of food and water and light."

Every day Nancy and I would hurry to the garden to see if the seeds were peeking through the black dirt. For several days, we were disappointed and heaved a deep sigh when we realized we'd have to wait a few more days to see tiny green shoots. Mom would say, "Be patient. Gardening takes time." She leaned over and plucked a weed from the black dirt. "Look at this! I was right!" she remarked, holding the scrawny unwanted plant for us to see. "The weeds have a head start on the vegetables. We can't let that happen."

A week later I was on hands and knees, searching for the new shoots to pop their heads from beneath the dirt. To my surprise, they were starting to grow. I shot up and pointed toward the green stems peeking out from underneath the earth. "Look! Mama, the carrots are growing." From that day on, the garden became the most important afternoon activity. The plants seemed to grow higher each time we looked at them. The weeds seen near the beautiful vegetables were plucked and thrown to the edge of the garden.

Whenever Nancy and I told Mom we were bored and we just couldn't think of anything to do, she shooed us out to the garden, and most days went with us. One day while we were weeding, I asked Mom, "Why do weeds grow faster than the vegetables?"

"It's not that they grow faster, it's because there are more weeds than vegetable plants. We don't want to let the weeds go to seed, because they will produce a thousand more weeds to be picked next summer. So keep pulling them out."

Before planting the oats, Mom made apron bags for the seeds. I opened the large pocket of my apron, and Dad poured oat seeds into it, filling it almost to the top. It felt heavy, pulling at my waist. The dirt was deep and thick around my feet while trudging through the freshly plowed soil. All four of us walked back and forth across the field scattering seeds. By the time we finally stopped for lunch, my legs ached.

When we went back to our job, I didn't want to spread any more seeds. Mom looked at me and made a suggestion that changed my mood. "Maybe, you can get your favorite doll and put her in your apron while you work."

I found myself flying across the field with renewed energy.

"Bring my doll too," Nancy yelled.

I grabbed our dolls from their spot on the porch, put both of them in my apron, and ran back to the field. Handing Nancy her doll, I laughed and said, "Let's show them how to throw seeds." The hard work seemed exciting once again.

It took thirteen months to fulfill our homestead agreement. When the man from the land management office stopped by to check on our progress, the oats had grown about ten inches high, and the vegetables in the garden were tall and green, growing in straight weedless rows.

Standing on the porch, we looked out over our accomplishment. The oats bent and glistened in the sunlight as a gentle breeze blew across the field.

Clearing the land and tilling the soil moved more quickly than Dad had anticipated. He had time to prepare a corner of the field for a vegetable garden, and the rest of it was seeded with an oat cover. Mom and Nancy are standing on the cleared land.

Dad screened the porch during early spring so we could open the door to let a cool breeze blow through the cabin and keep the summer mosquitoes out.

Mom in the driveway after a fresh snow had fallen the night before. She was probably helping Dad shovel the driveway.

Nancy standing with Dad's sister, Eleanor, who lived in Seward with her husband, Frank DeLoughery and family. She stopped to visit us on one of her trips to Anchorage for supplies. Since the road between Seward and Anchorage hadn't been constructed yet, all travel to Anchorage was by train.

When Dad received the land patent, he celebrated by placing a sign with his name on it at the beginning of our driveway. We took turns getting our picture taken beside it. There was satisfaction in Dad's voice when he said, "Our dream has come true. We finally own the land."

Mama's Apron
1948

My father always said that Mom was an amazing cook. She could juggle meat, potatoes, gravy, and a hot vegetable on a two-burner kerosene camp stove. I thought it was amazing, too, especially when we had warm pudding for dessert. She used the camp stove as we traveled the highway to Alaska and during the time we were building our log cabin.

When we moved into the cabin, Mom and Dad both agreed that a cookstove was a necessity. The new two-lid wood cookstove was beautiful with the shiny black top, white enameled oven door, and polished black legs. It had an oven that Mom said would be somewhat tricky to use because the oven temperature gauge was controlled by the amount of wood burned. She saw to the fire all day, anticipating our cooking needs. The best part of the new stove was the water reservoir. Mom told us we would always have hot water.

Dad ran the stove pipe through the roof and showed Mom how to operate the damper.

"What's it for?" I asked, pointing at the damper, watching as Mom turned the valve.

"Knowing how to operate the damper produces a more efficient fire," she told me. "It controls the amount of air that goes up the chimney."

Water was taken from the fifty-five-gallon barrel that stood alongside the cabin and poured into the reservoir. Finally, the stove was lit. I waited in the cabin for the water to heat. Mom suggested I go out to play, that she would call me when it was warm.

"No," I said, "I want to be the first one to feel the warm water." After a half hour passed, she told Nancy and me the water was probably beginning to warm. Because we both wanted to be first to touch it, she suggested that the three of us do it together at the same time.

"One, two, three," she counted. The three of us quickly dipped our fingers into the lukewarm water.

"It's barely warm," I said with disappointment.

"Give it time," Mom smiled. Grabbing a hotpad, she pulled the gray and black speckled coffee pot from the flame, replacing the lid over the crackling fire.

The next time we touched the water, it was starting to feel hot. Mom told us from now on, we could no longer put our fingers into the water. "There's the chance that you might get burned," she warned, "and I wouldn't want that to happen."

Mom always put the kindling and paper in the stove the night before and prepared the coffee so the morning was less demanding when the body was just waking up. The last thing she did in the evening was lay a freshly laundered apron over the back of the kitchen chair.

Every morning I woke to the sound of the grate being moved on the cookstove. Mom would dress immediately after striking the first match that ignited the fire in the stove. She hurried back to the kitchen pulling her apron from its resting place and tying it around her waist.

By this time the kindling was burning, and she grabbed some scrawny birch logs and gently laid them on the fire. Using her apron, she wiped pieces of bark from her hands.

The wood box was positioned between the cookstove and the barrel stove that was used for heating the cabin. It had a cover that could be used as a seat, and it supplied wood for both stoves.

It needed filling quite often, and that job was given to Nancy and me. It didn't take too long to bring in an armload from the pile on the porch. The fun part was when the wood needed to be cut. Nancy and I sat on the huge logs held in place by saw horses while Dad sawed them into smaller chunks. He used an ax to cut the smaller pieces of wood into kindling, leaving them for us to pick up when he had other things to do.

The post office was the place where we visited with neighbors who enjoyed a cup of coffee while mingling with one another. On one of those occasions, Mom learned a new way of preserving food. A neighbor shot a moose and was giving most of it away because it was the middle of summer and there was no way that he could store that amount of meat.

Mom had a long conversation with the neighbor's wife about the strangest way of preserving meat throughout the warm months. Even though she thought it was unusual, she listened to what the woman had to say. Others joined in the discussion, saying they had found it to be a surefire way of keeping meat fresh.

The next day, Mom used the hot water from the stove reservoir to wash and sterilize five-gallon Blazo cans. The cans held white gas that we used in our lamps. She worked outside where it didn't matter how much soapy, bleach water splashed about. After the final rinse, she wiped her hands on the apron tied snugly around her waist.

"What are you going to do with them?" I asked, leaning close to the cans savoring the fresh, clean smell.

"I'm going to put moose meat in them. Remember the lady who talked about preserving meat when we went for our mail? I'm going to try it. You and Nancy can help," she told me, walking slowly to the cabin, carrying the Blazo cans. "We'll leave them on the porch. That's where we'll do most of our work."

"What does preserve mean?" Nancy asked, looking up at Mama.

"It's a way to store food to make it last."

Mom told me that searing the meat was the first step in preserving it. The moose steaks sizzled as she laid them carefully in the frying pan and seared them quickly on both sides. She asked us to stay away from the stove as the meat hissed and popped. Finally, she had a large pan full of steaks and carried them to the porch. Returning to the kitchen, she removed one of the pans of bear lard that had been melting on the stove and brought it outside.

"What are you going to do now, Mama?" Nancy asked, peering into the can.

"Well, now I'm going to begin the last step of preserving the meat." She began by pouring a layer of warm lard into the can. Then she put a layer of meat on top and added another layer of lard. "I'll do this until the can is full. I pour the lard over the meat to seal it so that air can't reach it"

"Can I help?" I asked, moving closer to the steaks smothered in peculiar-smelling lard.

"Go in and get an apron for yourself and Nancy. You don't want to splash lard on your clothes."

I hurried to the drawer that held Mom's fresh-smelling, line-dried aprons. I grabbed my favorite yellow one with the two pockets and a green one for Nancy. I handed Nancy hers, and tied mine quickly around my waist. I stood with my hands in the pockets, waiting for my turn while I listened to the sucking sound of the lard wrapping around the meat.

"You can put the meat into the can," Mom told me, "but be careful."

The can was almost full, and Mom had just finished putting another layer of lard into it. Nancy was leaning over the can, waiting for her turn. I pinched the meat between my fingers and moved it swiftly over the lard when it slipped from my grasp, landing with a greasy splash and splattered a big gob onto my cheek. I shrieked and sprang upward.

Nancy jerked backwards out of the way as the splattering lard missed her by inches. I was closest to the can and could feel the warm goo on my cheek. I was about to scream again when I noticed Mom had a gob on her face, too. We looked at each other quite surprised. I saw Nancy's hand go to her mouth and her eyes wrinkle up. I knew she was starting to laugh.

"Mama," I wailed, "she's laughing at me."

Mom got up from where she had been sitting. "Oh, poor Darlene," she whispered, taking the corner of her apron and gently wiping my cheek. It was after I finally felt better that she sat down and dabbed at the greasy spot on her face.

Nancy tapped Mom on the shoulder, saying, "I'll put the next one in, Mama. I won't make a mess."

It took part of the morning and most of the afternoon to preserve our meat. Mom put the cans in a cool place and covered each one with a board telling us that damp air and the heat from the sun could cause the lard to spoil.

That evening, after the dishes were washed and dried, Mom finally took off her apron and laid it over the back of the kitchen chair. I snatched it and wrapped it around my waist tying the strings in front. Gently, I lifted my doll from her resting place and walked to the davenport. I sat with my legs beneath me and cradled her in my arms. "Oh, poor Molly," I said, tenderly swaying her. I caught the corner of the apron and carefully wiped her cheek.

Giant George's Bus

1948

It was a cool day in late August 1948. A slightly chilly breeze blew the yellow leaves from the birch trees. Earlier in the day, Mom had pulled the box of sweaters from under the bed, insisting it was sweater weather. She lifted the blue one, gave it a shake and held it to my shoulders. "Here, try it on and see if it still fits."

"It fits pretty good except the sleeves are too short. It would look better on Nancy," I said, stretching my arms.

"You can wear it until we can get you a larger size."

We left for the Moosehorn Trading Post after supper to check the mail. Mom wanted to talk to George, the bus driver, about taking us to school. The trading post housed the post office, coffee shop, gas, and wrecker service. It was also the halfway stop between Anchorage and Palmer, making it the perfect place for passengers on the bus to break up the monotonous trip back and forth on the dusty two-lane dirt road. They stretched their legs, moaned and groaned, and then settled themselves at the counter for quick cups of coffee.

The post office was in the back of the log building and the place where many of the neighbors stood around chatting. They talked about the crops they were growing and the type of fertilizers they were using. There was always talk about the latest stuff they found at the Army dump. The coffee shop, located in the middle, was usually crowded. All the latest gossip was shared in that area, while standing around enjoying a hot cup of coffee.

Nancy and I had a favorite spot by the door. The magazine stand was just inside the doorway, and that was where we spent most of our time looking through movie magazines. Mom would let each of us buy a magazine every now and again. Most of the time we would buy ones with Elizabeth Taylor on the cover.

Dad sat down at the counter beside one of the old-timers and ordered a cup of coffee.

The old-timer was saying it would be an early winter. I'm not sure how he knew all the answers about the weather, but everyone seemed to hang on every bit of information he revealed about it. "Yep! Winter will start early this year and stay late into the spring, like a cheechako that has overstayed his welcome," he informed Dad. Whatever in the world did that mean, I wondered, as I turned away from that conversation to the one Mom was having with George.

Holding Mom's hand tightly, I gazed up at George. He was deep in conversation with Mom, and occasionally he would look at me and smile as though he wanted to see how I might be responding to their discussion about me. The only thing on my mind was the tremendous height of his slim, yardstick body dressed in blue from head to toe. His hat had a shiny bill that reflected the light coming through the window and it sat sideways atop a tuft of gray hair. I smiled back as I squeezed Mom's hand. I was fascinated by his smile, wanting all the time to reach my hand upward to see if I could touch his clean-shaven face. I had never before, in all my eight years, seen a giant.

He held a cup of coffee unsteadily in his right hand. If the cup tipped just a fraction of an inch, I'd probably be flooded with black yuck all over my new plaid dress Mom had made for me.

I knew Mom had wanted to talk to George for a long time, because I overheard her talking with Dad about school and how worried she was about sending us all the way to Anchorage. We had already missed one year of school since moving to Alaska. She worried about all the things that could happen to us. I heard her talking to Dad one night when she thought I was asleep. "I worry about the people who stop at the bar after work for a drink or even several drinks before they board the bus. And some of them carry flasks in their pockets and drink while on the bus. I'm scared for my girls when I'm not with them, and I worry that someone might touch them."

I knew Dad was worried too. "We'll go for the mail tomorrow evening when the bus stops at the trading post, and you can talk to George. He'll keep an eye on them."

I was smiling back at George as he assured my mother that her two very special daughters would be safe as they traveled to school and back on his bus. I listened as he told her he would seat us directly behind him so he could look after us as though we were his own. All the while, I kept squinting at that tilting cup of coffee, waiting for the moment the contents might spill forth. Finally, he took one last gulp. I watched his Adam's apple bob up and down.

He tipped his hat at Mom and smiled at me. "I'll see you soon, young lady," he said to me. He walked to the door and called out, "All aboard. I'm leaving in five minutes." I watched through the window as he boarded the bus and started the engine. The passengers finished the last of their coffee and headed out the door. They boarded and the bus drove off in a cloud of dust.

Mom, Nancy, and I rode the bus to the depot in Anchorage a week before school started. She pointed out where we would sit and wait for the bus, where we could buy a snack, and where the bathroom was. As we walked the two blocks to Anchorage School, I held Mom's hand while Nancy held the other. "I'll be scared walking to school," I told her.

"I know you'll be scared on the first day. New things are usually scary. All the other kids will feel nervous, too. There'll be older kids walking with you from the depot. You won't be by yourselves. Soon you'll have a new friend and wonder why you were scared," she said, giving my hand a squeeze. "You'll be just fine."

We spent the rest of the day looking through the shops and buying some groceries at Piggly Wiggly. Arriving back at the depot, Nancy and I picked out a candy bar and each of us paid for it with the money Mom gave us. We were exhausted when we finally got on the bus and slept most of the way home. Now and then, the wheel rolled into a large pothole, waking us.

September came quickly, and we were looking forward to the first day of school. We were up early, eager to begin the day. Nancy and I wore new dresses Mom made for this special occasion. We had oatmeal for breakfast, but I couldn't eat very much. I was excited and nervous, thinking about the twenty-two-mile bus ride into Anchorage.

I didn't want to be out of the house so early in the morning. I clung tightly to Mom's hand, feeling very queasy and anxious about a trip to Anchorage without her by my side. I shivered, and goose bumps appeared on my arms even though I wasn't cold. I was glad I had my blue jacket on. The bus came to a stop beside our driveway at six o'clock in the morning.

Nancy and I stepped on board; George smiled and said, "Good morning, girls. Sit right behind me." He said something to Mom, probably reassuring her that we would be just fine under his watchful eye, but I wasn't paying attention. I was noticing that Giant George didn't seem to tower over me today. As a matter of fact, we seemed to be the same height as he sat in the driver's seat. I was scared as I sat down behind him and didn't want anyone to know.

After we were settled in, I took a moment to look around. I was in the aisle seat and turned my head to look behind me. The bus seemed empty, so I turned myself all the way around and looked over the top of the seat. The adults on the bus seemed to like the window seats even though their eyes were closed. They didn't look as if they were interested in the view from the window or catching a glimpse of who just got on the bus.

The kids from Eklutna were a few seats behind me. I recognized some of them I played with when Dad, Nancy, and I visited the village, and waved to them. Dad enjoyed chatting and swapping gossip with the railroad workers at the Eklutna Station. Nancy and I would walk to the old Russian Orthodox church and play with the kids who lived across from it.

I smiled and waved to Virginia when George startled me by saying, "Turn around, young lady, and sit down. I wouldn't want you to lurch forward if I had to stop fast. Your mother wouldn't be very happy with me."

I wondered how he knew what I had been doing. I looked at Nancy with a puzzling frown, hoping she could give me the answer. She shrugged her shoulder, apparently just as baffled as I was. The rest of the trip was spent looking out the front window and trying to figure out how the door swung open each time someone boarded the bus. The trip to Anchorage from Peters Creek took more than an hour and a half. The time passed slowly as I glanced at my watch a hundred times, wishing I could see the depot around every curve.

The bus wound down Peters Creek hill, crossed over the two wooden bridges and up the other side, hugging the edge of the hillside. The road bed was gravel and not very smooth, making travel slow and monotonous. It seemed that George was continuously twisting and turning the steering wheel, trying to maneuver the bus in order to avoid the hundreds of potholes that made up the road.

Eagle River hill was the most dangerous spot on the road. George inched the bus slowly down the hill, his foot pushed against the brake. The wooden bridge at the bottom groaned under the weight of the bus. Nancy and I took turns sitting by the window. When it was my turn, I held my breath and closed my eyes so I didn't have to see the water rushing beneath the bridge. In late spring, the water almost swallowed the bridge. I shivered every time the bus crossed the creaking boards, scared that it might break under its weight and terrified that the bus might not float.

The climb up the hill caused the wheels to spit gravel in every direction. The rocks shot out from beneath the tires and vibrated the small trees that lined the edge of the hillside. I watched as the yellow leaves broke away and sailed to the ground. The hill was well-known for having the worst accident rate, higher than any other place along the road from Anchorage to Palmer.

We stopped at the Fort Richardson gate. George opened the side window, taking a piece of paper from the soldier that he would display in the window until he returned it when leaving the military property. The road was smoother than the rest of the highway, and the speed limit was fifteen miles an hour through Fort Richardson and Elmendorf Air Force Base.

It seemed as though I had just fallen asleep when the bus finally slowed and made a wide turn, arriving at the bus depot located on a side street between Fourth and Fifth Avenues. George told the kids to stay in their seats while the other passengers left the bus. Then he motioned us to follow him inside.

The depot seemed much bigger than the last time we came with Mom. The few benches were empty because no one came into the depot in the morning. They were all on their way to work. I could smell the coffee from the small café in the corner as George gathered us together. He said there were older students that knew the way, and we were to follow them to Anchorage School and back to the depot at the end of the school day. We walked two blocks west to the only school in Anchorage that accommodated grades one through twelve.

Our school day was extra long. We arrived one hour before classes began and had to stay one hour after school because of the work schedules of the adults who rode the bus. A teacher was always assigned to keep us busy during those time periods. We sat in a circle taking turns reading with other kids until it was time to go to class or to go home.

One day, my teacher tucked a note into my pocket telling me to give it to my mother when I got home. "Did I do something wrong?" I asked.

"No, I'd like to talk to your mother about helping you with your reading," she told me, touching my cheek.

I gave Mom the note, which she handed to Dad after reading it. Mom wouldn't be able to go in and talk to the teacher because we only had the truck that Dad used for work. The next day, he took time off during his lunch hour. He drove supplies from the Anchorage dock to Elmendorf Air Force Base. The school was just a short drive from the dock, and so he could eat lunch while he drove, talk to my teacher, and not be late getting back to work.

Dad arrived at the door of the classroom and whispered with my teacher in the hall. I hoped the other kids didn't know it was my dad who knocked on the door. Maybe, they didn't when she asked me to write down the names of any kids that talked while she was out of the room. She told Dad she was worried about the long days I spent at school. She thought I might need a nap at some point in the day and discussed the possibility of the nap during morning recess. She told him I needed help with spelling and word pronunciation, and she'd send a study packet home with me.

After school she gave me word lists. "Study hard and you'll be a good second-grade reader," she told me. I was glad she put them into a bag so the other kids didn't know I was having trouble reading.

I don't remember the naps, but I do remember those long lists of words that I had to repeat over and over again. I don't think I would have learned to read well if the lists of words had not been drilled into me every single evening until they were memorized.

Dad helped me. He sat at one end of the table, and I sat at the other. He called Nancy and said, "You can learn the vocabulary words, too." I smiled as Nancy pursed her lips and sat down to the miserable job of remembering words.

Finally, the day came when my teacher said, "You've learned to read very well, Darlene. You worked hard, and I'm proud of you." I smiled, not knowing what to say. She patted my shoulder. "I have some pictures of my children. They learned to be very good readers, too, memorizing the same words," she said, pointing to the lists I had set on her desk. She took the pictures from the drawer and handed them to me pointing out and naming each child in the photographs. She didn't show any of the other kids the pictures, just me. I felt special, and from then on, I worked hard so she would always be proud of me.

There were days when we arrived home at eight o'clock in the evening. On those nights the bus had either broken down at the depot or along the road. George was always true to the promise he made to my mother. He looked after us like a father tending to his own children. He brought us something to eat and checked on us occasionally while we sat on the bench waiting for the bus to be repaired.

When the bus broke down along the road, George always had a candy bar for all the kids. Those breakdowns were miserable, because it always seemed to happen on a cold, dark winter night. He turned the lights on inside the bus, making the interior dim and eerie. All the men would leave the bus and try to figure out what was amiss. Each one had his own hunch, sometimes the problem was obvious.

The women huddled together and discussed chores that wouldn't get done that evening, and sometimes they touched the shoulder of a worried child, trying to comfort him or her. My sister and I would go to the middle section to visit with the other kids.

One evening as we waited at the depot, George walked up to us with a cat tucked away in his arms and asked, "Would you like to take it home?" He slowly lifted it so we could get a better look. Nancy was standing ready to receive the yellow and white cat. I could hear it purring and knew it wanted to go home with us as much as we wanted to take it home. Nancy grabbed the tiny bundle of soft fur from him. All the way home, we took turns petting and holding it. When we got off the bus, we thanked George for the precious gift.

We were sure that Mom and Dad would be just as delighted as we were to share our home with such a cute itty-bitty cat. We hurried into the house out of breath, both of us yelling at the same time, wanting to reveal our wonderful surprise before the other had a chance. I held the cat up for everyone to see. We hadn't given a thought as to how our dog, Queenie, would feel about a cat in the house. She took a quick look at it and lunged forward as though her life depended on ridding us of the unwelcome intruder. The cat screeched and shot like a rocket from the grip I had on it. It landed next to the davenport and made a dash to safety underneath. Queenie was able to get her head part way underneath, further terrifying the already frightened cat. She snarled, a clawing paw ready to tear into the yellow and white fur, driving it further into the safety of the darkness.

Dad bolted from the davenport where he was reading a book, relaxing after a long day at work. He grabbed Queenie by the scruff of the neck, and Mom turned from preparing dinner and dropped what she was doing as Nancy and I screamed. Dad finally got Queenie to the door and pushed her outside. We all took a deep breath and calmed down. Dad started to sit back down when I screamed again to warn him not to crush the cat that was hiding somewhere underneath. It didn't come out of its hiding place all evening. I'm not even sure if it ventured out during the night.

The next morning we were told that the cat couldn't stay and be a part of our family. We groaned and begged, hoping Mom and Dad would change their minds. Dad worked hard trying to retrieve the cat from beneath the davenport. He was finally able to grab it from its hiding place. Queenie put in her two cents as Nancy cuddled the cat in her arms, preparing for the walk to the bus. Queenie always walked with us and she looked miserable when she couldn't sneak through the partly open doorway as we left. Mom always wanted her with us to bark if there were moose around. "Poor Queenie," I cooed, waving goodbye to her as I squeezed through the door.

George smiled as we boarded the bus that morning. We took turns holding and petting the cat while we told him about our adventure with it the night before. At the depot, George took the cat and gently snuggled it up against his jacket saying, "Thanks, girls, for taking care of the cat last night."

I think back to how grateful my mother must have been to have someone like George looking after us for the two years we rode the bus back and forth to school. I will always remember Giant George as a guardian angel who kept my sister and me safe under his wing and protected us from all danger while we were in his vigilant care.

Moments in Time

Her soft, silky fingers delicate
as the wisp of a breeze
caress my cheek while she cuddles
me up in her arms.

You will have memories to cherish
as you grow, she tells me, enduring
moments rich in times past.

A log cabin that holds laughter
within its walls, filling days
with a sparkle of liveliness.

An orphan bear, your friend
for one remarkable summer,
leaving you with eternal sorrow.

The bus driver caring for you
every day upon stepping aboard
for the twenty-two mile ride to school.

All the timeless moments, memories
you'll impart to others one day while
remembering the difficult, yet gratifying
life as a homesteader's daughter.

Moose Horn Trading Post was a bus stop for weary people traveling the fifty miles between Anchorage and Palmer. It housed the post office, a coffee and snack area, and it became a gathering place for neighbors to catch up on the latest news.

Photo courtesy of the Chugiak-Eagle River Historical Society

Ice for Mama

1948

Dad stepped up onto the porch, slapping at a mosquito on his neck. "I'm going to screen in the porch this summer so we can keep the front door open on warm days and not have to beat off the mosquitoes," he said, while stacking an armful of kindling wood on the pile in the corner.

Mom walked from the cabin onto the porch, shaking the dust cloth and letting her hand rest on the icebox next to the door. "I'm glad that we brought the icebox with us. It sure would be nice if we could use it. Do you suppose it would be possible to have ice next summer? It would be a shame if we didn't use it after hauling it all the way from Wisconsin. It took up a lot of space in our cramped trailer."

Mom wiped the dust cloth over the top of the icebox, "We could have cold milk and cheese, and our eggs would last longer. Just imagine how convenient that would be."

"Don't forget about a cold beer or two. It sure beats drinking it warm," Dad replied, brushing splinters from his shirt.

I was reading on the wood pile and listening to them. I scooted myself from the stacked wood and moved toward the icebox. Using my foot, I brushed away some of the wood chips on the floor next to it. I hadn't paid much attention to the icebox until now. I opened the brown door and peered inside. "How does it work, Mama?"

"Well, it's sort of like the one we had in Wisconsin except it was much taller and it had a large box on the top half of the inside. To keep food cool, ice was put into the upper box. Then the ice circulates cold air down into the area where the food is kept.

This one is small," she said, rubbing her hand over the icebox, "and it won't hold very much ice. It has a small box inside of it. We'll probably have to chop the block of ice into pieces and put ice into it more often. There's a catch tray at the bottom to drain water." She pulled the tray from underneath.

I called Nancy. I wanted her to see the tray. It would be the perfect place to hide stuff and no one would know it was there.

I opened the top drawer of the icebox and pulled out some gloves. "It's sure a big mess."

"We'll clean it up when we are ready to use it," she told me.

Mom turned to Dad, smiling. "I can almost taste a cool custard pie and cold ice water."

"Bernie, if you want ice next summer, I'll make sure that you have it." He smiled, inviting her to help him pick the spot for the icehouse.

"We have a lot of land to clear and cultivate in the next couple of months, but after the trees are cut and the fields plowed, I'll make a nice-size ice house. I'll cut some trees, dig some trenches for drainage, build it using barrels from the dump, and put on a flat roof. I might even make a small room for meat when I pile the ice."

The next day I saw Dad cutting down trees and hurried over for a closer look. "Why are you chopping trees? We have lots of firewood."

"Your mother wants ice," he said, swinging the ax against the tree.

"Timber," I yelled as the birch tree crashed to the ground. I caught some of the green leaves as they drifted gently in the air.

Dad rested for a minute. "This is as good a spot as any to put the ice house. I don't want to carry heavy blocks of ice too far when I fill the ice box."

"I can help you carry the ice," I said, watching Dad sink the ax into the tree.

"Well, maybe you can help. I can load it onto your wagon, and you can pull it to the house."

I thought about pulling a heavy block of ice all by myself. What if it was too heavy to pull? I turned, jumped over some of the fallen trees, and ran toward Nancy, yelling, "Do you want to help me haul ice in our wagon next summer?"

After buying supplies in Anchorage, the Army dump was our last stop where we filled the bed of the truck with fifty-five-gallon barrels. On our arrival home, groceries were taken into the cabin, then Dad backed the truck to the spot where the ice house was beginning to take shape. He rolled the barrels from the truck and placed them in an area twelve by fourteen feet.

He filled the open-topped barrels with dirt, and planks were placed on top of the barrels. He put a second row of barrels on top of the first, filling them with dirt. Planks were placed on the second row, and a flat roof of spruce logs ran the length of the ice house. He left the front of it open so he could drive up close and push the ice off the bed of the truck. Dad dug several shallow trenches in the dirt floor for drainage.

Large amounts of sawdust were needed to cover the ice. Throughout the summer, we made several trips to the Goat Creek Saw Mill near Palmer. Mom, Nancy, and I always went with Dad. We enjoyed the scenery and the drive along Knik River.

The sawdust pile grew into an enormous mound. Dad stored it next to the ice house to be readily available to cover the ice when he brought it home from Mirror Lake. Nancy and I spent many hours making tiny ice houses out of twigs and using our toy trucks to haul sawdust.

By the end of July, the ice house was finished. While working on it, Dad cleared five acres of land and planted oats. He found time to build a cache to store meat through the winter months. There was a spot near the house where three trees were close enough together to use as posts to build a square platform on a triangle framework for the floor of the cache. The plywood floor was built nine feet from the ground. The walls and roof were also built from sheets of plywood.

Dad was glad when the cache was finished, because Mom worried about him falling, and Nancy and I begged for a chance to climb the ladder and help. Mom insisted that the ladder be taken down, so there was no chance of us getting hurt trying to climb in and out of the cache.

Dad said, "When the thaw comes, I'll pull what's left of the moose meat out of the cache and store it in the ice house. We'll have fresh meat all year around."

He told us the squirrels would never gain entry into the cache, because it was built so tight they wouldn't find a space big enough to squeeze through. Day after day, Nancy and I sat quietly on the porch step watching the yard squirrels leaping from nearby trees onto the top of the cache. He was right. They never found a way to get in.

The first snowfall came in early October. I heard Dad's footsteps on the porch and opened the door. "Did you see all the snow? Can we go for the ice?" I asked, grabbing his lunch pail and watching him remove his boots, coat, and hat.

"It just snowed. The lake hasn't frozen yet. We'll go when the ice on the lake is about six or eight inches thick. That means we have to wait for cold, freezing weather."

"When will that be?"

"Probably in about another month," he replied, walking over to Mom and kissing her cheek.

"How was your day at work?" she inquired, smiling at him. She moved the pot of potatoes to the cooler side of the wood stove and pulled the moose roast from the oven.

"It was a busy afternoon. I'll sure be glad when the railroad calls, telling me they have an opening," he answered, pouring a cup of coffee.

In late November, the ice on the lake was thick enough to drive the truck onto it. Our neighbor, Bob Stewart, went with Dad to help cut the ice.

The truck was parked, and a ramp was set in place to pull the ice up and into the back of the truck. Snow was shoveled off the area to be cut. Before he cut into the ice, Dad shoveled an area for Nancy and me to play.

"I want you girls to stay here while I'm cutting ice. It's too dangerous for you to be nearby." We both promised to stay away and began sliding on the ice.

Dad used a saw to cut two parallel lines through the ice about fifteen feet long, and then he cut across the ends. The first piece was shoved under the water. The ice was cut into eighteen-inch sections, and ice grips were used to lift and carry the chunks to the truck. They were pulled up the ramp and stacked on the bed of the truck.

I found myself unable to concentrate on anything except watching Dad. Every time I heard the saw tearing through the ice, I wanted to be there helping him bring the big chunks out of the water. I wasn't close enough to see how he was doing it. Finally, I couldn't stand it any longer. "Let's go peek at what Dad's doing," I said, knowing Nancy would follow me.

The hole was huge. I threw some small chunks of ice into the water and watched them disappear. My attention shifted to the ramp. Dad was on the bed of the truck when he saw us and yelled, "Stay away from the water. Go back to where you were playing."

At that moment, a block of ice broke loose, sliding down the ramp so fast that I was surprised when Bob stopped it as it slid onto the ice. Dad pulled it back up and pushed it against the rest of the ice blocks. He jumped from the truck bed and motioned us to go back to where he had cleared the spot for us to play. We began moving in that direction, but I was still thinking about sliding down the slippery ramp. I knew it would be fun to slide as fast as the ice chunk. I turned to see what Dad was doing. His back was toward me, and he was saying something to Bob. I walked quickly over to the truck, stepped up onto the running board, and pulled myself up and over the side into the bed of the truck. Glancing at the ramp, it looked really high, but I didn't feel scared. I scooted myself onto the board and let go of the sides.

When I reached the bottom, I kept sliding across the ice. I stopped at the edge of the hole with my feet dangling just above the water. I sat there staring into the black water. I looked up at my Dad. He had stopped cutting the ice, and he was staring at me. It seemed like such a long time before he spoke.

"Don't move," he said, lifting himself from where he was kneeling on the ice.

He moved quickly to where I sat and pulled me from the edge, lifting me upright. "You came mighty close to falling into the water. I want you and Nancy to wait in the truck while I finish. It's just about time to go home."

I don't know if Dad ever told Mom what had happened at the lake that day. There was never any mention of it, but Nancy and I never got to go with him again.

There were several trips to the lake before the ice house began to fill. Dad sprinkled a thick layer of sawdust on the ground and laid the rows of ice blocks about a foot away from the walls. He filled the space along the walls with sawdust and sprinkled it over each layer and between each ice block. As he layered the ice, he took time to build a small room within it to store meat.

When the ice almost filled the room, a thick layer of sawdust was spread over the top.

As the weather warmed, Dad took what was left of the moose from the cache and stored it in the ice house. Whenever we needed meat, he would slice a piece from a hind quarter.

On hot summer days, Nancy and I chiseled chips of ice from the large blocks and added them to our root beer. We would sit on top of the pile of sawdust that covered the ice and stay cool on warm summer days. It turned out to be the perfect place to play with dolls or to tell wonderful, imaginary stories.

Mom got the ice she wanted, and Dad enjoyed his frosty beer. A cool custard pie was always a treat. The powdered milk tasted much better when cold water was added to the mixture.

The ice lasted throughout the summer. Dad replenished it every winter and was glad that he was able to provide it for us.

The ice house (upper right) was unique. Everything Dad needed came from the Army dump. He used two layers of open-topped fifty-five gallon drums filled with dirt for the walls. He laid planks of wood over the first row and a second layer of drums, placing planks across them. A flat roof of spruce logs ran the length of the ice house. He left the front of it open so he could drive up close and push the ice from the bed of the truck.

Dad built a cache to store moose meat through the winter months. When the thaw came, he pulled out what was left and stored it in a small room of ice he built in the middle of the ice house.

Waiting for Santa
1948

I always looked forward to neighbors visiting. Most of the time, I'd sit on the floor and read until I'd hear words that sounded interesting. Hearing Gracie Tatro say "telephone" caught my attention. I put down the comic book, went over to Mom, leaned against her back, and wrapped my arms around her neck letting her rub my arm while my head rested on her shoulder. I liked the warmth of her soft hand against the coolness of my skin. Mom and our neighbor, Gracie, who lived two miles from us, talked about getting telephones to keep in touch. They worried about something happening while they were home alone and needed help, and they wanted to hear another friendly voice on a cold winter day.

"We don't seem to get out and visit as much in the winter as we do during the summer," Mom said, rubbing her finger over the flower pattern on the delicate coffee cup.

"I really miss the telephone," Gracie said. "I try to call my family back home every now and again. It would be so much nicer to sit down and relax with a cup of tea in the kitchen and make a telephone call."

"Do you think there'll ever be telephone lines in our area?" Mom asked.

Dad and Reese Tatro were talking about fishing, but quickly worked their way into the conversation, saying they would check the Army dump to see if there might be spools of surplus battlefield wire. "Maybe, we can string some wire right here in the neighborhood. Although, we would still have to go to Anchorage to call family back in the States," Dad told them. That's when I got tired of listening and went to see what Nancy was doing in the bedroom. I didn't want to hear about rolling spools of wire through the woods.

After our company left, I helped clean the cups and saucers from the table. "If we get a telephone, will it be like the one we had at our other house?"

"It'll be different," Mom said, stacking the dishes on the counter." There'll be just a few people to talk to on the telephone. It won't be like living in Wisconsin where we could call all over the world. We won't even be able to make a call to Anchorage."

"Who would we be able to call?"

"Only the neighbors that live about a mile or two from our house."

When Dad came home with huge rolls of wire, I climbed up onto the bed of the truck and stood next to one of the round rolls. "Wow! Is this a spool?" I asked, rubbing the thick wire.

"Yep," he said, lifting himself up onto the bed of the truck.

"Is this what you're going to roll through the woods?"

"Yep, it's going to be a big job."

"These rolls are almost as big as I am. Can I go with you and help roll them?" I asked.

"Maybe another time. It's going to take awhile to clear brush and lay a couple miles of wire. You can go sometime when I'm checking lines," he said, jumping from the bed of the truck. He reached his arms upward and let me fall into them, swinging me safely to the ground.

The day Dad nailed the hand-cranked telephone to the wall, Mom was first to call our nearest neighbor. Tugging her sleeve and eager for my turn to talk, she gave up the telephone. I put it to my ear and listened.

"Say hello," Mom said.

"Hello?" I whispered, gripping the black receiver and wondering how someone could hear my voice through the tiny holes in it. After that, I'd run for the telephone every time it rang. Sometimes Mom let me crank the phone when she made a call.

"Don't answer it," Mom called, when I made a dash for the phone. "That's not our ring. Remember, it's two shorts and a long."

There were times when Mom didn't wait for the two shorts and a long and quietly picked up the receiver and listened in. Sometimes, she picked up the telephone, said hello, and joined in the conversation. The day came when everyone ignored the rings and answered the phone, choosing not to care whose ring it was. Mom said it was because the ladies were home during the day without an automobile, and this was their way of visiting together in the afternoon. In the evening, they were more respectful about privacy.

Mom was chatting with one of the neighbors on the telephone a few weeks before Christmas saying, "It's just around the corner." I was going to ask her what that meant when Dad called from outside. I wanted to stay close to Mom and hear more about Christmas. I pretended not to hear him until he called several times. I knew he wanted help stacking wood on the porch.

Throwing on my coat, scarf, mittens, and boots, I stepped out into the chilly afternoon. "Do you think Santa will find us this year?" I asked, lifting a piece of firewood from the snow and stacking it on top of the three already on my arm.

"What makes you think he won't find us?" Dad answered, splitting a log in two.

"He didn't find us last year."

"Sure he did."

"No he didn't. All I got last year were presents from my grandmas," I said, looking straight into his eyes.

Dad put the long-handled ax across his shoulders, grabbed it at both ends and stared back at me. "He brought you a sled."

"Oh." I said, remembering the red sled we harnessed our yellow-haired dog, Queenie, to. "But Santa always brings lots of toys. I had a long list. Besides, the sled was for both Nancy and me. Are you sure he'll find us? Can I call him on the telephone?"

"You sent him a letter a month ago. That's all you need to do. Besides, our telephone lines only go to a few neighbors who live nearby. It would take a lot of wire to go all the way to the North Pole."

"Do you think Santa got my letter yet? Do you think my map was okay? Maybe, I should write again."

"He'll find you."

"How do you know for sure?"

Dad lifted the ax high above his head, bringing it down swiftly, slicing through the log. "Because we live close to the North Pole, and he's familiar with all the land in Alaska. He'll stop here before he goes other places. He won't miss you."

"You're sure?"

"I'm sure."

Picking up several pieces of wood, Dad gently added them to the load in my arms. Carrying the wood onto the porch and dropping it on top of the already stacked pile, I thought about Santa, I still wasn't certain he would find me. I didn't remember getting stuff that was just for me.

Dad spent a lot of time whittling the bark from small tree limbs during the evening, while we listened to stories on the battery-operated radio. Some pieces were long and others short. He sat forward on the davenport, letting the shavings land on a large piece of paper in front of him.

I sat next to him on the floor, leaning against the davenport, letting the bark fall onto the back of my hand while listening to Amos and Andy. Amos would say something funny, and I'd fall sideways giggling, pushing the shavings off the paper.

"Be careful," Dad said, leaning forward and brushing them back onto the paper and off of my sleeve.

"What are you making?" I asked.

"Just keeping my hands busy."

It seemed to take forever before Christmas vacation finally arrived. I made a paper ornament at school, and I was anxiously waiting for the day I could help put up the tree. I wanted to fasten my ornament onto a lower branch and sit on the floor watching it twirl around. I made it from strips of red paper dipped in glue and draped over a blown-up balloon and left to dry in the shape of a ball. I sprinkled lots of sparkly glitter on it. Then I got to pop the balloon and see the beautiful round design I had created. I was looking forward to the weekend when we would cut down a tree.

The next Saturday we walked the woods looking for a tree that had plenty of branches and was the right size to fit inside our cabin. I wanted one that had a nice long branch at the bottom for my red ornament with all the silver sparkles.

We found it just past the oat field and a short ways into the woods. Nancy spotted it first, and we all agreed it was perfect. Dad said it was full, and Mom thought it was tall enough.

Nancy said, "I think the top branch is long enough to hold the star." I walked around the tree, brushing my mitten across all the bottom branches, trying to decide which one would hold the sparkly ornament.

Dad put the ax up to his shoulder asking, "Are you sure this is the tree?"

We all yelled, "Yes," and the tree was laying on the snow after the ax whacked the trunk three times. Each of us took a turn pulling the tree home. I watched Dad lift the tree, shake it, and set it against the house. I wanted to bring it in right away, but Mom said we had to move some furniture around so we could put it in the corner by Nancy's and my bedroom.

Nancy and I found lots of things to keep ourselves busy. A favorite pastime outside was throwing snowballs at the rabbit pelts that hung against the back of the cabin. There were ten of them, and we'd make ten snowballs the size of apples and throw them at the fur pelts. My throw was so good that I could hit each of them. Nancy's toss was off until I showed her how her eye and hand could work together. Being expert shots, we massacred the pelts every day. Some days, we'd harness Queenie to the red sled and pitch snowballs at the pelts as we flew by. When Dad found out, he told us the furs were hung on the back of the house to dry, and every time we tossed a snowball at them, it would make the drying process longer. He never got upset, but he let us know that it better not happen anymore.

Dad came home from the post office on Saturday afternoon and told Mom the telephone line wasn't working to the north of our cabin. He was going to walk through the woods with another neighbor and see if they could find the break in the line.

"Can I go with you?" I asked, hurrying for my coat.

"Not this time," he told me.

"That's what you said when you strung the wire through the woods. You said I could go with you the next time you checked the line. Don't you remember?"

Following Dad to the door, I continued begging and hoping he would change his mind about letting me tag along with him. I wanted to see what happened when the telephone line didn't work. "Please, can I go with you?"

"There's almost a foot of snow in the woods."

"Do you think a moose pulled the wire apart again?"

"Probably, they're to blame most of the time."

"I won't grumble about being cold. I'll put on two pairs of socks and wear my snow pants over my boots so the snow doesn't get inside. Please, please."

Dad looked at me for a minute and didn't say anything. I thought for sure he wasn't going to take me along. I stared at him with the saddest face, hoping he'd feel real bad about not wanting me to tag along with him.

"Well, if you think you can keep up with me, and if you don't whine when you get cold, you can tag along," he said.

"I promise," I said, my sad frown turning to a smile.

We drove to the neighbor's house whose phone wasn't working and began walking from there. The snow wasn't deep along the path where the wire lay beneath the spruce trees. Dad reached down into the snow, lifting the wire and checking for breaks in the line. Sometimes I ran ahead, pushing my hand into the deep snow and lifting the line for him. In a place where there were lots of trees and very little snow, we found the line pulled apart.

"Do you think it was a moose?" I asked, looking at the pulled-apart wire.

"I'm sure it was," he said, bending to pick it up.

"Do you think the moose is still around?"

"Nope, it's long gone," he said, taking off his gloves and pulling the pliers and a knife from his pocket.

I stooped to watch his jackknife peel away some the covering around the wires and watched as he twisted them together with the pliers. "Wow! Where did you learn to do that?" I asked.

"Just a little trick or two I learned. It's an easy thing to do. Next time you come with me, I'll let you splice the line together," he said, removing black tape from his pocket and wrapping a piece around the bare wires.

I didn't know what splice meant, and I didn't care. I was going to use the pliers and stick the lines together. When I got home, I yelled across the room to Nancy. "I'm going with Daddy the next time a moose yanks the wire apart. I get to put them back together again, because now I know how to do it."

We decorated the tree a week before Christmas. It was beautiful even before Dad drilled holes in the trunk and added the extra branches in the one bare spot. The box of ornaments sitting on the floor had been looked through many times while we anxiously waited to hang them on the tree. In the afternoon they were finally unwrapped again and laid out on the floor. Mom had carefully packed and brought them with us when we left Wisconsin over a year ago.

I pulled a string of lights from the bottom of the box, rubbing my thumb over the slick glass. Gazing at the tiny bulbs, I laid them gently back in the box. "I wish we could string them on the tree. Wouldn't they look pretty all lit up?"

"Maybe we'll have electricity next year," Nancy answered, holding up a delicate red ornament in the shape of a raspberry in one hand and a handful of tinsel in the other. "Look! See how the tinsel shines when I wave it around. It might be just as pretty as the lights when we hang it over the branches."

Each of us found our favorite ornament and looked for a spot to hang it. We all chose a place right in the middle of the tree. Mine was silver and red in the shape of a Santa. Nancy chose the red raspberry, and Mom hung the red and green bell.

"Come on, Daddy," I coaxed. "Find the one you like best."

He pushed the chair back, laid his open book on the table and came over to where we were seated on the floor. Picking up a silver ornament in the shape of a house, he straightened and hooked it over a high branch.

"Why didn't you put it by our ornaments in the middle?" Nancy wanted to know.

"The higher branches are going to be mighty bare if all the ornaments are in the middle," he said, pulling a kitchen chair near the tree and stepping up onto it.

"Hand me the star, and I'll put it up now. Then the tree won't look so bare at the top."

Most of the ornaments had some kind of sparkly stuff glued onto them, except for a shiny silver one. Picking it up and laying it gently in my hand, I brought it even with my face, staring at the eerie mirrored reflection. Smiling made the face even scarier as the lips stretched out on the skinny long face. Placing it just right on the tree, I could walk up and stare at the funny-looking face anytime I wanted.

Finally, it was time to put the ornament I made on the tree. I spent a minute gazing at the tree to find the perfect spot for it. Suddenly, I realized that whenever I moved my hand, the glitter on my red paper ornament made the walls sparkle. "Hey! Look at what my ornament is doing," I said, swaying it back and forth in the sunlight.

Mom came over to where I was standing and said, "The sun is shining on it and casting reflections on the logs. Isn't it beautiful? Maybe, the tree isn't the place for your ornament."

"It's not?"

"Well, I'm just saying that maybe there is a better place for it. A place where its beauty can really shine," she said, looking toward the window.

"I can hang it in the window. Is that where you were thinking it would shine the brightest on the logs?"

"Let's get a piece of string and see how it looks hanging in the window," she suggested.

Several times I swung the red ornament back and forth along the window panes watching the colors light up the logs.

I woke early one morning, hearing Mom at the sewing machine. Slipping out of the top bunk, being careful not to wake Nancy, I walked into Mom and Dad's bedroom on tiptoes not wanting my feet to touch the cold floor, and sat on the bed with my legs tucked under me. "What are you making, Mama?" I said, yawning and pulling a blanket up and around my shoulders.

"I'm cutting up some of my pretty scraps of material. I don't know, yet, what I'll make with them," she replied, stacking the pieces on the machine.

"Can I have some to make Molly a skirt? What are you making with the Army blanket?"

"I made your snow pants from this wool blanket. Since it's already cut up, I've decided to cut it into small squares to use sometime when I have a need for them."

"Can I have that big piece for Molly's bed?" I asked, grabbing the largest scrap from the pile on the bed.

"Would you like to cut the jagged edges so she will have a nice blanket for her bed?"

"Yeah," I said, grabbing the scissors, "and I want to use some of that fur to make Molly some ear muffs," I responded, pointing at the rabbit pelt lying on the machine.

"Fur is very hard to work with. Maybe sometime I'll show you how to cut it, but right now you're cutting the blanket for your doll. Lets take it to the table so you can cut it evenly while I start the oatmeal."

The day before Santa's visit, the whole cabin smelled of sugar cookies. I sat on the bench in front of the window. It held the firewood, and when the cover was down it made a nice place to sit and watch birds or look at the pink mountain when the sun set.

I prayed every night that Santa would find me, and I promised to share my toys with Nancy and play with her. Surely, Santa would find our cabin tomorrow. There had to be some way to make sure he found us.

Staring at the dark, gloomy sky and nervously tapping my fingers against the window sill, I looked up and past the treetop wondering where the clouds started and if Santa's sled would fly below them. I spun my red paper ornament around and around, but it didn't sparkle.

Nancy tapped my shoulder, startling me. "Leave me alone," I said, pulling my shoulder away.

"We could harness Queenie and take a ride," she said.

Waiting eagerly for something to do, Queenie's ears perked up at hearing her name, and her tail thumped against the floor.

"I don't want to play." Then I remembered that I promised God that I'd be nice to Nancy and play with her whenever she asked. "What did you say you wanted to do?"

Then it hit me. I knew how Santa could find me on a dark gloomy night. I swung around and lunged for my coat and scarf and opened the door. Pushing past me, Queenie waited in the yard. "Come on, Nancy. I have an idea."

"Darlene," Mom called, "put on your boots, and if you're going to stay outside for any length of time, wear your snow pants. You too, Nancy."

"I won't be out there very long," I said, ignoring Nancy as she followed behind me.

"Hey, what are we going to do?" Nancy called, running to catch up with me.

"We're not going to do anything," I told her, looking up at the clouds and pacing in a circle around her. "How do you suppose Santa will see our house when he flies by? It'll be all dark inside and out."

"Santa sees everything. He'll see the smoke from our stove pipe," Nancy said, pointing at the roof. "Besides, he knows where everyone lives."

"How do you know? You're only seven years old."

"Seven and a half," she reminded me, "and Mama says it's true."

"You seem to forget. We didn't get any presents from Santa last year."

"We didn't?"

"No, we didn't, and I'm sure he still doesn't know where we're living. We moved at least a hundred miles from Wisconsin. You know what I'm thinking?" I asked, not paying much attention to what Mama told her. "We can put a lantern in the driveway. Santa will see it and know we live here."

"Just because you're nine doesn't mean you know everything. What makes you think Daddy will let us do that?"

"He will if I ask him. Think how bad he'd feel if Santa didn't find us again. I wish the telephone wire went all the way to the North Pole."

"Let's ask Mama what she thinks of your idea," Nancy said, turning and running toward the cabin.

Mom was making one of her delicious pie crusts when I got inside. I liked helping her but not today. I was too worried to do anything but try to figure out a way that Santa would find me. I was so anxious to tell her my idea that I didn't bother taking off my coat before sitting down by the table. "Can we put a lantern in the yard so Santa can find us?" I asked, watching the rolling pin make the dough grow on the tabletop. "Don't you think that's the best idea you've ever heard?"

Mom lifted the rolled-out crust from the table and set it in the pie dish, using her thumb to press the dough along the edges. "That's an interesting idea," she said, lifting her wrist and brushing a wisp of hair from her forehead "What makes you think Santa won't find us?"

"It's too dark and cloudy for him to see."

"Well, you're right about that."

"Do you think we could call Santa?"

"We'd have to drive all the way to Anchorage to do that," she told me, "and I think Santa has already loaded his sleigh and left the North Pole."

I couldn't talk fast enough when Dad opened the door. "Slow down," he said taking off his hat and coat, "let me get a cup of coffee and sit down, then we can talk." He finally plopped down on the double chair he had made from skinny birch logs, propped his feet on the coffee table, and took a sip of the hot black stuff in his cup.

He listened while I sat on my knees next to him. I told him about my great plan that couldn't fail and reminded him about the map and wanting to call Santa on the telephone. Then I told him what Mom said about Santa already on his way. He listened to every word. When I finally stopped going on and on, he said, "It seems you put a lot of time and thought into your plan." Then he looked at Mom, who was peeling potatoes at the table.

Leaning back against the kitchen chair, she gazed at Dad and then at me. She smiled at me, sat forward in the chair and said, "Would you be happy if we left the lanterns on inside the cabin? That way Santa would see the light through the windows." Raising her shoulders and eyebrows and tilting her head, she smiled at Dad.

"Yeah," I thought aloud. "If he saw just a small light outside, he might not see the cabin." I went to bed knowing Santa would have no trouble finding us on a cloudy night.

My eyes opened, all of a sudden, as if I'd never been asleep. The embers from the barrel stove cast red shadows on the log walls. The tinsel glimmered. Crawling from the top bunk, I wondered why the lanterns weren't burning. I crept quietly from the bedroom. I hoped the lanterns hadn't run out of kerosene before Santa found us. Glancing under the tree branches, my heart did a little flip when I spotted the log dollhouse, dolls, and toys. Wow! Santa found me and he turned off the lanterns on his way out. I quickly turned, yelling at the top of my voice, "Santa came! Nancy, get up. Santa came!"

Running into the bedroom, I grabbed her hand and pulled her into a sitting position. "Get up. Come see what Santa left us," I said excitedly, as she followed me to the tree. While staring at her shining eyes, her hand gripping mine, my heart did that odd little flipping thing again. "He found us," I whispered.

"Well, you're sure up early," Dad said, coming from the bedroom. "You never get up until I've stoked the stove and it gets too hot for you on the top bunk."

"Look at all the presents," I said, kneeling and reaching for the Eskimo doll. "Santa found us. He saw the light from the lanterns."

"Yeah, I guess he did," Dad agreed, lighting the lanterns and shoving small logs into the barrel stove.

"It was a good idea," I said softly, not caring if anyone heard me.

By now, Mom was up and lit the kindling in the cookstove and had the coffee heating.

Picking up the Eskimo doll, I carefully brushed the fur around the hood of the coat. The doll's black yarn braids rested on a snowsuit made from an Army blanket. A ruff of rabbit fur was sewn around the hood and the bottom of the coat. I let the softness of it brush my cheek and nose. Brown leather boots were pulled over the snow pants. I never had a doll with boots. She could walk in the snow and ride on the sled without getting cold feet.

I reached for the yellow-haired doll in a blue and white plaid dress. Fingering the blue silky ribbons at the ends of the braids, I noticed she wore black sandals and no socks. "I'll let you wear the boots too," I told her, staring at her big blue eyes. I twisted around to tell Nancy about the boots. She was smiling and sitting cross-legged on the floor with a doll propped on each knee. "Hey," I said, crawling towards her, "our dolls are twins."

I spied the dollhouse again, nestled under the branches close to the trunk of the tree. Lying flat on my stomach, I scooted under the tree and gazed into it. "Hey, my dollhouse looks just like our log cabin," I called out, feeling the smoothness of the logs against my hand.

"I think Santa expects the dollhouse to be for both you and Nancy," Mom said, kneeling on the floor with her cup of coffee held between both hands.

Again, I remembered my prayer to share. Reaching inside the dollhouse, I gently picked up the tiniest cradle I'd ever seen. Inside was a pink baby, as small as my thumb, wearing a white diaper. "Oh, my gosh! I've never seen a doll so small, and her pink skin looks real. Look! Her eyes open and close," I said, holding it in the palm of my hand. "Nancy, come here and look at it. I like the upstairs in the dollhouse. It will be the bedroom. I'm going to put the babies up there," I said, placing one of them on the dollhouse floor.

Nancy squirmed beneath the branches and lay beside me on her stomach. She set her dolls against the side of the dollhouse. Reaching for the cradle, she put it next to the tiny doll. "You can't just lay the baby on the floor. Put it in the cradle," she scolded.

"The baby can lay on the floor if she wants to," I told her.

"Look," Nancy said. "There's a window on each side of the dollhouse just like our cabin. I can make curtains for them."

"Did you see the lamp in the dollhouse?" Mom asked. "I just noticed that it has a tiny bulb in it that probably lights up. It even has a switch on it."

Nancy turned the miniature switch, and the inside of the dollhouse lit up. "Wow! Daddy, come see the light."

I scooted in and made sure I got my turn to switch the light on and off several times. There was a battery attached to a wire and placed outside of the dollhouse.

"Santa must think you're both pretty special to leave all these presents, plus a dollhouse with a light in it," he replied, sitting on the floor, ready to open gifts.

"Let's open the presents we got from our grandmas," I said, scooting from beneath the tree and pushing up onto my knees, eager to pull the ribbon from the colorful present with my name on it. Grandma Hixson gave us dolls. Mine didn't look like a baby; she had a little-girl look and had a cloth body and soft arms and legs made from the latest soft rubber material that felt like real skin. She had a plastic face with eyes that opened and closed and wore a beautiful white dress, bonnet, shoes, and lace socks. Nancy got a rubber baby doll. Mom and Dad got a set of drinking glasses and other household items from Grandma and Uncle Floyd's hardware store.

Grandma and Grandpa Stockhausen sent prayer books, story books, material for Mom to make matching dresses for Nancy and me, and all the sausage and cheese we had opened earlier. The candy, nuts, and cookies she sent were on the coffee table in a beautiful glass dish.

I slept happily in my bed Christmas night, surrounded by my dolls, and wondering why I had worried about the map. I was glad we didn't drive all the way to Anchorage on Christmas Eve to make a telephone call to Santa. He found me and that's all that mattered.

Mom made each of us an Eskimo doll dressed in snowsuits, made from an Army blanket trimmed with rabbit fur, and leather boots. The Dutch dolls had blond hair and brightly colored dresses, soft shoes, and a sweater to keep them warm when we took them out to play.

It was always great excitement to bring a beautiful tree into the cabin, arrange each ornament carefully on it, and hang the tinsel over the branches. The shiny tinsel glistened in the flickering light from the fire in the barrel stove.

Precious Gifts

She performs miracles using the old treadle
sewing machine. Her feet move swiftly back
and forth as the needle breaks through soft
material creating a masterpiece.

Cutting, pinning fabric, and bringing
together the edges of the cocoa beige cloth,
her delicate fingers fashion dainty Eskimo
dolls waiting to play.

She wraps up her love in the licorice
black yarn braids, her spirit in the cinnamon
and apple red embroidery stitches
of the round eyes and smiling mouths.

Cutting a taffy brown Army blanket, she sews
snow pants and jackets. Her silky hand smooths
silvery rabbit fur on the hood and edge
of the coats, giving the garments their final touch.

The pecan-colored leather boots pulled over
snow pants bring images of childhood
days frolicking through vanilla snow
on a frosty winter afternoon.

Smiling, she sets her precious gifts under the spruce
tree trimmed with popcorn and red and white
candy canes, anticipating the sparkle in girls'
blue eyes on Christmas morning.

Darlene enjoyed cuddling Queenie's puppies. Dad made a doll house from birch tree branches. It looked like our log cabin with its pitched roof. Inside was the tiniest cradle and doll. There was a teeny lamp that had a bulb attached to a battery with a miniature switch that turned the light on and off.

My Father's Hands

Sinewy, coarse hands, fingers stiffened, gripping the
plane gently as shavings of wood glance off like the
brush of blossoms on tender skin.

The creator envisioning a miniature of something already
fashioned, runs palm over smooth, diminutive logs.

His textured hands are rough with sprinkled dust like the
Alaskan volcanoes' gritty powder weaving the fabric of the land.

What sentiments shaped your cabin in this untamed land?
Is your heart happy here, or do you long for other distant places?
"My heart," he enlightens me, "is here in the building of a doll
cabin that will bring you the same happiness."

Nancy and I were playing by the road when a car stopped and a man got out and asked to take our picture. Mom heard the car slow down and come to a standstill and called from the cabin, "Girls, come on home." Nancy yelled back saying, "Mama, he wants to take our picture." Being the protective mother that she was, Mom rushed to the road and spoke to the man holding the elaborate camera. He was a photographer and said he'd mail us a photograph. We thought we'd never hear from him again, but about a month later, we received two 8x10 photographs.

Photo courtesy of H.M. Kurriger, 1948

Dad made the harness for Queenie, and she became our lead sled dog. After her puppy Slushy was born, he was second in lead. They pulled Nancy and me a mile up the highway and back home again. It was rare to ever meet a car on the road.

Rescuing Molly

Discovering my doll missing,
Nancy and I began a frantic search.
I won't sleep until I find her.

Already in her harness, Queenie
pulls against the sled, yipping
and barking, pawing the snow.

With golden hair flying, ears bobbing,
she carries us up sky-high mountains,
over frozen lakes and across glaciers.

Riding into the howling wind,
the sled shifts on uneven ground
as we trek onward to save Molly.

In the shadows of trees, we crisscross
the icy path, looking for the fork
that takes us back to the lodge.

Stopping the sled in a circle of light,
Mama hurries out with a knapsack
of cookies, a thermos of hot chocolate.

On the trail again, Nancy is calling.
She sweeps the air with her mittened
hand. "I found her," she shouts.

Swooping Molly up, I tuck her safely
into Nancy's arms. I yell, "Mush!"
Queenie's long strides bring us home.

A hug for Nancy, an Eskimo kiss
for Queenie, and a snuggle for Molly
as I sing her favorite lullaby.

Raising Chickens
1948-49

"I want to watch Daddy cut the heads off the chickens," Nancy said, climbing our favorite birch tree. It was the largest one near our homestead and was quite a long walk from the cabin.

"Me too," I said, settling on a lower branch. "Dad's not cutting their heads off. He's chopping them off with a giant hatchet. I heard Mama tell Daddy we had to stay in the house."

"Not me. I'm watching," Nancy said with determination in her voice. Pulling some yellowing leaves from the tree, she let them fall from her hand to the ground. "Aren't you just a little bit afraid?"

"I'm almost ten, and I think that's old enough to watch. Do you think you can look without covering your eyes?" I inquired.

"Sure, I can watch chickens get their heads hacked off. What's so scary about that? I'm eight and I can watch too," she stated firmly.

Throughout the winter, Mom and Dad sat at the kitchen table discussing dual-purpose chickens. "What are dual-purpose chickens?" I asked, shaking Mom's arm.

Turning toward me, she lifted her hand and straightened my barrette. "They're chickens that provide both meat and eggs," she answered, fluffing my hair.

"When will we get the chickens?" Nancy asked.

"In the spring," Mom said, continuing to look through the chicken catalog.

"What will they look like? Will they be babies?"

"Yes. They'll all be tiny yellow balls of fluff."

"We could make a few extra dollars raising chickens," Dad said, continuing to look through the catalog of different breeds, "but we need to decide how many we want. Maybe, about two hundred fifty to three hundred chickens to start with."

"Let's try it for a year, and if we don't like it, we don't have to stay in the chicken business," Mom answered.

When that was settled, they discussed the type of chickens best suited for the Alaskan climate and chose the Rhode Island Reds, because they are used for both meat and eggs.

Dad went to the co-op in Palmer and asked about the type of chickens the farmers used in the Matanuska Valley. Most farmers used the Rhode Island Reds and preferred them to many other breeds. He ordered three hundred chickens.

In early spring, the winter plans finally began to take shape. Dad built a chicken coop from scrap lumber he found at the Army dump. He used windows he bought from the Eklutna Industrial School when it was torn down. He was disappointed when he couldn't find any wire at the dump to use for fencing, and he had to buy huge rolls of it at the co-op.

Mom and Dad worked together stringing fencing around the chicken coop. I liked to watch and sometimes help as they sank the posts and nailed the fence to them. It also covered the top of the chicken yard.

"Why do you have to cover the top?" I called out to Dad.

He sat down on the roof, wiped his sleeve across his brow and told me, "Fencing the top keeps the hawks from flying into the yard and killing the chickens. It also provides a safe place where the chickens can get plenty of sunshine and fresh air."

"Why is the yard so big?"

"There will be three hundred chickens in the fenced area. Having lots of room to move around and being able to peck at the grass and shrubs will keep them healthy," he told me, pushing himself up from his resting place to finish the job.

"Three hundred chickens aren't going to fit in that yard. That's not enough room. You'll have to make it bigger, or they'll be getting in the garden eating the tops off the carrots and in the trees. We'll have to keep the screen door closed to stop them from coming into the house. They'll be everywhere. You'll need a bigger yard than that for all those chickens."

"It'll be big enough."

Dad scattered a bedding of wood chips and sawdust on the floor of the coop to absorb moisture and droppings. He built rows of boxes and nailed them to the wall. He hauled an old ladder into the hen house. "The hens can perch on the wood. It's rough enough for them to grip their claws around. I'll put the ladder in front of the boxes, so the hens have the choice of the perch or the straw-filled boxes. We want to make them as content as possible."

I spent lots of time in the hen house making soft round nests in each box so it looked like a hen had already been in it. I brought Molly in and sat her in one of the nests. "Doesn't it smell fresh and clean?" I asked, making her head bob up and down.

We spent a month preparing for the arrival of the chicks. The day came when we sat in the gravel at the entrance to our driveway waiting for Dad to return from the co-op.

About an hour later, Mom joined us. "Your father ought to be home soon," she said, waiting patiently for the sound of the truck in the distance.

Finally, the truck slowed and turned into the driveway. Dad stopped and let us pile into the cab. "Can I ride in the back with the chicks?" Nancy begged, turning to look out the back window.

"When we get to the cabin, you can help me carry the chicks to the coop," he said.

When the truck was parked, I got out on Dad's side and hurried around to the back of it. I could hear soft, quiet cheeping coming from inside the boxes as Dad lifted himself up and onto the bed of the truck. He handed the boxes to Mom, who set them on the ground.

I was down on my knees beside Nancy, trying to see through the tiny round holes. All I saw was yellow fuzz poking through. "Can I take off the cover?" I asked, poking my finger through the round hole feeling the fluffy back of a chick.

"Let's wait until we get the chicks inside," Mom suggested, reaching for the box Dad handed to her. She carried it into the hen house and set it gently on the floor. Dad followed with the last box.

We gathered around watching Mom remove the cover. There were twelve tiny chicks hidden beneath yellow downy fluff. "Ohhh! Can I pick one up?" I asked, reaching into the box, feeling the softness of the baby chicks on the back of my hand.

"Will they bite?" Nancy asked, kneeling beside the box.

"You don't have to worry about biting. Chickens don't have any teeth," Dad replied.

"How do they eat?"

"They swallow food whole, and they swallow little stones."

"They eat stones?" Nancy's eyes widened and her lips parted in disbelief.

"The stones are stored in a gizzard, and it's used to grind the food into tiny particles."

"What's a gizzard?"

"It's a second stomach."

I watched the hens grow over the months and waited with great excitement for the day I would find the first egg in one of the straw nests. The rooster was growing, too. Each time I went into the fenced yard with Mom, it became more fearless, racing forward and pecking at my shoes. As weeks went by, it was charging forward and flying as high as my shoulders, flapping its wings wildly around my hair. I watched it grow into an ornery red vampire that pecked violently at my legs. I made sure they were always covered. I clung desperately to Mom's arm, once inside the fence if the rooster was anywhere near. I was always happy when it was on the other side of the hen house.

The day finally arrived when we discovered the first egg. I hadn't been paying much attention to the chickens on that particular day. Molly and I went for a walk around the house and stopped near the chicken yard to watch Nancy push weeds through the fence. The chickens scurried around for their share of the greens. While they gathered around the weeds, Nancy and I hurried past them and into the coop. We closed the door behind us so none of the hens would follow us in. I set Molly on the window sill and began poking in the nests.

"Oh, look," Nancy whispered, carefully lifting an egg from the nest.

I ran over to where she stood holding a brown egg. "Its not white," I said, confused by the color. "Maybe, it's rotten. I'll carry it to Mama."

"No, I found it. I'm taking it to her," Nancy said, gripping the egg and heading toward the door.

"Well then, I'm going to tell her first," I said, running for the door, opening it, and heading in the direction of the cabin screaming, "Mama! Mama!"

"I want to tell her. I found the egg," Nancy yelled, running and catching up with me. "You left Molly on the window sill."

I almost twisted my ankle stopping in the slippery dirt. I grabbed Nancy's arm as she sped past me, almost toppling us. "Please, go back with me to get her," I begged. "I don't want to go by myself. The rooster might follow me."

"Only if you let me tell Mama about the egg I found," she insisted. We rescued Molly and made a hasty retreat before the rooster found us. I stood in silence while Nancy excitedly told Mom about her wonderful discovery.

"Why is the egg brown?" I asked.

"All of our hens will lay brown eggs. There are other varieties of chickens that lay white eggs," she told me, turning the brown egg in her hand.

The hens started laying in August. After the excitement of the first egg, we found ourselves collecting them two or three times a day. Mom said, "I don't want the eggs to get dirty or cracked. Water washes away some of the natural protection that helps to keep them fresh. They also might begin to spoil if they are left in the warm hen house." She helped us understand why we gathered eggs so often.

Nancy and I took turns holding the small basket used to put the eggs in. Mom would reach under the hens that were still sitting on their eggs. Sometimes her hand jerked back after being pecked. Giving the hens a gentle nudge, she quickly reached under them again to retrieve the eggs. She placed the pointed end downward into the basket telling us, "The yolks stay in the middle of the eggs when they are put into the basket properly."

The eggs were placed in the icebox immediately after checking for dirt and cracks. Dad had built an icehouse the summer before and filled it with ice from Mirror Lake during the winter. Mom always said the icebox was her one and only luxury she brought with us when we moved from Wisconsin. With the icebox full of huge blocks of ice, they both agreed it was a very valuable item to have since there was no electricity and, until now, no way to keep food cold. The icebox held the milk, Dad's homemade beer, and the week's supply of eggs.

Dad put a sign up by our road advertising eggs for sale. People would see the sign and drive up to the house, get out of their car, and introduce themselves. They were invited inside for a cup of coffee while Mom got their eggs ready. Our brown icebox was always a topic of conversation, especially with the women. "Oh my," they would say, "how fortunate you are. Not many people in these parts have a fancy icebox." Then Mom would tell her story about bringing it all the way from Wisconsin.

Mom approached the owner of the Piggly Wiggly store about selling her eggs to him. It took several weeks for eggs shipped from Seattle to arrive, and they weren't considered fresh when they were unloaded at the dock in Anchorage. People craving fresh eggs would make the dusty fifty-mile trip to the Matanuska Valley, knowing they could be found at the co-op in Palmer.

The owner of the Piggly Wiggly store was happy to buy Mom's eggs. "How much do you want to sell them for?"

"How much do you want to pay for a dozen eggs?" she inquired.

"I'll pay $1.35."

"That sounds fair," she told him. "I'd like to barter my eggs for flour, sugar, beans, and other supplies. When it's time to butcher the chickens, I'd like to sell them to you." He agreed and arranged for her to bring several dozen eggs to the store once a week.

When Dad found out about the deal Mom made with the store owner, he was almost ready to purchase another three hundred chickens. When we stopped at the coffee shop on our way home, he bragged about the great price Mom got for her eggs. He told everyone what a smart businesswoman she was.

On Saturday mornings, Mom gathered the warm eggs from the hen house and removed the cool eggs from the icebox. They were carefully packed into boxes that had been used to bring eggs from Seattle to Alaska. The four of us would crowd into the truck, and Mom, Nancy, and I held the eggs on our laps as we traveled twenty-two miles on the graveled, meandering two-lane road to Anchorage.

Every now and again, I'd hear bits of quiet talk between Mom and Dad about butchering the chickens. I was really curious about it, and every time they noticed me listening they would begin talking about something else. They got up early the morning they planned to butcher them and slipped quietly from the cabin while Nancy and I slept. When I woke, I heard the thump of the hatchet against wood. It didn't take long to realize what day it was. Still in my pajamas, I hurried through the cabin and out the screen door, noticing the pot of steaming water. Mom's back was to me, and she'd just pulled a chicken from the pot. She began plucking the wet feathers. They clung to her hand like gooey paste. She shook it vigorously in a desperate attempt to get rid of the sticky mess, letting them drop in clumps from her hand into a box beside her.

I walked to the side of the house and saw Dad grab one of the squawking chickens. I clamped my hands over my mouth to keep from screaming when he grasped both legs and held it upside down, letting its head and neck rest over the chopping block. My hands moved down and wrapped around my neck. Squinting my eyes, I lifted my shoulders almost to my chin. Dad raised the ax and brought it down with a thud against the block. I screamed as the chicken dropped to the ground. All of a sudden, it got to its feet and was running around the yard without a head. Dad turned in time to see me dash frantically around the corner of the cabin.

Mom dropped the chicken she was plucking and hurried to where I was seated on the porch step. She lowered herself to sit beside me. Wiping her hands on her apron, she gently wrapped her arm around me. "Your father and I got up extra early this morning. We wanted to be finished by the time you woke," she whispered holding me close.

Dad came from the side of the cabin removing his hat and wiping his forehead with his sleeve. Taking a handkerchief from his pocket, he brushed the tears from my cheeks. "That was a frightening thing for you to see," he said softly.

Mom helped me into the house and made a comfortable place on the davenport for me to sit until she completed the unpleasant chore waiting for her outside. She plucked the chickens after scalding them in hot water to loosen the feathers. When she finished, they were rinsed in fresh water and melted paraffin was brushed over them. She pulled the hardened wax off along with the pinfeathers. After the insides were removed, the chickens were ready for market. Mom put twelve of them in a box to be taken to Piggly Wiggly later in the morning.

When Nancy woke, Mom was making breakfast. I was sitting at the table reading a comic book and trying my best to fool her into thinking that I was calm. "You woke up too late to see the chickens being butchered," I told her.

"I wanted to watch too. Why didn't you wake me up," Nancy demanded, with her hands tight against her hips.

"You're not old enough to watch. You would've been afraid."

"Were you afraid?"

"Me! Why would I be afraid? I already told you I was old enough to watch chickens get their heads chopped off."

Mom was listening to our conversation. She turned toward me as I told Nancy the big lie. I saw her watching and decided

I'd better change my story. "Well," I began, hoping to convince Nancy that I was brave even if it wasn't true. "It's kind of scary," I told her, shrugging my shoulders, "so I only watched one chicken get its head chopped off. Next time, I'll be sure to wake you."

I watched Nancy smile as she sat down at the table, seeming perfectly content, knowing she wouldn't miss out the next time and feeling confident that she would be as brave as me.

Mom standing by the chicken coop, and Nancy making sure the water and food dishes are full. Dad built the chicken coop from scrap lumber he found at the Army dump. He was disappointed when he couldn't find wire at the dump for fencing and had to buy huge rolls of it at the co-op in Palmer. He purchased windows from the Eklutna Industrial School when it was torn down. He ordered three hundred Rhode Island Reds from the co-op.

Rooster's Domain

1949

One of our favorite times of the day was listening to stories on the battery-operated radio. There were two programs that we really enjoyed, *Lorenzo Jones* and *Helen Trent*. Nancy and I made sure we huddled beside the radio as soon as we heard their theme songs. Each story lasted fifteen minutes. Mom always found something to work on while listening. She would mend, iron clothes, or work on supper.

Mom was making a pie. Her crusts were delicious, and when we raved about them she said, "The crust is so soft and flaky because I use bear lard. Mrs. McDowell told me about the many uses of the lard when we were at the post office." Mom always told us the cooking hints she learned from our neighbors.

I had my chin resting in my arms on the kitchen table watching the wind blowing the trees, and Nancy was busy coloring a picture. We were involved in the life of Helen Trent and her family when a movement in the yard caught my attention.

"It's them!" I screamed, startling Nancy and Mom.

"Who?" Mom asked, peering out the window.

"It's the twins, Jane and Joey and their mother. I don't want to miss the last of the story. Can I please listen to it while they're here?"

"It'll be over in a minute or so, and it will take them that long to walk up the driveway. The story will end just as they reach the yard." Mom was right. "I'm glad I didn't miss it," I said, relieved.

"I want you and Nancy to play outside with them, today." Mom said, turning off the radio.

155

"I don't want to play with Jane. She's so snotty, and she thinks she's so grown up," I said, shuffling out the door.

Out in the yard, I told Jane about the wonderful pie crust made from bear lard.

"Yuck. Do you really eat bear lard? I wouldn't. That's sickening," she said with her nose all wrinkled up.

Feeling a little smug, I said, "There was bear lard in the pie you ate when you were here last week."

Jane's brown hair was chopped off at the ears, and her brown eyes stared at me in disbelief. She was nine years old, a year younger than me. Her arms were always folded in front of her as if they were stuck in that position. I wondered if she unfolded them when she went to bed. The folded arms was the one thing I truly disliked about her. Why didn't her mother make her stop doing that? Every time Jane saw me, she folded her arms and would say, "And how are you today, Darlene?" Oh, how I hated it. But I liked Joey. He never acted snooty and never folded his arms. He always walked around with his hands in the back pockets of his pants.

The four of us walked toward the fenced-in area where we kept the chickens. The chicken coop was a scary place every time I opened and walked through the wire door. Even when I was with Mom during egg collecting, I would scan the fenced area before going in. The rooster could be anywhere. One time I thought it was behind the hen house, but once inside the chicken coop, it flew onto my shoulder from behind. The rooster was able to fly high enough to attack my hair, and its claws would pull at my hair until it could free itself. If it wasn't in the mood to fly, it would peck at my feet and ankles. I always made sure I was wearing overalls when I went through the wire door.

The chicken coop was made from scrap lumber Dad found at the Army dump. Wire fencing was strung around the coop, and fencing covered the top of the yard to keep the hawks out. There were lots of windows in the hen house. Mom said, "If there isn't enough light, the hens will stop laying eggs in the winter." When they weren't laying eggs in the warmth of the hen house, three hundred chickens pecked and scratched the ground all day long.

I'm not sure why we chose this particular day to think about venturing into the coop. Maybe we felt safe because there were four of us. Maybe, a small part of me felt it would be great fun to see Jane run from the rooster, but I could never get her past the gate, no matter how hard I tried. I stared at her and knew there was no way she was going to follow us in. Her eyes were wide, and she was pulling on Joey's jacket with one unfolded arm, keeping him outside the fence.

Oh, Jane, I thought, how I'd like to get you through the gate and see the rooster running and flapping its wings at you for a change. You'd have to unfold those arms to defend yourself from that scary flying bird. It would be your turn to scream when the rooster clawed at your back and hair. I'll bet your unfolded arms would be flying everywhere. I see it all happening right now. Maybe, just maybe, one little push through the fence door and we'd be running for the henhouse. Yes, I see it happening.

Nancy and I gazed in every direction to make sure the rooster was somewhere else, unaware of our invasion into its world. There were chickens by the fence door. I opened it, giving myself just enough room to squeeze through, and gently moved the hens with my foot, not wanting to upset them. Joey came through next, pulling free of Jane's grip and eagerly wriggling his way through. Nancy came in right behind Joey, keeping an eye out for the rooster. She was nine and the bravest of all of us.

Jane stood outside the fence with her arms folded. She seemed very cautious about coming through the wire door. I wasn't sure why, because all three hundred hens were on their best behavior. It was almost as if they knew guests were arriving.

"Come on, Jane. The chickens are trying to get out," I said, trying to coax her inside.

Finally, she pressed her way through the opening. Her arms were still folded in front of her, only now they were moving upward toward her chin while staring wide-eyed at the hens. Nancy closed the door and glanced around the chicken yard one more time to make sure the rooster was nowhere in sight. The hens gathered in a circle around us, hoping we would feed them.

"Run!" Nancy hollered. The hens scattered in every direction. Their wings were beating wildly against their red bodies, and they were cackling their fool heads off.

We took off in the direction of the hen house, reaching the ramp that led to the open door. Jane was running behind Joey with her arms flapping in the air like a chicken with broken wings. She was wearing a brown sweater and was beginning to look a lot like the reddish-brown rooster. Her long, skinny chicken legs shot past Joey.

"Hurry up before the rooster sees us," I called from the door. Jane screamed and looked over her shoulder. She stumbled, catching herself just short of toppling forward onto the ramp.

Once we were safely inside the hen house, Nancy slammed the door. Together we chased the hens out the small opening in the bottom section of the door. There was one chicken that didn't want to leave its nest. I lifted the broom that stood in the corner by the door and used it to coax the hen from her nest. I chased her around the room until she scurried out the door. With a sigh of relief, Nancy dropped the board over the opening.

Jane gazed around the hen house looking at the rows of straw-filled nests. The windows let in sunlight, making the room very warm. She used her thumb and finger to pinch her nose, and she covered her mouth with the other hand. "Oh! Open the door. It stinks terrible in here. I can't stand it," she choked.

"You'll get used to it. Come and see what's in this nest," Nancy said, turning to see Jane and Joey stepping gingerly, lifting their legs and eyeing the bottom of their shoes.

"Ick! There's poop all over my shoes," Joey moaned.

It was thick underneath his shoes, and I laughed. "Don't worry about it. We'll clean them with a stick later. Come look in the nest."

He and Jane walked carefully across the room, but it was impossible to avoid the squishy mess on the floor. It had been several days since the gooey stuff had been shoveled from the floor.

"Let's count the eggs. Some are still warm. Feel how warm this one is," Nancy said, passing it to Jane who finally unfolded her arms, cupped her hands together, and accepted the egg.

We counted fifteen eggs. Nancy grabbed the basket from the corner. "Let's gather the eggs, but be real careful laying them into the basket or they might break." she said, putting a handful of straw on the bottom to hold the eggs in place while we gathered them from the nests.

"I don't want to stay in here any more. It's hot and the smell is horrible. I can't stand it any longer," Jane complained. "Let's play on the swings."

"Can I carry the egg basket?" Joey asked.

"No," I told him firmly. "I know how to carry the basket so none of the eggs crack."

"Let's go," Jane said, impatiently.

"We have to make sure the rooster doesn't see us," I told her. "Nancy, peek out and see if it's safe. Jane, if you run real fast, maybe the rooster won't peck at your bare legs." I wanted to frighten her, and my attempt paid off. I saw the horrified look on her face. Her folded arms tightened against her chest.

"I don't see the rooster. We can go," Nancy said, opening the door slightly and peering out.

"Move, so I can look too." I searched the yard in all directions. I didn't want us to be attacked as we made our dash to safety. "Okay, when I open the door, run as fast as you can. Jane, you go first. When you get to the fence door, reach around to the outside of the door and push the latch up so we can run out. Do you understand what I said?"

Jane's head bobbed up and down. Her folded arms were tight against her chin.

I clutched her arm and moved her in front of me. I turned to Nancy saying, "You and Joey get behind Jane, and I'll be last and guard all of you."

I opened the door quickly and saw two chickens starting up the ramp and several others trailing close behind. Jane hesitated. "Go!" I shouted and gave her a push.

She charged forward, leaping over the two chickens, causing them to spring from the ramp, clucking in dismay. Once she began running, the only thing on her mind was reaching the fence door. She dodged and darted around the chickens that got in her way. They scrambled in every direction, making a terrible racket.

There were about fifty chickens huddled together by the fence door. Pandemonium broke out as Jane closed in on them. Wings were flapping, feathers flying, and the clamor of the clucking was deafening. The chickens scattered in every direction. The lone rooster was left defending the entrance to its domain.

Jane glanced at the rooster as she charged toward the door. She reached through the fence, lifting the latch upward. The rooster seemed to be caught off guard. She pushed the door open, shot through, and slammed it shut before the rooster had a chance to attack her legs.

We stopped short as the door swung shut. The rooster eyed us and began to move in our direction. Nancy and Joey were in front of me. They began moving backward, bumping me and causing all of us to topple to the ground. I was surprised that I was still clutching the handle of the basket and the eggs were safe. I scooted myself backward and rose to my feet.

"Open the door! Open the door!" I shouted to Jane, while helping Joey to his feet with my free hand. The rooster was after Nancy, flapping its wings violently as it circled her. I thrust the basket at it without letting go of the handle, grabbed Nancy's sleeve, and pulled her toward the door. Suddenly, the rooster was in the basket, its wings beating frantically. I could feel the feathers touching my fingers as I gripped the handle. In my panic, I flung the basket, not realizing it flew straight for the fence where Jane was standing on the other side. While the basket was still in the air, the rooster flew from it, landing and running toward the doorway. The basket toppled to the ground. The eggs tumbled out, splattering near the entrance.

When we were a few feet from the door, I saw Jane begin to open it just a crack and then close it again. "Open it. Hurry!" I shrieked.

Nancy grabbed the door and pushed it open. We bolted through, and Jane slammed it shut. From the corner of her eye, Jane watched the rooster scramble amongst running feet and come to a standstill beside her. She screamed and kicked it away from her. With its wings flapping wildly, the rooster flew a foot into the air and settled a short distance from her. All of a sudden, in a crazed frenzy, it charged toward her. Jane's eyes were huge, her arms stretched out in front of her to ward off the attack.

The rooster flew forward and landed on her left arm. Her arms shot out sideways, and she ran in the direction of the cabin screeching at the top of her voice. Her arms were beating frantically. The rooster seemed bewildered and tried to fly from her arm, but its claw caught in her brown sweater. In a wild attempt to free itself, the rooster pulled Jane to the ground. Finally, untangling its claw, it headed in the direction of the chicken coop, looking very distraught.

Jane was quite a sight sitting on the ground with her clothes all rumpled. Her knees were full of dirt, and her eyes looked dazed. The three of us stood frozen in shock staring at her. Then Joey started laughing, quietly at first, with a hand over his mouth. Nancy and I looked at him and then at Jane. I ended up on my knees on the ground laughing hysterically. Nancy was curled up in a ball holding her stomach, which was beginning to ache from laughter.

Jane stood up, folded her arms, stomped her foot and yelled, "I hate you. I hate you. I hate you. I'm going to tell." She turned and stomped off in the direction of the cabin.

Oh, Jane, You're lucky today. I got to hear all of Helen Trent. *How funny it would have been if we had actually...*

A hard poke against my arm startled me. My hand clung tighter to the fencing. My eyes flew open, staring down at the folded arm that jabbed my ribs. Jane's lips were so tightly pursed that the words barely came out of her mouth. "Didn't you hear me? I'm not going in there," she said, "and you can't make me. So there."

"Guess what, Jane, I don't want to go in there either."

Remembering how comical she looked with the rooster on her arm, set me off on another round of laughter. She stared at me as though she thought I was crazy.

Nancy and Darlene rarely went into the fenced area of the chicken coop unless Mom or Dad were there as protection against the red rooster. It attacked us each time we walked through the fenced gate. Dad would close the rooster in the hen house when we wanted to feed and hold the hens.

Keepers

1949

Our third summer found us ready to become farmers. Dad plowed the winter's left-over oat crop under and readied the soil for planting. He used Mr. Tatro's tractor again to prepare the ground. That was the best part of gardening, because Nancy and I got to ride with him down the seemingly endless rows. Nancy begged for the chance to drive the tractor until Dad finally gave in. Then she wanted to do the driving all the time. By the middle of May, it was getting warmer and planting time was getting closer.

Dad found a fishnet at the dump, and said it was one of the best things he came across to help him live off the land. He put it into the inlet at the mouth of Peters Creek. Each day when the tide was low, we drove the Birchwood road to Cook Inlet to check the net. Usually there were about ten or fifteen fish laying in the sun. They were untangled from the net, picked up by the gills, taken to the waters edge, and cleaned.

We had more stinky fish than we knew what to do with. Mom canned fish, Dad smoked it in a small shed, and we ate fresh fish almost every day. The leftover cut-up pieces and heads were chopped up and put in a tub and saved to fertilize the ground.

Mr. Tatro gave us several gunnysacks full of healthy potatoes with several new green sprouts beginning to grow from the large potatoes. Dad cut each one into four sections with a sprout left in place on each piece. We planted them in hills of soft dirt about twelve inches apart. We traded jobs about every fifteen minutes to make the work less boring. Dad dug the hole, I threw a stinky fish head in for fertilizer, and he topped it with more dirt. Mom carried the bucket of cut-up potatoes, dropping one on top of the fresh dirt that covered the ugly head. Nancy came along behind us with the shovel, pushing the velvety black dirt over the hole.

The very worst part of the job was grabbing the heads from the bucket and seeing the fish eyes staring at me when I tossed the slimy things into the hole. When I got tired, I'd crawl along the ground dragging the fish bucket and moaning, hoping Mom would see how I was suffering. Fish scales would stick to my skin, looking like little diamonds shimmering in the sun. No one wanted to take time to look at the sparkling diamonds flashing when the sun caught them. "We'll look later," Mom said, dropping potatoes behind me.

"But, my hand looks like I'm wearing a fancy shiny glove. See?" I stood to show her, waving the sparkly specks of light in the air.

"Wow! They do give off brilliant, glittering flashes of light."

When Dad and Nancy finally took time to look, the shiny spots were covered with dust. The dirt would work its way through the knees of my slacks and onto my skin, and dust crept into my nose. My fingernails were grubby, even the few times I wore the gloves that were too big for my hands.

"Can we change jobs, Mama?"

"Yes, you can carry the potato bucket. It's not so heavy now," she said, setting the bucket next to me.

"Pack the dirt tightly to keep the tubers covered," Mom told Nancy, moving slowly ahead of her. "The new potatoes grow above the seed pieces, not underneath."

I was just starting to get up. I turned, sat flat on my rump, and asked Mom, "What are tubers?"

"Tubers are underground stems. New plants develop from the eyes of the potatoes."

Nancy stopped spreading dirt over the potato pieces. "Eyes! Potatoes have eyes?" she asked, staring into the hole. She bent, bracing her hands against her knees for a closer look.

"Well, sort of." Mom explained, "The eyes are also called buds, and the new plants grow from them."

"Eyes," I muttered quietly to myself, repeating the word over and over, imagining potato eyes and fish eyes in the holes under the ground. "That's spooky," I said aloud, hoping to scare the tar out of Nancy. Suddenly I was startled from my world of eyes.

"Look, Darlene, this is an eye," Mom said, tapping my shoulder and pointing to a small spot on the potato. "That's where the tuber grows."

Nancy stood up gawking at the spot Mom was pointing at. "That's not spooky," she said, hands on her hips and giving me one of her famous slit-eye looks.

"You're lagging behind," Dad called out. "Let's get the ball rolling again. I need a fish head in the four holes ahead of you. We have lots of work to do today."

We watched the new shoots peek through the dirt, eagerly waiting for the pretty flowers Mom promised would bloom on the potatoes. At the same time, we began to see the chickweed sneaking in and winding its way through the lush black soil. Dad said, "By golly! Those weeds aren't going to stick around in our garden." He pulled on several of them, yanking the roots clear out of the ground, then tossed them to the edge of the garden and reached down and grabbed one after the other. Then he looked at Nancy and me and told us, "That's what I want you to do. Every day I want you to come out here and walk along the rows and pull out every weed you see." It wasn't long before the chickweed was everywhere, and Dad handed a hoe to each of us. I knew I was going to hate this job as I stared over the three acres of potatoes.

Nancy liked being outside and didn't seem to mind getting her hands dirty in the garden. Not me. I'd rather be in the cabin helping Mom. I'd do anything to just be able to stay inside and away from the potato patch, even sweep the floor, which wasn't an easy job with the miserable groove in each board.

Mom would make cookies almost every day, and Nancy would sprinkle and stir the chocolate chips or raisins into the batter. I spooned the dough onto cookie sheets and we both licked our fingers after running them around the inside of the bowl. Then Mom would say, "If you go out for twenty minutes and hoe the weeds, the cookies will be warm and out of the oven and ready to eat. I'll call you when they're done."

"I don't want to pull weeds, Mama," I complained. "Let Nancy do it. She likes being outside."

"I don't want to pick weeds by myself," Nancy said, reaching into the bowl for the last big chunk of dough and shoving the whole thing into her mouth.

"Why do I have to help?" I whined.

"When the two of you work together, you get a lot more done. You make up such wonderful stories as you work to entertain each other, and the job is done before you know it. You ought to be able to finish two rows in twenty minutes. I'll call you when the cookies are cool enough to eat, and I'll make two tasty glasses of Ovaltine to dunk the cookies in."

I grabbed my slacks that were left by the door, pulling them on and dropping my dress down over them. I liked wearing dresses, and most days I'd put one on, thinking I wouldn't have to go outside if I looked dainty, but it usually didn't work. On the really bad mosquito days, we pulled on garden gloves and wore netting over our heads that tied at the neck. The buzzing sound drove me crazy. The mosquitoes would stick to the netting, waiting patiently for a chance to attack. I'd take a deep breath and blow most of them off. When Mom called, "Cookies are done," we didn't care if the two rows were done. We dropped the hoes and ran hungrily for the warm cookies and tasty Ovaltine.

The hoeing always went faster when we sang songs we memorized from the radio. Dad usually joined us on the weekends, pulling the weeds and whistling as we sang. We had just finished the first row of the day when Dad bent over looking at something. Running toward him Nancy shouted, "Daddy, what are you looking at?"

Dad dug around a potato plant, carefully uncovered it, and looked closely at the tiny potatoes, then gently put the dirt over the plant. We followed as he stepped over several rows and did the same thing. "See these potatoes? They're big and healthy. We're going to have a good crop this year. Do you think it was the stinky fish we used for fertilizer?" he joked, while the three of us slowly walked back to where we had left the hoes. He bent to pull some weed and said, "The patch is growing so well because of all the hard work the two of you do every day to keep the weeds from choking the potatoes."

"Weeds choke potatoes?" Nancy asked, wrapping her hand around the front of her neck and bending for a closer look at the chickweed that was dangerously close and starting to wind around the flowering plant. She grabbed the weed and pulled it out and carefully touched the flowers. "You're safe now," she whispered.

"Yep, we have a crop of keepers," Dad said, taking off his hat, wiping his forehead, and surveying the field.

Nancy looked at him. "What are keepers?"

"It means we are going to keep them all. They're healthy, and no bugs are eating them. Look at all the white flowers on them. A beautiful sight. They definitely are keepers."

I looked across the acres of white flowers and felt proud that I had a hand in creating healthy potatoes with eyes. Nancy took Dad's hand and together walked toward the cabin. With a sweeping wave of her arm, Nancy glanced over her shoulder saying, "Our very own flower garden. Let's go see if the cookies are done." We took off running, leaving Dad to follow slowly behind.

Farming became a way of life during our third summer: tilling the soil, fertilizing with fish heads, and planting row after row of potatoes. Nancy and I pulled weeds every day. We learned about tubers and what chokes potatoes.

Dad, Darlene, and Nancy admiring one of the many fish that were caught in our net at the mouth of Peters Creek. We used the fish heads to fertilize the potato field. We ate fresh fish, and canned and smoked the rest.

Garden Under the Ground

1949

Mom poured a cup of coffee for herself and one for Dad. I watched them walk together out the door and leisurely stroll toward the hill. I finished my oatmeal and ran to catch up with them.

Nancy waved from the hill where she was staring into the huge hole that the bulldozer carved out of the top. I hurried ahead, rushing up the hill to stand beside her. "I wonder if the hole is big enough for all the potatoes?" I asked, glancing at the acres of plants full of white flowers.

"It's not big enough. That's a little hole," Nancy said, carefully working her way down the hill. "Look at all the potatoes. There's probably millions of them."

I was almost ten years old, but it seemed that everywhere I went, I followed along behind my eight-year-old sister. She always walked faster than me, even on the rocky mess the bulldozer left after digging the hole in the side of the hill. Reaching the bottom, we hurried to where Mom and Dad were sitting on tree stumps enjoying their coffee.

"That'll be the best place to build the root cellar, because the hill faces north," he told Mom. Then pointing toward the hill, he said, "The entrance can be there on the north side."

"The potatoes won't fit, Daddy," Nancy interrupted.

"Sure they will," he told her. "With your help, we'll make them fit. Do you want to work with me to build the root cellar?"

"Yes," we shouted.

"We're going to the dump to look for barrels. We'll use as many as we can find to build the walls."

When we arrived at the dump Dad scanned the area, searching for fifty-five-gallon oil drums. "There they are. Over there." He pointed toward a spot heaped with barrels and moved the truck closer to them.

It had been a long time since Nancy and I had been to the Army dump, and we always looked forward to finding the treasures Mom said were hidden among all the stuff. We helped roll barrels to the truck, and Dad loaded them onto the truck bed. "How many more do we need?" I asked, laying over the warm barrel. I wanted Dad to notice how tired and out of breath I was.

"I don't think we can get another barrel onto the truck. You did a good job."

I perked up when I heard the job was over and done with. I rolled off the barrel, ran over to Mom and put my hand into hers.

Mom smiled and look down at me. "I'm going to look around and see if I can find something we might be able to use. Do you want to walk along?"

The best part of going to the dump was looking around. Mom found some jars and passed them to Nancy and me. With our arms full, we turned to go back to the truck. I heard Nancy stumble and I turned to see her land heavily on top of the jars, shattering two of them. Lifting herself, we noticed immediately that she came away without a scratch. Suddenly I saw what made her trip. I guess we all spied the box of candy bars at the same time.

"Who would throw away candy bars?" Nancy asked, setting the jars carefully on the ground and grabbing the box.

"I can't imagine who would do that," Mom replied.

We drove home perfectly content, passing the box of candy bars and enjoying every bite. There were enough bars leftover for dessert that evening and for several snacks throughout the week.

Dad figured he had an area big enough to build a sixteen- by twenty-foot root cellar. He shoveled dirt away from the place the doorway would be. We began rolling barrels into the dug-out area, and Dad arranged them around the dirt wall, leaving an opening for the door. He laid long boards on top of the barrels and set a second row of them on top of the first ones.

The roof was difficult for Dad to build by himself; Mom helped as much as she could. The barrels supported what was beginning to look like a roof. Nancy and I pulled the heavy boards through the doorway, and Mom handed them to Dad. Slowly, the dirt hole began looking like a room.

Dad used the bulldozer to backfill along the sides. He was concerned about the weight of the dirt that would cover the roof. He pushed four feet of dirt over the top, and when completed, the roof stayed firmly in place.

When he finished, I could see it was dark inside. Walking through the doorway, it wasn't the pitch black dark I was hoping it would be. "I want it to be real dark," I said, following behind Mom.

"It will be, once your father puts the door in place," she told me.

The entrance was framed and the door hung. Just when I thought we were all done, Dad said, "I'm going to need you girls to bring me some more boards so I can build shelves for some of the vegetables."

Nancy and I dragged long boards to the cellar, feeling more exhausted with each trip we made. It wasn't because the boards were far from the cellar, it was the bumpy ground we had to pull them over. "I'm tired of working," I moaned crumpling onto the dirt floor.

"You'll be glad you helped plant the vegetable garden and work on the root cellar when you eat carrots and potatoes during the winter months," Mom said.

When the shelves were finished, I asked Mom why they weren't pushed against the wall so there would be more room. "There needs to be space between the wall and the shelves so air can go around them."

Now I was sure the cellar was done. I took Molly to look at the dark room, keeping the door open so I could see. Setting her on the shelf, I told her how I helped build the cellar. "Do you want to see how dark it is when I close the door?" I asked.

Molly stared at me with wide eyes, begging me to close it. And so I did. Turning back in the direction of the shelf, I stretched my arms, searching for it. "Where are you, Molly?" I called, feeling shaky. She didn't answer. I wasn't sure which way to turn in my search for the door. It was pitch black, and I didn't like it. Suddenly the door opened, letting the sunlight stream into the room. Running swiftly for the door, I slammed against Dad.

"Are you okay? Did the door shut? I remember putting a rock on the ground to use as a doorstop."

"No, I closed the door. I wanted to show Molly how scary it is with the door shut, and when I saw how black it was, I didn't like it. Molly couldn't find me," I sobbed while Dad comforted me.

"If you want it fairly dark but not completely dark, be sure to put something between the door jam and the door. Like this thin board," he said, lifting it and placing it between the door and jam. "I'll close the door and we'll see how much light comes in."

Hanging onto his sleeve in case it was pitch black, my eyes adjusted to the dimness in the room. Racing toward Molly and snatching her from the shelf, I held her tight in my arms. "You're okay now. I'll bet you were scared, but I'm here now," I whispered tenderly in her ear.

Dad pulled out his tape measure. "Do you want to help me measure the cellar?" he asked. "I'm going to build some bins to store the potatoes."

I enjoyed the easy task of holding the tape while Dad measured the cellar. I didn't mind a job like this one.

"I'm going to ask you to do one more job for me, then you'll be done for the day. I need just a few more boards," he said, rolling up the measuring tape and putting it into his pocket.

I stood staring at him. "I can't haul another board. My arms will fall off." My shoulders slumped forward; my arms drooped toward the floor. I groaned and hoped I looked pitiful.

"You're a hard worker. Maybe we can finish the job today if we work together for another hour. I'll cut the boards into small sections so they'll be easier to carry. Let's ask your mother and Nancy to help us."

After hauling the boards, I asked, "Is the root cellar done now?"

"We'll be finished when the bins are put together."

"Why do we need so many bins?"

"The potatoes need to be placed in small piles," Dad said. "If we pile all the potatoes together, it will bruise them and air won't get into the middle of the pile. They'll heat up and won't last as long."

"You sure know a lot about potatoes," I said, heading for the door before Dad found another job for me to do.

"Thanks for helping today. You did a good job."

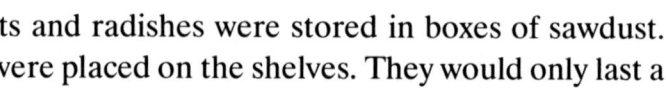

The carrots and radishes were stored in boxes of sawdust. The cabbages were placed on the shelves. They would only last a short time. The potatoes took more care before they were stored.

Dad told me, "They need to strengthen their skins. We'll do this by putting them in a safe place out of the rain and sun before we put them in the cellar. It gives their skin a chance to thicken. When we put them in the root cellar, they will keep for six months or maybe longer. They'll be in the dark so they won't sprout before we're ready to plant them next spring."

When the potatoes and vegetables were finally stored away in the cellar, the door was always kept closed. When entering, we opened the door just enough to squeeze through. Mom told us, "The sunshine and the warmer air from outside will cause the potatoes to sprout, and the light will also spoil some of the other vegetables."

We used a kerosene lantern when we went inside. It cast strange shadows along the barrel walls. Sometimes I'd dance between the lantern and barrels, watching the twisted shapes play along the wall of curves.

We had so many potatoes that we weren't sure if they would all fit in the root cellar. Mom suggested that we sell some of them. The next time we drove to Palmer for supplies, Dad bought burlap sacks at the co-op for the extra potatoes.

Mom painted a sign that read "Potatoes For Sale." Dad nailed a post to the sign, and we all walked together to the road and watched Dad pound it into the ground next to our driveway. A lot of people stopped by to purchase potatoes. Some would stay for coffee and tell us interesting things about themselves. They'd leave and we'd never see them again. Others stopped to buy a sack of potatoes every time they traveled between Anchorage and Palmer.

We visited the root cellar every few days. Mom planned our meals, and we'd take the basket to collect potatoes and carrots to put in with the moose roast. During late fall we ate the last of the cabbages with caribou steaks.

When the snow piled high and drifted across the driveway, we didn't have to worry about getting to the store. Our underground garden brought us through the winter.

There was a good-sized hill a short distance from the cabin that would house the perfect root cellar. Dad always found what he needed at the Army dump. He hauled home all the fifty-five-gallon drums he could find and built a sixteen- by twenty-foot root cellar. He stacked dirt-filled barrels on top of one another for the walls, finished it with a flat roof, and bulldozed the dirt over the top. He had mounds of potatoes to sell to neighbors and enough leftover to plant the following year.

Dad standing in the cleared area that became our vegetable garden for many years.

Darlene, Dad, and Nancy showing off the wheelbarrow full of cabbages. They were stored in the root cellar along with the other vegetables and potatoes. We ate a lot of moose and caribou meat along with cabbage, finishing up the last of the cabbage in late fall.

Runaway Dough

1950

My Grandmother Hixson was excited about her first visit to Alaska. She never dreamed she would ever experience such a far-away land so out of the ordinary realm of what she was familiar with.

When the letter came telling us she was coming for a visit, our ho-hum existence changed as we anticipated her arrival by air from North Dakota. It was her first airplane flight. Dad wasn't able to pick her up, because he couldn't get time off from work. It was arranged for her to travel by bus from Anchorage to Chugiak. At the airport, she took a taxi cab to the bus station in Anchorage. She arrived early, waiting for the business day to end at half past four. It took people half an hour to walk from office buildings to the station and buy coffee and snacks to take with them before George hollered, "All Aboard."

We knew that the bus traveling every day between Anchorage and Palmer would be arriving at our house around six o'clock in the evening, if there wasn't a breakdown. We were anxiously waiting her arrival. George tooted the horn several times to let us know our long-awaited visitor had arrived.

Nancy was taking her turn watching from the window for the bus. "She's here! Nonnie's here," she hollered, pushing herself from the bench next to the window and heading for the cabin door.

George brought Nonnie's luggage across the road and deposited it in our driveway. By that time we had run the distance from our house to the road. She hurried toward us, reaching for Mom. "Oh, Bernie, I'm so happy to see you and John and the girls," her eyes filling with tears, hugging her tightly.

She turned, heading toward Nancy and me, wrapping her arms around us. Her short brown hair brushed my face. Tears were brimming in her blue eyes. She stood back, her whole face spread into a smile. "You both have grown so tall and beautiful." She hugged us again, spreading kisses on our cheeks and foreheads.

She turned to Dad and broke into an open and friendly smile. "It's good to see you, John," she said, affectionately.

"It's good to see you too, Em. It's been a long time. I'm glad you're here to see what life is like in the wilderness," he said, embracing her in a bear hug.

"It was a long tiring trip, but I'll feel like my old self after a good night's sleep," she remarked, walking arm in arm with Mom to the cabin.

Grandma moved slowly across the floor boards toward the kitchen table. She clasped her robe tightly around her waist with one hand, rubbing her aching hip with the other.

"Are you all rested, Nonnie?" I asked, watching her sit down heavily on the kitchen chair.

"Oh, I ache all over," she replied, pushing her brown hair away from her face with fingers itching to wrap around the handle of the first cup of coffee of the day. "It was a long airplane ride and it wore me out. The seat wasn't very comfy, and I didn't get up and move around often enough. Today, I feel older than my fifty-three years. I'll work the ache out when I start moving around. A cup of hot coffee ought to make all the difference."

"Mama's French toast will perk you right up," Nancy told her, draping her arms around Nonnie's neck, squeezing her tight.

"I'm sure your mother's French toast will be yummy right after I've had my coffee," she told Nancy, pinching and then kissing her cheek.

"Especially with the homemade blueberry syrup Mama makes," I said, pulling my chair closer to her.

"Let your grandmother have a few minutes to enjoy her coffee," Mom said, pouring Nonnie's coffee into the cup

"Are you glad you're here, Nonnie?" I asked.

"You bet I am. It's been a long time since I hugged you," she said, pulling me on to her lap. "I've missed all of you the past three years, and I counted the days this month, knowing I'd see you soon. I enjoyed the letters you've sent and all the pictures you've drawn for me."

Our kitchen area was small and next to the front door, which was the only door into the cabin and was always called "the front door." The cupboards were built along the front wall. The cookstove sat along the side wall next to the bench beneath the window that held wood for it and the barrel stove that heated the cabin. The table was in the middle of the room with Mom's beautiful rag rug underneath. A kerosene lantern hung above the table. The living room was by the back wall.

Mom used the last of the bread to make French toast for breakfast. After their fourth cup of coffee, she and Nonnie cleared the breakfast dishes and began making bread.

"The cabin sure looks cozy," Nonnie said, wiping the oil cloth and putting the large yellow bowl on it. "When you wrote about your double chair that John made, I couldn't imagine it being comfortable. Since relaxing on it last night, I know what you meant when you said it had a snug comfortable feel to it."

"It's the first piece of furniture John made. The folding chairs we brought with us were all we had to sit on." Mom put the cookbook on the cupboard and began reading aloud the ingredients. "Let's see, yeast, liquid, and flour. Let's make a double batch.

Then we won't have to make bread for a while. I'll fix the yeast, and you can measure fourteen cups of flour."

Nonnie pushed the measuring cup deep into the flour sack, pulling it out several times dumping the contents into the large sifter she placed over the heavy yellow bowl. "The cushions are so colorful."

"Mama, can I help?" I asked, watching her drop the yeast cakes into the water she saved from the pot of potatoes she had boiled for last night's supper. She said it added more flavor to the bread rather than using plain water. Mama was listening to Nonnie talk about the double chair. I knew it wasn't polite to interrupt, but she didn't seem to hear me the first time. "Mama, can I put this in?" I asked again, pointing to the yeast and pulling impatiently on her sleeve trying to get her attention.

"In a minute, Darlene," she said, still talking to Nonnie while looking at me. I took it to mean yes, as she continued her conversation. I carefully lifted the yeast cake from the counter. I liked the feel of it crumbling between my fingers and watching it fall and dissolve in the warm water.

"We call the chair our love seat. John reads, and I mend and finish projects that I didn't get done during the day. We found so many Army blankets at the dump, I folded some and made pillow covers for them," Mom told her, measuring the salt, sugar, and shortening. She poured cups of coffee for Nonnie and herself. "John spent a lot of time peeling the birch trees and varnishing them so they would always have the shiny new look."

"Well, it must have taken a long time to finish your love seat. The pillows are bright and add beauty to the room," Nonnie said, admiring Mom's handiwork. She dipped into the flour sack and poured another two cups of flour into the sifter.

"We decided to keep it after we got our davenport. It holds a lot of memories for us. We had many discussion about building an addition to the cabin someday and the size of the garage and greenhouse. And we planned the garden while sitting on it in the evenings. We would sit there and remind each other how fortunate we were to have chosen Alaska to be our home. It has brought us great enjoyment living here on our own land."

I always enjoyed helping Mom make the bread. Most of the time she baked during the week, but sometimes she waited until Saturday when I could help her. I'd get to wear one of her aprons, and she'd tie a ribbon around my hair to keep it out of my face. I'd shake cups full of flour from the sifter into the bowl, watching it swirl into the yeast mixture that Mom was stirring. Punching the risen dough was the best part. I'd gently lower my fists into the white mound, feeling the warm dough surround them.

I was disappointed as I watched Nonnie tie one of Mom's aprons around her waist and help with the job I always got to do. I walked to the drawer that held the colorful aprons and lifted out one that was yellow and green plaid. "Can I punch down the dough?" I asked, tying the apron around my waist.

"Yes, as soon as it rises. I wouldn't want you to miss your favorite job."

Mom turned back to Nonnie. "I'm glad you came to visit. I missed you and our long casual talks about ideas and everyday matters, and I have so many things to show you. Tell me what made you decide to move to North Dakota?" she asked.

"After you and John moved, Floyd and I felt there was no reason to stay in Wisconsin. Floyd had a brother in North Dakota, and we decided it would be nice to live by family again. We put the restaurant and bar up for sale, and when it sold, we were carefree and decided to pull up stakes, move on and try something different. We ended up in North Dakota in a small town outside of Bismarck called Carson. An appliance store had a FOR SALE sign on it, and we bought it. There were living quarters in the same building, which helped to make up our minds to buy. We thought,

'Wow, we won't even have to drive to work.' That was a real buying point for us. Like I said, it was time to try something new. After we were settled in, Floyd got involved in the community, helping design many of the new streets as Carson grew."

Nonnie pushed the cup deep into the sack. When she pulled the cup from it, I tapped her arm. "Can I pour it in?" She handed me the cup and I sprinkled it into the sifter, shaking it through the screen and into the yellow bowl, watching the flour land on top of the rest of the powdery white stuff, exploding into a smoky cloud.

Nonnie lifted the spoon saying, "Bernie, the consistency doesn't seem right. It's too sticky."

I got to sift the remaining flour until the dough cleaned the bowl, then Nonnie covered it and set the clock for fifteen minutes. She lightly floured the bread board that almost covered the table. When the clock alarm rang, she lifted the dough from the bowl, placing it on the board. Mom and Nonnie divided the dough and kneaded it for ten minutes. When they finished, it was turned into the clean, greased bowl and turned greased side up, then covered with a white cloth.

"It seems like a lot of dough for a double batch," Nonnie commented, while filling the dishpan with warm water from the reservoir on the wood-burning cookstove. "I set the clock for an hour," she said. Mom washed while Nonnie dried the dishes.

"You wrote about John's job on the railroad. How does he like it?" Nonnie asked, putting the dishes into the cupboard.

"He's really happy with the job. There was an opening at the Birchwood station. The men live in the section house. The best part is that he only has to drive four miles to the Birchwood station, so he comes home every night. He never liked the long drive to Anchorage. He works with six to eight men, and he likes the section boss, Gilbert Rosenberg. There is a young man, George Ondola, that John enjoys talking to during breaks and lunch. He said George is very knowledgeable about Chugiak and the surrounding areas."

Nancy turned to Nonnie, "Daddy is a gandy dancer. Do you know what a gandy dancer does?"

"No, I don't," Nonnie replied. "Why don't you tell me."

"Daddy said that sometimes the train can move the tracks when it goes around corners. He makes sure the tracks are nailed down. We got to walk along the railroad tracks and he showed us some wooden ties that were rotten that he had to change. He makes sure that the train is safe on the tracks."

"It sounds like he has a very important job," Nonnie told her.

"Can we show Nonnie the pigs?" Nancy asked, running her fingers over the damp table that Mom had just wiped off. "We have five pink pigs, Nonnie, and one of them has black spots. When they get bigger, Daddy said we're going to eat them."

"You can even help us collect the eggs," I said, "and you'll want to be careful because it really hurts when the hens peck your hand."

After showing Nonnie the pigs, I didn't want to walk around the garden while Mom talked about vegetables, and I didn't care to go into the stinky chicken coop on a hot day. "I'm going in and read for awhile," I told them and headed for the cabin.

"I'm going with you," Nancy called from the garden, running to catch up with me.

I yawned and looked up from the Nancy Drew book, feeling very relaxed lying on the love seat. My hand was propped against my head on the armrest. I laid the open book over my hip and watched the dough bulging over the rim of the bowl. It was covered with the white dishcloth Mom made from a flour sack. It seemed to spring to life, determined to reach the tabletop. That's odd, I'd never seen the bread do that before. It looked silky smooth as it stretched from the bowl like elastic. Staring in fascination, I sat up straight, watching it.

Maybe I should call Mama; I don't think its suppose to do that, I thought. I pushed myself from the love seat and walked slowly to the table, put one knee on the chair, then slid down on my folded leg. Maybe it's time to punch it down.

"Hey, Nancy. Do you think the bread is supposed to do this?" I asked, moving my head forward for a closer look.

Nancy got up from the floor, carrying her book with her to the table. She inched her arm toward the dough, laying her open hand under the glob that was about to sag on to the tabletop. "I've never seen the dough grow like that before."

I poked my finger twice into the dough making two eye holes. "Now you look like a face," I told the dough, "with a scarf on your bald head."

"Maybe I'd better call Mama right now," Nancy said, pushing herself away from the table and rushing toward the door, "she'd want to know about this."

The door opened, startling me. Nonnie was the first to walk through the doorway "Oh! My gosh, Bernie," she screamed, moving quickly toward the table.

I pushed my chair back and moved away. "I didn't do it. I was getting ready to call you, but Nancy beat me to it."

"Quick!" Nonnie yelled, taking charge of the runaway dough. "Get another bowl. What in the world happened! Hurry! The dough is everywhere."

Mom grabbed a bowl from the cupboard, and Nonnie whipped off the towel and began scooping the dough up. Mom pushed the bowl under the dough in Nonnie's hands, letting her set it carefully into it. Mom lifted more of the sagging dough that already touched the table and let it fall lightly into the bowl.

"I'll punch it down," I called out, but nobody was listening.

"What happened?" Nonnie repeated, wiping her hands on the dish towel.

"I don't know," Mom answered. "Oh, my word! You don't think we could've made a triple batch? I measured the same amount of yeast that I usually do for four loaves of bread, I'm almost positive."

"I'll punch it down," I said, pulling on Mom's sleeve.

"Okay."

"I think I put in fourteen cups of flour," Nonnie replied. "I'm almost sure of it, yet I guess I really don't remember how much was mixed in. We were so engrossed in catching up on each other's lives that I guess I wasn't paying attention to bread-making. I do remember it being sticky and we needed more flour."

I looked at the bald head of dough and watched what was left of the eyes disappear into the mound, my fists sinking deep into the warm dough. At that moment, I remembered putting in the yeast cake and not getting Mom's okay. Pulling my hands from the dough, I realized it was my fault that the bread overflowed the bowl. I grabbed Mom's arm. "Mama," I whispered, pulling on her sleeve. "Mama," I repeated, quietly trying again to get her attention. "I think it might be my . . . "

"Not now, Darlene," she said, ignoring me. "Well, we certainly have more dough than we have pans." Mom sat down on the kitchen chair, hands on hips, shaking her head back and forth. Frown lines grew deep between her brows.

Wrapping my arms across my chest, I stared at the dough. What a mess I've made of the bread. What will Nonnie think of me if I tell about the extra yeast I slipped into the bowl. Maybe,

I shouldn't say anything. Mama will scold me in front of her, and Nancy will laugh and tease me.

"What a predicament. It wouldn't seem so bad if we had all the pans we need to get this mess into the oven," Mom said.

Nonnie glanced at Mom. "What are we going to do with all this dough?"

I watched a half-hearted smile pass between them, so maybe it wasn't as bad as I thought.

"I have a muffin pan in my doll dishes," Nancy said, wanting to be helpful. "You can use it."

Mom burst out laughing. Nonnie stared at her for a few seconds and saw the hilarity of the situation and began to laugh, too.

I wasn't laughing. "Mama, I think it's my fault that the dough fell over the sides of the bowl." I said, hardly loud enough for her to hear, my heart pounding like the Little Gingerbread Boy running away from the baking pans.

Mom put her arm around my waist and pulled me toward her. "It's not your fault, honey," she said, squeezing me close, easing the scared feeling.

"But I put a yeast cake into the bowl."

"An extra yeast cake wouldn't make as much dough as we have in the bowls. It's something your grandmother and I did. It's not anything you did," she said, freeing me of worry.

Nonnie covered the dough, leaving it to rise another thirty minutes. "We're going to have plenty of bread, that's for sure," she said, pouring a cup of coffee for herself and one for Mom. "How about some cinnamon rolls? Or maybe some butterhorns? I know, some nice cloverleaf rolls with supper tonight. Doesn't that sound good?"

"I want to roll up the butterhorns," Nancy told Nonnie, "and make the frosting."

In the meantime, Mom pulled five bread pans, two cake pans, two cookie sheets, and a muffin pan from the cupboard and greased them. "I'm sure we'll need all the pans."

They finished their coffee just as the thirty minutes were up since punching down the dough. Pieces were sliced from the dough, laid flat, and the air pressed out. Mom placed the bread into the five pans, greased the top of each with oleo, and left them to rise until the dough reached the top of the pans.

Mom's two-lid cookstove was beautiful with a shiny black top, white enameled oven door, and polished black legs. It had a big oven that Mom said was somewhat tricky to use, because the number of logs she carefully laid on the fire would control the oven heat. The temperature gauge revealed the need for less wood to cook a roast and more to bake bread. It didn't take very long for her to know the exact number of logs to have the perfect oven heat for anything she planned to bake.

The kitchen filled with the aroma of yeasty bread. When the bread was pulled from the oven, Nonnie immediately put the two pans of cinnamon rolls on the top rack and slid the two cookie sheets of butter horns on the bottom, closing the door quickly to keep the heat from escaping. The cloverleaf rolls were overdue for the oven and rose high above the rim of the muffin pan. Nancy made tiny rolls of dough and placed them in her own special muffin pan from her set of dishes.

Mom brushed the warm, golden loaves of bread with oleo and covered them with a towel for a couple of minutes to soften the crust. She laid the cutting board on the table and took the sharp knife from the drawer. We waited patiently for the crunch of the golden crust as the sharp knife cut the hot fresh bread.

Grandma Emma Hixson, Mom's mother, moved to the small town of Carson, North Dakota, in 1948 after Mom and Dad left Wisconsin. Her husband, Floyd, bought a building and put in a hardware store with appliances such as refrigerators, stoves, and furnaces. He installed them in area homes when electricity came to Carson. He was on the city board and helped with the layout of streets and sidewalks. Grandma worked in the store. They knew all the people in town and spent the rest of their lives there.

Wishing for Water

1950

Cupping my hands around my mouth and peering into the deep hole in front of me, I shouted. "Helloooo. Can you hear me?"

"I can hear you," Dad yelled back.

"I can't hear you very well. You sound far away," I hollered. I heard sounds of another shovel of dirt being dumped into the bucket.

"The bucket's full, and in a minute it'll be ready to haul up," Dad shouted, tying the handle to the rope and slowly hoisting it upward.

When the bucket reached the surface, Mom swung it toward the dirt floor of the basement and gently lowered it.

"How deep do you think the well is now?" Nancy asked.

"It's probably around thirty feet deep," Mom told her, pulling the bucket to the foot of the stairs and dumping the dirt into the long box Dad had built. Setting the bucket down, she walked to the well. Leaning over the black hole she called to him, "John, it's time to come up. You've been down there for almost an hour."

"I'm on my way up," he shouted.

Dad climbed the ladder to the surface and lifted himself from the well. Pulling a handkerchief from his pocket, he wiped the sweat and dirt from his face. He fastened the truck's winch to the sled-like box, climbed the stairs, and started the truck. He used the winch, bolted to the front of the truck, to pull the sled full of dirt up and out of the basement. Driving a short distance from the house, he dumped the load on an already growing mound of dirt.

I was looking forward to the day the water would start trickling into the well. I didn't like going outside to get water from the barrel beside the house. I always splashed it on my clothes when I pulled the bucket out of the fifty-five-gallon barrel. I would always tell myself this is the day I won't splash any water on myself, but no matter how hard I tried to lift the bucket carefully over the top, somehow it always hit the rim and droplets would spray out, landing on my face and clothes.

I was also waiting for the day Dad would chop down the outhouse and cover up the hole. I hated sharing the toilet seat with the mosquitoes in the summer and the frost in the winter. None of us liked the frosty seat covered with ice crystals. We used what Mom called the best modern convenience of all time: the inside winter bucket with a toilet seat.

I'm not sure when it was that Mom and Dad began feeling cramped in our cabin. The cabin had been adequate for the past three years, but now it was time to expand. Mom wanted more cupboard space for pots and pans, and there never seemed to be enough room to store all the canned goods she had preserved.

Nancy and I didn't have any room left in the small space we called our bedroom. All our toys were tucked away under the bunk bed. Everything was jumbled together, and whenever we wanted to play with a particular toy, piles of stuff had to be sorted through and then shoved back under the bed. Dad mounted a wooden pole to hang clothes on, and underneath we stuffed what didn't fit under the bed.

Dad borrowed Mr. Tatro's bulldozer and dug a basement behind the house. His plan was to dig a well in the basement after the addition was built. He wanted to bring the water pipe straight up into the new kitchen so we wouldn't have to worry about frozen pipes in the winter.

The twelve- by sixteen-foot addition was also a log structure with a kitchen and porch on the lower floor and the entire upstairs would be a bedroom for Nancy and me. The kitchen was huge with lots of cupboards. Dad bought a brand new kitchen sink, knowing it wouldn't be long until Mom would be tossing out the small aluminum pan for washing dishes. The ice box was brought in from the front porch and set in the corner by the back door. He built a table and placed it next to the window, and Mom made red curtains for the large window. Dad had a neighbor help him move the heavy cookstove into the kitchen. We finally had a modern, roomy kitchen, and spent most of our time in it.

With the kitchen finished, we were looking forward to having a large living room in the original part of the cabin. Dad tore out the old cupboards and put in a floor furnace. I was glad when the barrel stove was moved outside. It was always such a dusty, dirty mess when the ashes were removed from it. With the two stoves gone and the cupboards removed, it left us with a bare living room. The folding table and chairs were taken upstairs to Nancy's and my room. I could finally see Mom's beautiful homemade rag rug. Now it was in full view, and the sunlight brought out the soft red, brown, and green colors.

On weekends Dad invited the men who worked with him on the railroad to help dig the well. He offered them a home-cooked meal and his special home brew. They were eager for something to do on their days off and always looked forward to Mom's fried chicken dinners.

We enjoyed visiting with all the men that came to help, but out favorite was George Ondola. He lived in Birchwood with his family close to the railroad station. He was about nineteen years old. Dad said, "George is a good friend and a hard worker."

George always had time to talk to Nancy and me. "Do you think we'll see any water today?" he'd ask.

"Daddy said it should be any day now," Nancy replied.

George had lots of brothers and sisters, and once in awhile he would bring a sister with him to visit with us. Dorothy had the most beautiful long black hair worn in French braids. Nancy's hair was just as long, but her braids always started below her ears, and by the end of the day, strands of loose hair escaped from the braids and drooped by the sides of her face. One day Nancy saw George and his sister coming down the driveway, and she tugged at Mom's sleeve and begged her to ask Dorothy if she would show her how to make beautiful braids. After Mom poured each of us a glass of homemade root beer, she asked, "Would you show me how to make French braids?"

"Sure," Dorothy said. "I braid my sisters' hair all the time."

Mom practiced braiding the right side of Nancy's long brown hair while Dorothy braided the left side. It didn't take long for Mom to get the knack of French braiding, and after that, Nancy's hair always looked neat.

Dad finished our bedroom by the end of summer. He made a frame for the double bed that Nancy and I would share and bought a brand new mattress for it. We were glad to give the bunk beds back to the dump where they had come from three years before. He built a long desk the length of the wall for all our books and the many odds and ends we were always collecting.

The railroad workers kept digging on the weekends, hoping each day we might be celebrating a well full of water. When the well was sixty-four feet deep, Dad said it was time to quit digging. He and his helpers climbed the basement steps, feeling downhearted after all the backbreaking work. They relaxed with bottles of Dad's home brew and Mom's rhubarb pie.

"Maybe if we dig a few more feet, the water will be there," one of the men suggested.

"No, we've dug deep enough. The air is thin and it's time to call it quits," Dad replied.

Mom said Dad always finished projects he started, even though it might turn out different than the original plan. She was still going to have her water flowing into the kitchen sink. She said he always came up with inventive ideas to make everyone happy.

Dad put several fifty-five-gallon barrels in the basement and used a hose that could be transferred from one barrel to the next as the water in each emptied. He brought the hose through the kitchen floor and into the cabinet under the sink. He fastened a well pump on the counter beside the sink and attached the hose to it.

Dad built a trailer frame and added wheels he found at the dump. He made a large box, bolted it to the frame, and lined it with canvas. He filled it with water from Peters Creek and drove home slowly so water wouldn't spill over the top. The truck was parked by the back door, and a hose was used to transfer the water to the barrels in the basement.

We gathered around the sink as Dad primed the pump and water splashed into it. I pushed my hand under the water flowing into the new white sink, shrieking with delight as the cold numbed my fingers. Pulling my hand from the stinging cold water and wiping it on my shirt, I turned to Dad asking, "What are we going to do about the outhouse?"

"I guess we're still going to use it," Nancy said, looking up at Dad.

Dad looked at Nancy and me with a downturned mouth and a sad face. Gazing at one another, we copied his gloomy expression. We burst into laughter, even though our wish for an inside bathroom would have to wait until Dad had another nifty idea.

The addition was built in 1950. Dad hauled water for three years and decided a good place for the well would be in the basement where he could bring the water up and into the new kitchen. The well never produced water, so Dad improvised to everyone's satisfaction.

The outhouse was a permanent fixture in our lives for the five years we lived on the homestead. We dreaded using it in the winter with its frosty seat and sharing it with mosquitoes in the summer.

Family Comes to Chugiak

1951

My Grandpa Stockhausen and Dad's brother, Gerry, came for a visit in July. They drove Uncle Gerry's Studebaker truck from Wisconsin. He sent a letter to Dad saying he wanted to sell his truck cheap and would Dad be interested in purchasing it. The plan was to drive it to Alaska and fly home. Dad agreed. He was looking forward to seeing family and needed a truck to drive. He felt it was time to sell the 4 x 4 truck because he didn't have much use for it anymore. He had bought a car a year earlier, and it was used most of the time.

When they arrived, Grandpa pulled two bicycles from the bed of the truck. Now, I knew this was going to be the best summer ever. My uncle was going to help Dad with the final touches in the upstairs bedroom, and then our room would be perfect. Dad also wanted help finishing the roof on the back porch. Grandpa was helping in the garden, making weed-pulling a less grueling job. Then, just maybe, Dad would find the time to build a bathroom in the cabin even though we didn't have a well full of water.

Nancy and I spent most of our time on the bikes. I was almost twelve years old, and it took just a few minutes to learn to keep my blue bike upright. After that, Nancy and I spent most of our time peddling back and forth in the driveway.

We had a great time riding through dirty brown mud puddles, laughing as the water splattered around our uplifted legs. Some of the puddles were as big as lakes. Nancy would be right beside me riding through the biggest puddles, screaming as she tried to avoid the splashing water that drenched our jeans.

Grandpa sat at the table sipping coffee. Between noisy sips, he said, "Are you ready to do some gardening? It's still early enough so the sun won't beat down on us."

I was washing breakfast dishes and eagerly looking forward to helping Mom make a cake. The last thing I wanted to do was go out and pick weeds. "Nancy and I go out in the afternoon."

"Why not get it done in the morning? Then you have the whole afternoon to play."

"We're going to help Mama make a cake," Nancy said.

Uncle Gerry agreed with Grandpa, but he added a whole new twist on the job that needed to be done. "I think if we all went out and worked in the potato patch, we might get two days work done. Then we can do something fun tomorrow. Wouldn't it be nice not to have to think about weed-pulling and do something enjoyable instead?"

"A day off from pulling weeds?" I asked, taking my hands from the water, drying them, and handing the dish towel to Mom. Now, he had my attention. "I like that idea. We can make the cake later."

Grandpa laughed. "I know a way that will make weed pulling less of a chore." He lifted the square black suitcase from the corner by the table and headed for the door.

At that very moment, a small earthquake startled and silenced all of us. Grandpa turned and looked at Mom, asking, "Was that a moose running across the yard?" He seemed stunned by the rumbling of the ground and headed toward the window to catch a glimpse of the moose.

"No, Grandpa," Nancy laughed. "It was an earthquake."

Grandpa sat down on the chair again. "I need just a minute to relax," he said nervously. "I've never felt an earthquake before. Wait until I tell everyone back home about this." He took a deep breath and let it out slowly, got up, grabbed the black case and headed for the door.

Uncle Gerry grabbed the camp chair from the back porch as we headed for the garden.

Grandpa reached for his hat on the hook by the door. Both Grandpa and Uncle Gerry wore white shirts every day. They put on a tie and suit jacket whenever we went to Anchorage or Palmer.

When I asked Dad why they dressed like that, he said, "That's how people dress in the big cities in Wisconsin."

Then, I asked, "Why don't you wear a suit when you go to Anchorage?"

"I'd look mighty odd when I stop to rummage through the Army dump on my way home."

Uncle Gerry set the camp chair down in front of the cabin while Grandpa took his concertina from the case, sat down and fanned it out, letting the instrument moan a long musical sound. "What do you want to hear?" Grandpa asked.

"My favorite song," I said excitedly. "Do you know what it is?"

"I hear you humming it all the time," he said, and began playing "You Are My Sunshine" while we all sang along.

After a round of clapping and cheering, Uncle Gerry pointed toward the garden and asked, "Where shall we start?"

Nancy looked up and into Uncle Gerry's eyes. "Is Grandpa going to stay here? Will we be able to hear the music from way over there?" she asked, pointing in the direction of the garden.

"I'll grab the sawhorse from the yard," he answered, "and then if we can't hear Grandpa's concertina, we'll call him to come closer."

"You'll hear me," Grandpa said, running his fingers over the keys on the concertina. "Run along now and pull weeds."

Grandpa was right; weed-pulling was less of a chore that day. We sang lots of songs, and finally coaxed him to come closer and the hour passed quickly. I never thought to ask what time it was. Mom brought out glasses, a pitcher full of ice water, and cookies. When Grandpa started playing again, we went back to work for another half hour.

We cheered when Uncle Gerry stood and stretched. "I think we've accomplished two days' work," he told us.

Feeling satisfied with all we had done, we turned our thoughts to cake baking and the joy of dipping fingers into the bowl after the cake was in the pan.

The next day was just as Uncle Gerry said it would be. We never once gave the garden a thought. Mom packed a picnic lunch, and we drove five miles north, turning off the main road to Eklutna Lake. The car bounced in and out of potholes carrying us ten miles up the mountain to the lake. We pitched skipping stones into the water and ate until our stomachs could hold no more.

We received a letter from Aunt Eleanor in Seward saying they had sold their house and were riding the train to Anchorage. Grandpa and Uncle Gerry were planning on going to visit them, until they learned about the sale of the house and changed their minds, staying with us and visiting Uncle Frank, Aunt Eleanor and their four children at our house. Dad and Grandpa took the Studebaker truck the twenty-two miles to the station. Everyone piled in the front and back of it for a wind-blown trip home. We spent a lot of time on the swings with cousins Lenore and Tom, and took turns pushing each other in the wheelbarrow. This was the first time since leaving Milwaukee that we had cousins to play with. They stayed with us for two days. Uncle Frank bought a car in Anchorage, and their plan was to drive to Fairbanks and visit Uncle Ed and Aunt Kay and then drive the Alaska Highway to Wisconsin.

Grandpa was sure proud of Dad. He was a carpenter and taught him a lot about building. Dad had built a garage the year before, and all the tools my Grandpa had given him when we left for Alaska were neatly placed on the workbench. The saws hung on the wall.

The twelve- by twenty-foot greenhouse was built at the beginning of spring, using all the leftover windows purchased when the Eklutna School was torn down. Tomatoes and cucumbers were just beginning to ripen in the rich black soil. I planted some petunias and my very own cucumber to take care of.

Grandpa brought a box of angleworms with him. He dumped them into the dirt in the greenhouse. I watched the tangle of worms wiggle free and find safety deep in the black soil. I was very careful when I watered my cucumber and petunias. I never had the nerve to put my fingers into the soft black dirt, knowing that a long icky worm might be waiting to wrap itself around them. They died during the cold winter months, and the following spring I felt free to dig deep into the soft dirt I was preparing for my petunia seeds.

Grandpa was impressed with the blocks of ice in the ice house and the root cellar full of last fall's potatoes.

The day Grandpa and Uncle Gerry left for the airport, our bedroom was finished, the back porch had a roof, there were fewer weeds to pull, the new truck was parked in the garage, I got to play with my cousins, and Dad had fastened a wire basket onto the front of my bike.

Christine

Genevieve

Dad's sisters, Christine and Genevieve Stockhausen, drove the Alaska Highway to Fairbanks in the spring of 1951 to deliver a car to their brother Edward. They took the train from Fairbanks to Birchwood where Dad met them for the four-mile trip to our cabin. On their three-day visit, we caught up on all the news from Wisconsin. The best news they told us was that Dad's father, Nicholaus, and brother, Gerhardt, known as Gerry would be visiting this summer.

Mom, Grandpa Stockhausen, Uncle Gerry, and Darlene standing by the truck. Grandpa and Dad's brother, Gerry, visited in July. Gerry drove his Studebaker truck over the Alaska Highway and sold it to Dad. Mom and Dad looked forward to their visit, and they were eager to show them all they had accomplished in the four years since the move to Alaska.

The best thing about Grandpa and Uncle Gerry's visit was the surprise of receiving bicycles from our grandfather. Nancy and I had years of fun on the bikes. Actually, we finally wore them out.

The twelve- by twenty-foot greenhouse was built in the spring, using all the leftover windows Dad had purchased when the Eklutna Industrial School was torn down. The bed of the Army truck was loaded with windows when he arrived home. He used them for the cabin, garage, chicken coop, and greenhouse, and I think he still had windows leftover. I'm not sure if he even knew what he was going to do with all of them, but he definitely found a use for them.

Dad's sister, Eleanor DeLoughery, wrote saying that they had sold their family home in Seward and were leaving the Territory of Alaska. They would stop and visit with us before traveling the Alaska Highway back to Wisconsin. It happened that Grandpa and Uncle Gerry were here at the same time, so it turned out to be a great family reunion. Cousins Lenore and Tom are in the wheelbarrow and cousins Mike and Nancy are standing. Dad is by the back door of the new addition.

Photo courtesy of Lenore DeLoughery Mickelson

School Days

1951

It was a chilly, windy October morning as Nancy and I waited for the school bus. The leaves had fallen from the trees, and the wind swirled them around our feet. We walked in circles, making footprints in the melting snow.

I felt warm in my new winter jacket. It was almost the same color blue as the dress Mom made for me. My blue barrettes matched my dress. I bent down to wipe some of the snow from my new saddle shoes.

Nancy hated dresses and refused to wear them, so Mom bought her slacks and blouses for school. She always wore her hair in braids.

"Here it comes!" Nancy shouted. I caught the first glimpse of the bus as it rounded the corner of the hill a mile from our house. I watched as it disappeared from sight at the bottom of the hill and then came into view again as it crested the smaller hill. It stopped to pick up Cheryl and Bobbi. They were our closest neighbors, and we played together when their parents came to visit,

"Our bus, our very own bus!" I couldn't stop my excited laughter as the bus came to a stop beside us. I hopped up the two steps and stopped when I didn't recognize the bus driver. "Where's George?" I asked, looking at the stranger driving the bus.

"He's driving the bus that took you to school in Anchorage. I'm Paul, and I'll be taking you to your new school from now on." He smiled at Nancy and me.

I sat down, and Nancy pushed in beside me. I waved and said hi to Julia, Virginia, and Daniel who lived at Eklutna. Then I turned and said, "Hi, Cheryl. Hi, Bobbi."

Cheryl nodded her head and turned to stare out the window. Bobbi moved forward one seat so she could talk with Nancy.

I glanced at the new bus driver and knew I would miss George. For three years, he had driven us the twenty-two miles to school in Anchorage on the bus that traveled between Palmer and Anchorage twice a day.

During the summer, the first school was built in Chugiak for grades one through eight. My thoughts focused on what it was going to look like. I had often seen the outside of the building as we drove by, but had never been inside.

The school wasn't finished when September arrived. That was okay with Nancy and me. We were excited about going to school only four miles from home, and we were also glad to have the extra time to enjoy the last days of summer and to miss a whole month of school.

The bus parked alongside the school. I got off and ran to the school door, opened it, and hurried inside. I had waited patiently for so long to see what the inside looked like. The school was beautiful. There were shiny new tiles on the floor. The walls were painted a nice, light color. There was a classroom upstairs, and a large, empty room downstairs. The windows were huge! They ran the entire length of the building. The brightness of the classroom lights made it seem like the sun was shining every day. We had electricity at home, but our lights didn't shine as bright.

I knew the school had toilets that flushed. I heard neighbors talk about them at the post office. I hurried downstairs to see for myself. I was fascinated by the water rushing through the small opening in the bottom each time I pushed down on the handle. I stood there watching the water swirl around in the shiny white bowl. I hated going home to the outhouse after seeing the magic of toilets with swirling water.

The principal told us we could play in the room downstairs until the rest of the kids arrived. We had a great time tossing balls across the room to one another. It was a dream come true to have a school with a huge playroom. When they finally arrived, Mr. Thompson, the principal, gathered all of us together in the giant room and said, "I want to welcome all of you to your new school. I was expecting forty-five pupils, and I've counted sixty-six. I've decided this large room will have to be a classroom instead of the multi-purpose room. There isn't enough room for all the classes upstairs, so the fourth- and fifth-grade classes will move to this room."

I couldn't believe what I had just heard! I was in the fifth grade and would have to share the classroom with a bunch of little fourth graders. Suddenly, the playroom was gone, and I wasn't happy!

Mr. Thompson explained to us that he and his wife were the only teachers hired by the Territory of Alaska to teach at the Chugiak School. We needed one more teacher, and he was going to look into the matter right away. I was hoping Mrs. Thompson would be my teacher. She had beautiful blonde hair just like a fairy princess.

Sitting on the floor of the giant room, I received the biggest shock of all when Mr. Thompson stood in front of us and said in a matter-of-fact voice, "I'm sure all of you enjoyed having the whole month of September free to play instead of doing schoolwork. However, the Territory of Alaska has rules stating that you must spend a certain amount of days in the classroom. You have missed twenty days of school, and you'll have to make up those days. Starting this week, school will be held six days a week instead of the usual five. That means, you will be attending school on Saturdays until the missed time has been made up."

My mouth opened wide as I turned to see the expression on Nancy's face. We stared at each other wide-eyed. Nancy whispered, "He's teasing us." I knew that when I told Mom and Dad, they would never allow this to happen. It turned out he wasn't teasing.

Mrs. Thompson told us she would be teaching the first three grades, and Mr. Thompson would have the sixth, seventh, and eighth grades. So, now I knew for sure, the new teacher would be for my grade. I was hoping that my teacher wouldn't be old and she would be beautiful just like Mrs. Thompson.

Before the day ended, we gathered together in what I had thought was going to be the playroom. Mr. Thompson explained, "There is only one bus to take you home from school. This week the boys and girls from Chugiak will go home first, and the following week Eagle River pupils will be the first to go home. This routine will alternate each week, but the morning schedule will always stay the same."

This was something else I was going to have to discuss with Mom and Dad. I didn't want to stay after school.

The school day ended at four o'clock, and I was glad to be on the bus home. I knew I was going to hate the after-school wait next week. The bus went to Birchwood first, then back out to the highway, continuing to Peters Creek and then Eklutna. I was glad to finally get off the bus. I waved and said, "Bye, George." Realizing what I said, I turned and looked at the bus driver.

"That's okay. It'll take some time to get used to a new driver." He waved and closed the door.

Nancy already had a head start, and I wanted to catch up with her so I could be the first to tell Mom everything that happened today. We burst through the door at the same time.

"Mama, George won't be driving our bus anymore, and we have to go to school on Saturdays, and I don't have a teacher," I blurted out in one breath.

Nancy hugged Mom, took off her coat, and calmly said, "I met a new girl that just moved here,"

"We had a great, big, giant room to play in, and now it has been changed into the fourth and fifth grades," I continued, hoping she'd understand the disappointment I felt about my first day in my new school.

"Her name is Judy," Nancy said, "and she lives in Eagle River, and wants me to come to her house to play. Can I, please?"

I was upset. "Saturdays. I won't go to school on Saturdays. Tell the principal that I don't have to go to school on Saturdays."

Mom gave us both a hug. "Come on over and sit down. Let's talk about your day. I made some chocolate chip cookies. You can put Ovaltine in your milk for a special treat."

"I want Mrs. Thompson to be my teacher," I whined.

Mom poured canned, evaporated milk into two glasses, diluting them with water. She brought them to the table and set the jar of Ovaltine between us. I put two heaping spoonfuls of the powdered mixture into my glass and stirred it around until the white milk turned chocolate. Taking a big swallow, I ran my tongue over my lips to get all the chocolate powder that didn't get mixed into the milk in my hurry to taste it.

Mom looked at me and said, "The first few days of school are always hectic. Give the teachers a few days to get things organized, then I'm sure everything will work out. You've always liked every teacher you've had. I'm sure you'll like the new teacher just as much as you like Mrs. Thompson."

When I heard Dad's truck coming down the drive, I ran out to meet him. Before he had a chance to slide off the truck seat, I told him my account of how horrible the school year was going to be. He sat quietly and listened to what I had to tell him. Finally, he slid from the seat, grabbed his lunch pail, and we walked toward the house together. He put his arm around my shoulder saying, "I have something to tell you that might change the way you feel about school on Saturdays. When we get inside, we'll talk about it."

"Tell me now! I want to know now!"

Dad gave Mom a kiss, sat down on the davenport, and propped his feet up on the coffee table. "I saw Mr. and Mrs. Thompson at the post office. Mr. Thompson told me about school on Saturdays. Did you know you'll only be going to school for half a day on Saturdays?"

I smiled and was happy to hear that.

"Saturdays will be more of a fun day than a regular school day. He said he has lots of exciting things planned to do."

Now I was interested. "What kind of things?"

"He didn't say. I guess you'll have to wait and see, but I'm sure you'll like spending your Saturdays at school.

"Did you hear that, Nancy? I wish it was Saturday already!"

The next morning the desks and books came from Fort Richardson. The boys helped bring the desks downstairs, and they were situated so the fourth grade was on one side of the giant room and the fifth on the other. There weren't enough desks for everyone, so we shared, sitting together until more desks arrived. They didn't look new. My desk had several scratches on it. I thought all new schools would have new desks, and when the books were passed out, they weren't new either, and there weren't enough books for everyone. I wasn't very happy about this either. How could a new school have old books? When the first book landed on my desk, I didn't take one. I said to the girl who handed it to me, "I don't want one. I'll wait for the new books."

Soon the new teacher arrived. She stood in the doorway of our classroom and greeted us as we passed by. I quickly seated myself, eager to get a better look at her. Her name was Mrs. Oleson. She was tall, had light brown hair, almost blonde, and she spoke very softly. I was disappointed that she didn't look like Mrs. Thompson. I noticed she hadn't taken off her coat yet.

She walked to her desk and sat down on it, wrapping her coat tightly around her. "This room is cold. Does it ever get warm?" she asked. Everyone said, "Nooo." She laughed, and then told us how much she always enjoyed teaching fourth and fifth graders.

Nancy was in the fourth grade and was seated at the opposite side of the room. We were sharing the same teacher. I looked in her direction to see how she was reacting. She glanced quickly at me and then back at Mrs. Oleson. I could tell she liked her right away when she smiled at me and nodded her head positively.

Mrs. Oleson told us the Territory asked her to teach the fourth and fifth grades at our school. She said, "My husband is in the military at Fort Richardson. Because it is quite a distance to drive, he and I will be moving into the furnace room at the school."

I had seen the furnace room. The door was always opened to give added heat to the downstairs. I knew there couldn't possibly be enough room for a table or bed but, at least, she would be warm in there. At recess, I always tried to peek in, but the door was barely opened now that she lived in there, so I never got a good look inside.

She asked us to read silently from our geography books while she looked at the papers on her desk. One of the girls raised her hand and said, "Mrs. Oleson, there aren't enough books. We have to sit and read together." We seated ourselves with our reading partners, and the room grew silent.

I had a hard time concentrating on geography. I kept looking at Mrs. Oleson. Why couldn't she look like Mrs. Thompson? But, I was glad she wasn't old. Suddenly, she looked up and caught me staring at her. She continued to look at me for a few more seconds, smiled, and then looked down at her paperwork. I liked her immediately, and from then on she didn't have to look like Mrs. Thompson anymore. I thought she was the best teacher in the whole world.

A day later I walked into my classroom and there were more desks in each row and Mrs. Oleson's desk was stacked high with books. Finally, I was going to have my own books. When I took a look at the desks, I realized they were in worse shape then mine was, so I decided to stay with my desk. I waited, anxiously, for the new books to be passed around. Mrs. Oleson assigned several kids to hand them out. As each book landed on my desk with a loud thud, I took special notice, hoping for a new one, but that didn't happen. I looked at the books on the desks beside me and in back of me. I asked to trade one book with the girl beside me, but she said no.

Saturday found me eagerly looking forward to a day of fun. Mrs. Oleson began reading the last three chapters of a book she had been sharing with us when there was a thundering noise on the staircase along with shouting boys pushing through the outside door. We heard them in the yard along with horrible squealing sounds. Heading for the windows, we didn't know what we might see. The seventh- and eighth-grade boys and Mr. Thompson were racing toward a bunch of pigs on the playground. The pigs were running in every direction, trying to get away from them.

One of the boys in my class asked, "What are they doing out there? Where did the pigs come from?"

"The pigs are from across the road and belong to Mr. Swanson. They must have escaped from their pen," Mrs. Oleson said, peering out the window along with the rest of us.

"Can we go out and help round them up?" another boy asked.

"No, I think Mr. Thompson wants us to stay inside."

I stood at the window, wishing I could chase pigs. The older boys were laughing, shouting, waving their arms and running around the pigs, forcing them across the road and back into their pen. They looked like they were having such a good time, and I was missing out on all the fun.

"Can the girls help next time?" I asked, watching the boys running back toward the school. I was disappointed that the girls never got to help during the many times the pigs wandered back to the playground. All I could do was watch with envy as the whole adventure unfolded from the classroom windows. They were having such a good time and I was missing all the fun.

Mrs. Oleson finally had the class settled at their desks and finished the book she had started just before the noisy interruption. We had waited until Saturday to do our art project. We had our choice of either going out for recess or making decorations for the school windows. Halloween was three weeks away, and I wanted to make cats and pumpkins out of the orange and black paper.

At lunch a girl from Eagle River told me she and the other kids played softball while they waited after school for the bus. I spent the rest of my lunch hour imagining what I was going to do when I had my turn to stay after school. Nancy said she was going to play softball, and the more I though about it, I decided it would be more fun than jumping rope or watching the boys shoot marbles.

When I arrived home Saturday afternoon, my mood had changed. I liked Mrs. Oleson. I didn't mind going to school on Saturdays, and I was looking forward to the fun I would have when it was my turn to wait an hour after school for the bus. The first thing I was going to do was show Mom the pretty colored paper Mrs. Oleson gave me to make pumpkins for our windows.

There were nineteen Saturdays of fun left.

The Chugiak Terrirorial School opened its doors to students from Eklutna, Chugiak, and Eagle River in 1951. The school was built with extra growth capacity, allowing room for forty-five students. When the school opened its doors in October, sixty-six students arrived, eager for the first day of school to begin. It was a day of celebration for them because they would no longer have to make the long trip to Anchorage for their education.

An addition was added to the school, doubling the capacity to accomodate the growth of the area. Quonset huts were brought to the school site to assist with the overflow of students as the community continued growing. (Information from Between Two Rivers *by Marjorie Cochrane.)*

George Thompson–First principal and teacher, upper grades.
Fran Thompson–teacher, lower grades.
Mrs. Oleson–teacher, middle grades.

Photo courtesy of Virginia Kirk, 1958. The photograph was taken after the addition was built.

Perfect Shot

1951

Fifteen minutes had passed since Dad and I left the truck parked behind the Birchwood Railroad Station and started walking the railroad tracks. My hand was cold from holding the gun on my shoulder. The other hand was snug in my pocket. I was wearing Mom's black snow pants for the first time. As I walked, I concentrated on the swishing of the fabric as the movement of my legs rubbed against it.

At twelve years old, I was as tall as Mom and favored her snow pants over the ones she had made for me from an Army blanket. The blanket ones were nice and warm, but they couldn't compare with the grown-up feeling that comes with wearing ladies' store-bought clothes.

Nancy planned on coming with us until the last minute when she asked, "What are you going to do today, Mama?"

"I plan to have a nice warm batch of chocolate chip cookies ready when you get home," she told her, tying a clean apron around her waist.

Nancy pulled the mixing bowl from the shelf. "I'm going to stay home and help Mama make cookies," she announced.

I was sure Nancy was more interested in eating the chips and dough than helping with the baking. Actually, I was glad she wasn't tagging along. I liked having time by myself with Dad.

The sky was a huge, murky gray fog that hung over the top of the hill along the tracks, and scattered snow flakes fell like feathers onto the shoulders of my new blue plaid jacket from Minnesota Woolen Mills.

"I hate walking on the railroad ties," I told Dad, who was several steps ahead of me. "It's like taking baby steps. I don't get anywhere very fast, and I'm out of breath."

"Try skipping every other one like I'm doing," he suggested.

"I can't stretch my legs that far," I complained. My shoulder was beginning to ache as the gun pinched deeper into it. "I need to rest for a minute. We've been walking forever." I stopped, taking my gun from my shoulder and resting the butt on the same railroad tie I was standing on.

Dad turned, straddling two ties. "We're going to scare away any rabbits that might be around if we keep talking. We'll stay warmer if we're moving. Do you want to turn around and go back?" He removed his khaki gloves, cupped his hands around his mouth, and blew warm air onto them.

"No, not yet," I replied, starting to walk again. "Let's go a little farther and then turn back."

I was absorbed in counting the railroad ties to myself when Dad touched my shoulder, stopped suddenly, and pointed toward the woods. My eyes followed the movement of his arm. I surveyed the hillside in search of the rabbit that he had spotted, then scanned the nearby woods looking for it. There were patches of snow among the brown leaves on the spruce-filled hillside, making it almost impossible to see the furry white rabbit. Suddenly, it came into view, and I wondered why it took so long to find it on the rock under a thick spruce tree.

"Do you see it?" Dad whispered.

Nodding my head, I stared at the rabbit frozen on the rock.

"Do you want to shoot it?"

I pulled off my turquoise mittens, jamming them into my pocket. Lifting the gun, I watched the rabbit's ears twitch as it listened to the bolt move back and forth, sealing the cartridge in the chamber. I shifted the butt against my shoulder, aimed until the rabbit was in the sight, and stood motionless staring down the barrel at it. My finger touched and gradually pressed on the freezing cold trigger.

"Take your time," Dad whispered, "and try to place the bullet in the head."

Every time Dad brought out his shotgun to practice shooting at targets, I was the first in line begging for a turn. I remember the day he taught me to use a gun. "Since you're right-handed, you'll want to put your left foot forward," he instructed.

"Like this?" I asked, as I moved my left foot in front of me, stumbling in the clumsy position.

"That's good. Now lean forward," he said, moving my shoulders frontward. "That's better."

"Why do I have to do all that?" I whined, straightening and stretching my shoulders upward.

"Aim at that can over there," he smiled, "and stand the way you feel most comfortable and shoot it off the stump. Let's see how good you can do." I stared up at him as he raised his eyebrows saying, "Go ahead, lift the gun to your shoulder, aim, and shoot."

I lifted the gun, leaned back, aimed, and fired. The can was still on the stump. "I'll hit it this time," I told Dad confidently, raising the gun and leaning back. I fired and missed again. "I know I can hit it."

"The way you stand helps you relax, and you can move your weight back and forth easily from one leg to the other. Then, as you swing your gun upwards, aim at the target and fire; you'll be steady on your feet. If you remember to use good form and aim with your feet before you raise the gun, you'll probably hit the target every time. It's a good habit to get into as a beginner."

I heaved a loud sigh, dropping my shoulders. "I just want to shoot the gun."

"You'll hit the can if you do a few things right. Otherwise, you won't hit anything, especially if you don't use the good form I was just telling you about," he reminded me again. "Also, if you're not holding the gun properly, you'll miss hitting your bird or rabbit or even the can on the stump over there," he told me, pointing at the can I had been trying to hit.

"Okay," I sighed again. He showed me how to put the gun onto my shoulder and next to my face.

"Try to hit the can now," he said, standing next to me, "and keep both eyes open."

I put my left foot in front as Dad moved my shoulders forward. He positioned the gun next to my face. I aimed and pulled the trigger. "I did it. I did it," I shrieked, watching the can fly from the stump.

I handed the gun to Dad and ran over to the can, picking it up and examining the hole in it. "Look, I hit it," I yelled excitedly, waving the can in the air.

"That was a perfect shot," Dad told me.

I was finally able to spot, aim, and fire, hitting the can every time. After that, Dad started throwing them into the air. "You're another Annie Oakley with a gun," he told me, voicing his pride in my skills as a sharpshooter.

"Can I have my own gun?" I begged over and over.

I grabbed the Sears Roebuck catalog from the window seat, carried it to the kitchen table, and shoved the chair close to it. Sitting on my knees, I pushed the catalog to the middle of the table and lay across the top with my hand under my chin, flipping through the pages until I found the guns.

Grasping the catalog, I pushed myself from the table and walked over to the davenport where Dad was reading one of his favorite western books, his legs stretched casually on the coffee table. I snuggled up beside him. "Look, Daddy. I want a gun like this one," I said, nudging his arm with my elbow.

Dad set the open book on his lap, took the catalog, and looked at the gun I showed him.

"That's a mighty powerful gun you're looking at. You can kill a grizzly bear with that gun. It would probably knock you down. Now, this gun," he said, pointing at one on the opposite page, "might be one that you could handle."

"What kind is it?"

"It's a shotgun. Not as powerful as the one you were looking at, he replied, handing me the catalog.

"Can I have it?"

"Maybe."

"Can I have it for Christmas? I don't want anything else. Well, maybe just a few other things. Please, can I have a gun?"

"I want a gun, too," Nancy said, leaving the dishes she was drying. Squeezing between the armrest and Dad, she settled into the deep mahogany leather davenport. "Move over so I can sit here, too," she told Dad, as she crowded in beside him.

Dad shifted himself toward me making room for Nancy. I sat forward and looked at her intently. "You're squashing Daddy and me," I complained, scooting to make room for all of us. "I was here first."

"I'm the one getting squashed," Nancy grumbled. "I want a B-B gun."

With an unenthusiastic motion, I passed the catalog to her. "I don't want a gun from the catalog," she stated. "I want the one we saw at the store when we were in Anchorage last week. I like that one."

"That was a nice looking gun," Dad said.

Leaning her head back, she focused on his face. "Will it shoot holes in tin cans?"

"It might make a dent, but I doubt it would shoot through it."

"That would be okay," Nancy replied, in a matter-of-fact tone. She pushed herself up onto the armrest, slid off, and shook out the wrinkled dishtowel lying in her lap while chatting with Dad. "I'd like to have my gun now. I don't want to wait until Christmas." She turned and went back to drying dishes.

"Can I get this one for Christmas?" I asked again, pointing to the gun we had been looking at when Nancy interrupted us.

Dad looked at me and smiled. "Well, maybe Santa will remember to leave a gun under the tree.

"Don't forget about me," Nancy reminded him. "I want a gun for Christmas, too, if I don't get one sooner than that."

"I know you're Santa," I told Dad, with a knowing grin, "and I'm counting on you to leave a shotgun under the tree for me." I moved closer, hugged his arm, then settled back alongside him to read about the gun Dad thought I could handle.

Electricity came to Chugiak in 1951. Dad strung electric wire between the logs of the cabin when he first noticed the electric poles going in along the road. It was going to be our first Christmas with lights on the tree. When we moved to Alaska, Mom brought our tree lights, brightly colored ornaments, and silver tinsel along. The strings of lights remained in the box each year, although we always lifted them out, fingered the slick bulbs, then carefully returned them to the box, hoping the next year we'd be stringing them onto the branches.

On Christmas morning, the tree lights made the ornaments glisten and the heavy silvery tinsel shimmer. The walls of the cabin took on a warm red glow that reminded me of the red hot embers sizzling in the barrel stove.

Sitting on the floor, Dad reached for the smaller gun. "This one is for Nancy," he announced, handing the gun to her. "It's the B-B gun you wanted, and this one is for you," he said, passing me the heavier, bigger gun.

"Wow! My very own gun. What kind is it?"

"It's a .410 shotgun. You can hunt rabbits and birds."

I sat cross-legged on the floor, rubbing my hand up and down the cold barrel of the gun.

"Can we practice shooting at targets, today?"

"It's kind of cold out."

I laid the gun under the tree and crawled over to him, wrapped my arms around his neck, and kissed his cheek. "This is the best present. When can we go hunting?"

"Maybe when it warms up. Sometimes rabbits are smarter than we are. I doubt they are out and about when the temperature is as cold as it has been the last few days. They're probably keeping warm in their burrows."

"I want to go with you," Nancy told us, somewhat unenthused, more interested in the Mickey Mouse watch she was trying to attach around her wrist.

"Hey! Did I get a watch?" I asked, looking for a small box under the branches.

The echo vibrated against my ear as the bullet blasted through the silent snowflakes. The rabbit shot into the air, then disappeared from sight.

"Great shot. Your aim was perfect."

"Where is it?"

"Behind the rock," Dad replied, walking toward the woods. "Let's get it."

I wasn't sure if I wanted to look behind the rock. What if the rabbit was still alive? I knew I couldn't shoot it again. What if there were more rabbits behind it, maybe even baby rabbits? "I think I'll stay here and wait for you."

I stood with my feet spanning two rails and tugged my still-warm mittens from my jacket. Laying the gun across the rail, I pulled them on and shoved my freezing hands deep into the pockets. I straightened to relieve the ache in my shoulders. I could hear the crunchy snowy leaves under Dad's boots as he started up the hill. I kept hoping the rabbit had leaped from the rock before the bullet reached it. I even hoped Dad wouldn't find it.

"Here it is," he said, holding up the rabbit.

My stomach clenched tight as I stared, hypnotized by the bobbing head. My eyes followed the wiggly body as Dad came from the woods, carrying the rabbit by its feet. I struggled to wrench my eyes from its blood-spattered, red head. My eyebrows drew together in a sorrowful expression, and a shiver swept through my body as I watched Dad drop it into the gunnysack.

We walked without saying anything for awhile until I broke the silence. "I didn't like seeing the dead rabbit," I told him, watching my feet move from one railroad tie to the next.

"First-time hunters always have a hard time. Sometimes they never hunt again."

"I think from now on, I'm going to shoot tin cans," I told him, wishing the rabbit in the gunnysack was still running free in the woods.

I saw Nancy sitting on a sawhorse as Dad parked in front of the cabin. I jumped from the truck, not wanting to remember the white rabbit with its red head.

I hurriedly walked to where she was sitting. "Hey, guess what? I shot a rabbit!" Nancy didn't even look at me. Her B-B gun was laying on the snow beside her, and her arms were clutched tightly together. She seemed to be staring straight ahead at nothing in particular. "Hey, didn't you hear me?" I said, "I shot a rabbit."

Nancy continued to stare at whatever it was she was looking at. "See the tree over there?" She pointed to the one by our swings.

"Yeah."

"Do you see the dead squirrel under it?" She swallowed hard, biting back her tears. "I shot it out of the tree."

I drew in a deep breath and dropped down beside her. "You shot that little squirrel?" I was stunned as I turned from the squirrel back to her. "You shot it with your B-B gun?" I saw a tear forming in the corner of her eye and knew instantly that she ached with the same inner pain I was feeling.

I reached out and touched her arm. "Did you tell, Mama?"

"No, not yet. I just shot it a few minutes ago."

"I don't ever want to shoot another rabbit," I confessed. "Dad said it's always hard for first-time hunters. I don't want to be a second-time hunter." That was all I could think to say to her.

"Me either," Nancy said, mopping away the tear with her red mitten as it slid along her cheek.

I let my fingers trail down her shiny brown braid, gave the end a flip, and said, "Let's go tell Mama and Daddy what we decided."

I was twelve years old when I received my .410 shotgun for Christmas and Nancy got her wished-for BB gun. Before that, I practiced for several years shooting Dad's gun. I became an expert, hitting the target every time. Dad called me Annie Oakley.

Changes

1951-1952

I was twelve years old when my mother told Nancy and me she was going to have a baby. It surprised me, but I wasn't quite as excited about it as Nancy. Maybe, it was because I knew I'd never be able to share all the fun that Nancy and I had together with a brother or sister that was twelve years younger than me. Nancy was ten and thought it would be fun to have a live doll to play with.

Mom wrote to my Grandma Hixson in North Dakota, telling her about the baby that was arriving in March 1952. I guess my grandma was as excited as we were. She began making nightgowns, blankets, and bibs and sending them to us in big boxes that were ripped open immediately. Everything was yellow, green, and blue.

"Grandma didn't make anything pink," I said surprised, holding up a yellow blanket in one hand and a green nightgown in the other.

Mom smiled as she sat with a lap full of flannel nightgowns. "Your grandma didn't make any pink things, because the baby might be a boy, and boys don't wear pink."

"Do baby girls wear blue?"

"Yes, somehow it's okay for girls to wear blue, but when boys wear pink, people mistake the baby for a girl."

"That's silly," I said, sitting down beside her.

"You're right; it is silly," Mom answered, smoothing my hair with her fingers.

I came down the steps from the bedroom Nancy and I shared to get my Nancy Drew mystery book. I noticed Nancy in Mom and Dad's bedroom with her hands full of baby clothes. I watched her dump them onto the bed.

"Are you dressing that make-believe baby of yours again?"

Nancy didn't answer. She usually ignored me when I teased her. She laid out all the clothes on the bed and began dressing the imaginary baby. The baby wore a diaper pinned to an undershirt. On top of that, she laid a flannel nightgown and lifted the bottom to place a pair of socks so they partly peeked out. The outfit wasn't complete until a sweater was placed over the nightgown. Then she would call us into the bedroom so we could see how beautiful her baby looked.

"She does look pretty," Mom told her each time she came to see the make-believe baby.

"How come you always call the baby a girl?" Nancy asked.

"Well, I have both of you, and I will probably have another girl."

"You don't think it will be a boy?"

"I'm sure it's going to be a girl."

"Why not a boy?"

"It's just a feeling I have."

"If you have a girl, what will we name her?" Nancy quizzed, looking intently at Mom.

"I'm sure we'll pick a lovely name for her. I like Laura. What name do you like, Nancy?"

After thinking about it for a minute, she said, "I like the name Beth. Nancy Drew has a friend named Beth who helps her solve mysteries."

"I don't like Beth. I want her name to be Molly," I said.

"That's your doll's name." Nancy wrinkled her nose, squeezed her eyebrows together in a frown, and looked back at Mom. "What if you have a boy? What are we going to name him?"

"If we have a boy, he will have your father's name, John, and we will call him, Johnny."

"I want the baby to be a girl," I told Mom.

"Me too," Nancy agreed.

Every week we drove twenty-three miles to Palmer to do the banking and grocery shopping. We always went to the restaurant in the variety/drug store for lunch. It was our favorite place to eat. They made the best hot dogs. Mom said it was because they steamed the buns which made them extra soft.

There were other fun things to do besides eat lunch and go home. We looked for baby clothes, and Mom always bought more diapers. She was still using her washing machine with a gas engine. She knew that with a baby there would be extra wash to do and hoped that more diapers meant fewer wash days. Without running water, she had to heat the water in buckets and dump it into the machine.

I was put in charge of picking out embroidery thread for designs on the bibs Mom had just finished. I picked purple, pink, and yellow. In my heart, I knew I was going to have another sister. I wouldn't have any fun with a brother. Mom smiled when I showed her the colors.

"Don't you think they'll look nice on Baby Molly's bibs?" I asked her, as she put her arm around my shoulder, and we moved toward the counter to pay for our purchases.

The snow was collecting on the mountains, and I was waiting for the first snowfall so I could harness my golden-haired dog,

Queenie, to my small sled and let her pull me back and forth in the driveway. It was about this time of year when Dad mentioned he would like to move.

Mom was making cookies and the spoonful of dough seemed to freeze in the air. She looked up and stared at Dad. "Move? Why would you want to move?"

"I wasn't thinking about moving from the homestead. I'd like to build next to the road and start a business."

"A business! You've never talked about a business." She dropped the dough from the spoon onto the cookie sheet and sat down heavily on the chair. "How come you never mentioned this before? How long have you been planning to do this?"

"I've been thinking about it for awhile."

"What kind of a business?"

"Everyone along the road has animals. Rather than going all the way to Anchorage or Palmer for feed, we could start a feed store right here in Chugiak."

"A feed store?"

"Sure, why not? It would sure be handy when someone runs out of chicken feed or …"

"A feed store?" With one elbow on the table, her fist under her chin, she stared at him.

After that conversation, the plans began to come together as Mom warmed to the idea. They discussed a building with a living area on one side and the store on the other side. Mom seemed as enthused as Dad after she thought about it. It seemed to be their main topic of conversation throughout the winter months. Dad designed the building, and Mom worked out the floor plan for our living area.

"Are we really going to move?" I asked, looking over Dad's shoulder as he worked on his building design.

"I think your mother likes the idea. Do you want to move?"

"I guess so."

The winter months passed quickly as we prepared and looked forward to the baby's arrival. In the middle of February, our neighbor, Gerri Jahr, from across the road told Dad she was planning a baby shower for Mom and wanted it to be a surprise. She made him promise not to say a word to her about it When Nancy and I were outside with Dad, he told us about it.

"Jerri is having a baby shower for Mama?" I was turning toward the cabin ready to run and tell her.

"Wait a minute. You can't say anything to her about the shower."

"Why? She'll be so glad to hear about it."

"I know she would, but I promised I wouldn't say anything. Jerri wants it to be a surprise."

"When is the shower?" Nancy asked.

"Next Saturday."

"Maybe we could tell her about it, but not who's giving it," I suggested.

"Nope."

"What if we told her something exciting is going to happen that she'll really like." Nancy offered, staring at Dad who was already shaking is his head.

"Nope."

Nancy and I knew Saturday would be the best day for the shower because most families owned one car. The men would be home so the ladies would be able to get to the shower. We were very excited. Our imaginations began to run wild as we thought about all the presents.

Nancy smiled. "Do you think anyone will give the baby a pink dress?"

"I'm sure someone will buy a dress, but it probably won't be pink. You know what Mom said about colors."

"But that's just about boys."

"I still think Mom's right. Sometimes baby boys wear dresses."

"When would a boy wear a dress?" Nancy asked, with a doubtful look, her head bent sideways and squinting her eyes.

"They wear a white dress when they get baptized."

"Oh, I guess they do."

"Are you going to keep the make-believe baby when the real baby is born?"

"No, I'll dress the baby every day. I think a brother might not be so bad. We can show him how to make roads in the dirt for his trucks and cars."

"I want a sister named Molly."

"Her name isn't going to be Molly. Mama likes Laura and so do I."

Two days before the shower, Dad had a fever and didn't feel very well. Mom tried her best to bring the fever down. She watched over him all night. The next morning when she woke us for breakfast, she was unusually quiet. "Your father is still very sick, so I want you to be extra quiet this morning. We don't want to disturb him. He finally was able to sleep."

"What's wrong with him?" I asked, quickly sitting up in bed.

"He has the measles."

"Are his cheeks all swelled up? Can I go look?" Nancy asked, throwing off her covers and swinging her legs off the side of the bed.

"Cheeks swell up with the mumps. Your father has the measles. He has red spots all over his face."

"I want to see the spots."

While Mom was making breakfast, Nancy and I peeked into the bedroom for a glimpse at the red spots, but Dad was laying on his side facing away from us, so we were going to have to wait until after school to see them. Everything seemed to change in an instant now that he was sick. The shower was going to be the next day.

"We need to talk to Daddy before we go to school. It's really important." Nancy said, anxiously.

"Not now. You need to get ready for school and eat breakfast. Your father needs his sleep. You can talk to him after school," Mom told her.

"Please, we have to ask him about something," I begged.

"Girls, nothing is that important. It can wait until after school."

I folded my arms on the table and laid my chin on them. Nancy copied me, and we stared at each other until the oatmeal was ready to eat. I fixed my eyes on the mushy stuff and began stirring it around in the bowl. The only thing I could think about was that being so sick, Dad wouldn't be able to drive Mom to the shower.

Arriving home from school, we dashed into the cabin, pulled off coats and boots, waved to Mom, and headed for the bedroom.

Dad was sitting up in bed reading one of his favorite western books. His face, neck, and arms were full of bright red blotches. Mom followed us into the bedroom.

I turned to her, saying, "We have something to say to Daddy that you can't hear."

"If that's the case," Dad replied, "it might sound better if you ask your mother to please excuse us for a minute."

"Mama, would you please excuse us for a minute? We have to talk to Daddy about something real important, and you're not suppose to hear about it."

Mom smiled and left the room as we climbed onto the bed to talk about the secret. "How's Mama going to get to the shower if you're sick? She'll need you to help her up the hill to Jerri's house," Nancy whispered, examining the red spots on Dad's arms.

"I promised Jerri I wouldn't tell your mother."

"I'm sure she would understand, seeing that you are so sick and all," Nancy reminded him.

"Can we please tell her?" I pleaded, then added, "She would be so happy to know about the shower."

"Yeah, can we please?" Nancy begged. "The shower is tomorrow, and she'll want to fix her hair and wear her prettiest smock. She's not going to want to be surprised. Mama doesn't like surprises. We all know that."

"Well, I suppose she would like to know about it. Why don't we call her in and all yell surprise at the same time."

"Mom," we called together, anxious to unload our secret.

When she entered the bedroom, we all yelled, "Surprise!"

Nancy jumped from the bed. "There's going to be a baby shower for you tomorrow." She hugged Mom around the waist. "Aren't you excited? It was going to be a surprise. We weren't supposed to tell, but Daddy got sick, so now we have to get someone else to take you there."

Mom looked at Dad who shrugged his shoulders and explained, "It's kind of hard to keep a secret under the circumstances."

The shower was a huge success. It was the biggest baby shower the community had ever had. People came from as far as Eagle River. They were tired of being cooped up all winter. The ten-mile drive was worth the effort, since the shower was an opportunity to visit and catch up on all the gossip. The best gift was a bassinet. Mom had looked at one at Northern Commercial Company, but it wasn't as pretty as the one she got with a white lace ruffled skirt around it. It was going to be the perfect place for Molly to sleep when Mom brought her home from the hospital.

The doctor predicted the baby would be born in early March, possibly the fourth or fifth. It snowed the night of the fourth, so early in the morning Dad went to Birchwood and asked some of the railroad workers he knew to help him shovel the driveway. Mom started getting her labor pains early on the morning of the fifth. We gave her lots of hugs and begged to go with her and Dad.

"The hospital won't let children come inside, so it's best that you wait at home. I'll be back sometime tonight," Dad assured us.

Late in the afternoon, we heard the familiar whine of the engine and ran to meet Dad as he slid from the seat of the truck.

"What did Mom have, a boy or girl?" Nancy asked, running towards him.

Dad's face was beaming when he said, "You have a brother."

"We're not going to have a sister named Molly?" I asked, somewhat disappointed.

"Nope. You have a brother named Johnny."

"What does he look like? When can I see him? When is Mama coming home?" Nancy wanted to know everything while grabbing hold of Dad's hand.

"Let's go in out of the cold, and I'll tell you more about him. He has brown eyes, fuzzy light-colored hair, and weighs more than seven pounds," he began, as we walked toward the cabin.

The day Mom came home with Johnny, we thought we'd burst from the excitement of waiting to see what he looked like. I stepped up on the running board when Mom opened the door, and Nancy scooted into the truck as Dad got out. Mom lifted the yellow blanket from Johnny's face, and we both got our first glimpse of the tiny baby. His face and hands were all wrinkly, and he had soft wispy hair.

"Oh, can I hold him?" Nancy asked, touching his hand.

"Hello, little baby," I cooed, running my fingers through his soft hair. "We have the bassinet all ready for you."

Once inside, Nancy and I took turns holding Johnny. He slept through all the squeezing and kisses. After a while, Mom laid him on her bed while we got supper warming and the table set.

"Can I change his clothes?" Nancy asked.

Mom came over to check Johnny's diaper. "He's not wet. Let's wait a while longer to change him. The doctor circumcised him just before we left the hospital. He cried for such a long time, and I'm sure the crying exhausted him."

"What does circumcise mean?" Nancy inquired.

"It's a hygienic measure."

"What does that mean?"

"That's enough questions for now. Let's finish setting the table and eat the soup your father made for us."

After supper, Nancy made another check for a soaked diaper. "He's still not wet. I thought babies were always wet, and he hasn't woke up yet. Isn't he hungry? He should be starving and wet by now."

Mom came over drying her hands on the dish towel. She looked at him and loosened the blanket. "He's been sleeping for quite a long time, but he looks very content. If he's not awake when the dishes are done, we'll wake him."

"Can I pick out clean clothes to put on him?" Nancy was already on her way to the dresser to make her selection.

I headed for it at the same time bumping into her. "Why don't you choose something for your make-believe baby to wear, and I'll find something for Johnny."

Mom was still gazing at Johnny and listening to our argument. "Darlene, you pick out a fresh blanket, and Nancy can choose a nightgown."

The dishes were finally washed, dried, and put away. Nancy closed the cupboard door and moved toward the bedroom. "I'll wake him up."

We all headed for the sleeping baby. "Come on, Daddy." I called, as he pulled his feet from the coffee table, set his book down, and followed.

Mom picked Johnny up and sat down on the edge of the bed. With eyelids squeezed tightly together, he stretched and let out an earsplitting bellow. "He's awake now," she said, rocking him back and forth.

As much as I had wanted a baby sister, I was beginning to realize it might not be so bad having a brother. After all, boys get to have lots of toys that girls don't usually play with. Nancy had been begging for a train and just possibly this might be the year she found it under the Christmas tree.

Dad's brother, Ed, lived in Fairbanks and was a strict Catholic. He wrote right after Johnny was born and asked when he would be baptized. In the church, baptisms are done almost immediately after the birth of a baby. He wanted us to come to Fairbanks for the special ceremony. Dad's family embraced the church, every one of them, except Dad.

He said he was the black sheep of the family.

"What's a black sheep?" Nancy wanted to know.

"Someone who doesn't go to church and—"

"John!" Mom cautioned, shaking her head back and forth, warning him not to say another word on the subject.

Dad wrote back saying we would come in June. Nancy wanted to know if Johnny would be wearing a white dress when he was baptized. Mom told her no. She was going to dress him in his blue short pants with a shirt to match. We dressed in our finest clothes for the train ride to Fairbanks. Mom lined us up in the yard and took pictures.

Dad had free train passes because he worked for the Alaska Railroad. I was excited about my first train ride. It was fun crossing from one railroad car to the next on a ramp that covered the linking locks that fastened the cars together.

It was the first baptism I had ever attended. I was curious about what was going to happen. Dad told me about my baptism and the sprinkling of water on my forehead. I waited impatiently for the drops of water to fall on Johnny's face. I hoped he wouldn't be scared and cry. I didn't understand why the priest had to bless him and give him a name when he already had a perfectly good name.

On our arrival back home, Dad concentrated on his plans for the feed store and our new house. Mom's days were full of activity. Even with all the diapers she bought, wash days came often. My job was to hang and remove them from the clothesline which I didn't really mind. They smelled better than new after the breeze puffed them with airy perfume.

Nancy forgot all about her make-believe baby. She was true to her word, continuing the never-ending job of keeping Johnny in dry diapers and clean clothes. I think that's why Mom was forever washing clothes; Nancy changed Johnny's clothes several times a day, more than she ever put clean clothes on the make-believe baby.

Dad worked on the new building every spare moment that he had. Being right alongside the road, neighbors were always stopping by and watching the progress from day to day. Sometimes they helped, and other times their visits gave Dad a chance to relax and offer them a bottle of his home brew.

Dad worked on the feed store every day after work. When he was just about ready to order the supplies, there was news on the radio of a feed strike. It came as a shock and disappointment. The neighbors continued to stop by to discuss the latest news on the strike. A few men sat in the finished store drinking Dad's mouth-watering beer, and together came up with the suggestion of a liquor store. They speculated that most neighbors enjoyed a nip now and then, so why not make it easier for them to buy and take it home right here in the neighborhood rather than driving the long distance to Anchorage or Palmer. The evening ended with everyone raising their bottles of beer to a new business for Chugiak.

Dad walked back to the cabin and crawled into bed late that night. "What do you think about a liquor store instead of a feed store?" he said to Mom who was almost asleep.

"I think you've had too much to drink, John." She rolled over and tried to go to sleep.

He knew he could convince her if he made an effort to explain how profitable the sale of liquor could be. "We could make a lucrative income selling liquor. I think it would be much more profitable than selling feed for animals. People drive by in both directions all day long, and we're right smack in the middle. A perfect place to stop for a rest and buy something to take home to wet the lips."

"Go to sleep, John."

"We could name the business after you and call it Bernie's Liquor Store, and you could be the proprietor."

Now he had Mom's attention. She sat up in bed. "John, you finally convinced me a feed store was the business you were interested in, but now a liquor store? The feed strike will be over before you know it. Please, go to sleep."

"Just say you'll think about it."

"Go to sleep."

Dad brought the subject up at breakfast and supper and again in the evening as they enjoyed some of his home brew.

Finally, the moment arrived when Mom said, "Okay, John. I just hope you're not making a mistake and regret it later on down the road." Mom mailed the paperwork for the liquor license, and Dad ordered the liquor and beer. He made a few adjustments to the shelving. Mom agreed to the name of the business, and in a few weeks, they would be ready to open.

Moving from our homestead cabin was difficult for all of us. We spent five years enjoying a quiet life. The only noise was from the birds, chickens, squirrels, and the occasional bark from our dog, Queenie. Cars were infrequent the first two years, and when one passed by we'd look out the window to see if we recognized it. It was peaceful and just what Mom and Dad looked forward to when they left Wisconsin in 1947. Now it was time to leave our cabin and move to our new home.

Every day Mom would walk to the cabin to collect more of our belongings and set them in boxes by the door for Dad to pick up in the evening after work and bring to our new home. Dad finished putting the last of our belongings onto the bed of the truck.

Mom had cleaned and prepared the cabin to be rented and was reluctant to leave. When she had it neat as a new pin, she slowly walked through each room.

"Are you sad about leaving?" I asked, as I walked beside her.

"Yes, I am. I got a lot of pleasure living here. Your father and I built this cozy cabin, grew our own food and learned to do many things that other people only dream of doing." She closed the door as we walked out of the cabin.

Nancy carried Johnny down the steps and plopped him down in the basket on her bike. "Can I take him for a ride on my bike?"

"I think he's too young to ride in your basket. Maybe, when he's a little older, but I'll take a picture of him sitting in it while you hold him there." She picked up the camera from the step, asked for a big smile, and snapped the picture.

We walked slowly down the driveway. I held Johnny, and Nancy pushed her bike. Mom slowly turned for another quick look at the cabin she cherished. "I know we'll be happy with our decision to move. It won't take us long to settle in, and soon we'll feel right at home, knowing we are where we're supposed to be now, but I'll sure miss living in the cabin."

I turned to Nancy and asked, "Do your want to move?"

"Yeah, I got to help Daddy build our new home. Anytime I felt like it, I would run over the hill, climb the ladder, and ask him if he needed any help. He always said yes. I helped put the floor boards on and pound them in place. I got to climb up on the roof and pound nails. I helped with the siding by holding the boards in place. I'm going to be happy in the house I helped Daddy build."

"But I'm really going to miss the tractor," Nancy said, "because Daddy always let me drive when we plowed the field. He said I knew exactly what to do the minute I stepped up onto it. I'm going to miss the cabin too, and helping Mama get vegetables from the root cellar and bringing ice chunks from the ice house. Besides all that, we will have running water in our new house. I sure won't miss the outhouse."

I wasn't sure what I was feeling. I didn't know where I should be. I loved the cabin. I helped stuff moss between the logs that kept us warm all through the winters. I worked in the garden, hauled wood for the stove, I found and lost Moe, my pet bear. Nancy and I played with our cars and trucks in the dirt and told imaginary stories to each other while we sat on our swings. I spent hours exploring the dump and calling Mama to come and see the treasures I found for the cabin. I got my gun for Christmas and went hunting with Daddy. Now everything was changing, and I wasn't sure I wanted it to. I turned to see if Dad was following us, or if he had changed his mind and decided we would all stay at our cabin after all.

"Mama," I said, turning to look back, "I'm going to see what Daddy's doing."

"Let's let your father have a few minutes by himself," she said. "I need you to carry Johnny for me. Your Dad will catch up with us in a few minutes."

Dad didn't leave when we did. He stood gazing out at the two acres of potatoes that needed harvesting in the next couple of weeks. Last year's potatoes had sprouted in early spring and were this year's harvest.

He looked in the direction of the root cellar that was dug in the hillside and thought about the tons of potatoes and vegetables that it held over the past few years.

He slowly turned to take in the greenhouse that had given both him and Mom so much pleasure, growing many varieties of tomatoes. He moved toward the garage that he built for the truck his father and brother drove from Wisconsin for him and remembered how proud his father was when he saw the homestead. He took the ladder from the cache and laid it on the ground, chuckling as he thought about the squirrels that had tried so desperately to find a way inside but could never work their way through. He fixed his eyes on the large ice house, made from dozens of fifty-five-gallon drums he found at the Army dump. He cut ice on Mirror Lake every winter because Mom had convinced him how great a cold bottle of beer, from the icebox, would taste on a hot summer day. It was September, and only half the ice had melted.

Walking towards the chicken coop, he brushed his foot over a feather on the ground and remembered all the chickens and eggs they had bartered and sold to Piggly Wiggly since purchasing the first three hundred chickens in 1949.

It had been his dream to move to Alaska and file on the forty acre homestead. The log cabin was what he was most proud of. It was the first home he built for his family. He never regretted the move. Saying good-bye to five years of hard but rewarding work was difficult. He was satisfied with what he had accomplished and looked forward to having his own business.

Our new home was smaller than the cabin, but we did have a well with lots of delicious-tasting water. We finally had our indoor bathroom with a blue tub that could be filled to the top with lots of hot water and smelly bubbles, and a toilet that flushed. We brought along our brown davenport. Dad hung the velvet camp scene picture above it. I'd sit next to him, stretching my arms up and brushing my palms over the rough scratchy paint on the soft velvet. The davenport held a lot of memories for me. Dad and I sat together on it making lots of decisions. My favorite time was sitting next to him and browsing through the Sears Roebuck catalog for the gun I wanted for Christmas.

Mom and I would cuddle on the davenport while she taught me embroidery. I sewed fancy colored stitches on dish towels and pillow cases. It kept my hands busy while listening to evening radio stories: *The Green Hornet, The Shadow, Lone Ranger, Sergeant Preston,* and *Gang Busters*. Sometimes, I'd forget about the dish towel, letting it drop into my lap while resting my head on Mom's shoulder, my arm wrapped through hers engrossed in *Dragnet* as Sergeant Joe Friday learned about a crime, chased the suspects, and solved the case. I'd finally breath a sigh of relief when the story ended.

Mom's antique oval mirror hung over her dresser, and the fat white lamb cookie jar with the red scarf around its chubby neck had a special place on the kitchen counter. She bought it at the Northern Commercial Company soon after we moved into the cabin. The sewing machine was brought to our home with the first load of furniture and carefully place next to the kitchen table where Mom would cut material and then swing around, seating herself at the machine.

It wasn't too long after moving in the new house that Dad bought a floor-model television. I was so excited. "When can we turn it on?" I asked.

"I'll have it working in a jiffy," Dad replied, "just as soon as I get the two pieces of wire hooked up that sit on top of the television." It took a little longer than a jiffy as Dad adjusted the wires in every which direction, trying to get the best possible picture to watch. We got used to watching the snowy image. I didn't care about the snow; now I could watch *Dragnet* and see Joe Friday catch the bad men.

We ate a lot of popcorn on the evenings of our favorite shows. Dad didn't make home brew anymore. He'd get a cold Schlitz beer from the cooler in the liquor store and settle on the davenport asking, "What are we going to watch tonight?"

"Let's watch *Ozzie and Harriet*," I'd tell him, reaching into our kitchen refrigerator, grabbing two bottles of root beer for Nancy and me. "Do you think we'll ever make homemade root beer again? It was so yummy."

"When we empty the boxes and get everything put away. Then there'll be time," he said. "Why don't you turn on the television since you're up."

The one thing that I really liked about living right next to the road was being able to wait in the house for the school bus on a freezing cold morning. I'd stand by the window until I saw it stop at the driveway next to ours. I had time to give Mom a hug and kiss and walk out the door just as the bus stopped by our driveway.

It didn't take too long for me to finally feel settled again. I now knew that this was where I should be, just like Mom told us while walking from the cabin to our new home. Besides, I could take the short walk up the hill behind the house to the cabin whenever I wanted and just sit peacefully with my memories, letting time go.

Mom holding brother Johnny, March 1952

Nancy holding Johnny in the living room of the cabin. The velvet wall picture came with us from Wisconsin. Mom made our cabin cozy with throw pillows, rag rugs, and sheer curtains for the windows.

Nancy holding Johnny in front of the screen porch with Mom proudly watching. On the left is a nice view of the dollhouse that Dad secretly made for us and was found under the tree on Christmas morning. The fifty-five-gallon drum caught rain water from the gutter attached to the roof. The water was used for hair washing, baths, dishes, and laundry. The wood barrel on the right was probably used to make home brew.

Nancy wanting to take Johnny for a ride in the bicycle basket. Mom said he was too young for such a hair-raising ride. She took a picture instead.

Mom snapped this picture of Nancy, Dad, and Darlene all dressed up. We were ready to leave by train for the trip to Fairbanks for Johnny's baptism. Dad's brother, Edward, and his wife, Kathleen, became his godparents.

Bernie's Liquor Store was built in 1952. It was originally going to be a feed store, but just about the time Dad was ready to order the supplies, there was news on the radio of a feed strike. Dad's friends began stopping by suggesting the possibility of a liquor store in the area. He was in the ideal spot halfway between Anchorage and Palmer.

After the decision was made to change the feed store to a liquor store, Dad reconfigured the shelves, put in a large refrigerator, ordered the alcohol, and opened his business.

Cabin of Memories
1952

The cabin was just over the hill from our new home. Sometimes, over the next few months, I'd see Dad walking off in that direction, and I'd hurry to catch up with him. "Are you going to the cabin?" I'd call.

"No, I'm just out for a walk," he'd say. That walk always ended at the top of the hill overlooking the cabin and fields.

I took his hand, pulling him forward. "Let's go and look around."

He'd hold back, and I knew he was missing the cabin, too. He'd look out at the two acres of potatoes that needed harvesting. "We'll be renting the cabin this year, so we won't be doing any more planting. This is the last time we'll be picking potatoes."

"Well, that's one thing I'm glad about. I hated pulling weeds," I told him, turning to go back to our new home. I left him standing by himself. I knew how he felt, because I liked standing at the top of the hill too, wanting to hurry to the cabin, pull open the door, and touch the logs while walking through the bare rooms.

A couple of weeks earlier Dad had put a sign at the driveway letting people know the cabin was for rent. My secret wish was that no one would want to live in it, then I could visit anytime I wanted. But then one day we heard the loud engine of a truck coming down the driveway and pulling alongside the cabin. A family of four quickly got out. The two young boys pushed their way out, glad to be free to move around.

It was September and time to harvest. Mom, Nancy, and I were picking carrots and radishes. I looked up, hoping they wanted to buy some of the potatoes that Dad was selling. I was disappointed when they said they were interested in renting and asked to see the inside of the cabin.

Mom cleaned her hands on the towel we used when working in the garden. She didn't want us wiping our grubby hands on our jeans. She introduced herself to the family, inviting them to see the interior of the cabin. The woman said they were looking for a place between Anchorage and Palmer, because they liked both towns and couldn't make up their minds, so maybe living between the two would make it easy to go either way.

Following everyone up the step onto the screen porch that runs the length of the cabin, I could still smell the spruce. It was swept so clean, no one would ever know how much birch, spruce logs, and kindling was stacked all year around.

I was the last to enter the cabin. The smell of spruce filled the room. Rubbing my hand along the wall, I walked the length of it. It was so bare and I felt so sad to see everything gone. I moved toward the wood box. Sitting down, I took a deep breath, rubbing my hands over the top of my knees. Why can't we live here forever? The living room doesn't look the same with the furniture gone. I looked at the floor and still hated to think about sweeping it. It was spotless now, not a speck of dirt on it.

Nancy and I had so much fun hauling the moss in our wagon and stuffing it tightly between each log to prevent heat from escaping during the cold winter months. When the moss ended up drying and falling out, Dad said, "That's enough of that," and he cemented it in place. I pressed my fingers against the cement. It moved easily, pushing into the dry, hidden moss. I decided to leave it alone in case it fell, breaking into pieces all over the clean floor.

The coziness was gone. The white sheer curtains still hung on the window, and I fingered the edge of the soft material. When Mom made the curtains, she gave me some of the thin see-through material to make a bride's dress and veil for Molly.

Mom and Dad didn't have a door on their bedroom. It was a long open wall. Mom made a beautiful drape for it. Nancy and I pretended it was a stage with a curtain that opened during the many plays we acted out for them and for some of Mom's friends. They laughed at our antics and always clapped at the end. Queenie was always the hero and spent most of her time sleeping through the play. When it was her turn to take a bow, I would wrap my arms underneath her belly and lift her. She never complained.

I pushed myself from the wood box and rubbed my shoe over the spot where the sparks from the barrel stove left black burn marks on the floor, in spite of the grainy sand spread in a thick layer underneath it to keep sparks from igniting the wood floor. The sand was gone. Nothing was the same anymore.

I walked to the opposite side of the room where we always put the Christmas tree. I found my first gun under it. How I had wished for it and how proud I was to carry it when Dad and I hunted. Now that Dad worked during the day driving the grader for the Alaska Road Commission and worked in the liquor store at night, I wondered if there would be time to target practice or roam through the woods, searching for anything that was moving? The best part of being in the woods with Dad was that he never shot anything when I was with him, even if it meant letting a moose wander slowly by, stopping here and there, munching on leaves. He'd just say, "Look how magnificent he is." We'd watch the moose eat for awhile, then turn and quietly walk away.

I turned to where Mom's treadle sewing machine used to be pressed against the wall. It was always opened with cloth folded neatly and a pattern lying on top of it. Sewing was Mom's way of relaxing. She hummed while guiding the needle through a long piece of material that mysteriously turned into identical dresses for Nancy and me. She let me pull the pins from the sewn fabric, jab them into the pin cushion in fun designs. She always gave me the leftover pieces so Molly and I could be twins.

The living room was my favorite place in the cabin. It's here where I listened to the battery-operated radio. Programs such as *Amos and Andy*, music, and the news. I learned to sew and embroider bibs for Johnny. I read Nancy Drew mysteries sprawled out on the brown davenport, and sat on the grooved floor with my dolls and doll house. I cut out paper dolls and made special houses for them on the treadle of the sewing machine. I rolled on the floor with Queenie and came away brushing yellow hair from my sweater, and she'd shake vigorously, smoothing her hair before settling beside me for a nap. Now Queenie was dead, but I have lots of memories, especially when we harnessed her to the sled and she pulled Nancy, me, and Molly back and forth in the driveway and around the house. All the wonderful memories never to be relived but always remembered.

The laughter from the kitchen caught my attention. I was missing out on something funny. I hurried in, not wanting to miss whatever it was they were talking about. Mom was telling the lady she didn't want to buy an electric stove. She liked cooking on the wood stove because she knew exactly how much wood was needed when baking something in the oven. The lady was laughing and said, "The first thing I'm buying is a stove that does all that for me. I don't want to guess at the temperature of the oven."

I remember Mom opening the oven door and removing five or six loaves of bread. Sniffing the air and taking in the yeasty aroma, I waited patiently for the first piece of the golden-crusted bread slathered with oleo and Mom's homemade jam. The new lady didn't deserve to live in our beautiful cabin.

The man and woman liked the cabin. They wanted to have their own garden and were glad the land was cleared and plowed, so all they had to do next spring was plant the seeds. Just wait until they see all the weeds they have to pick around each plant, I thought to myself, they'll change their minds about gardening.

"Why do we have to let someone we don't know live in our cabin?" I asked, while walking home with our bags of vegetables.

"No sense in letting it stand empty," Mom said, shifting the bag in her arms.

"But I don't want anyone else living in our cabin. I miss being there."

"Over the past five years, we've had happy memories living there," she said, smiling and rubbing my shoulder. "Maybe, the new family will remember good times while living in our cabin too. What are some of the fun things you remember?"

"Oh, it was so funny to watch the squirrels," I laughed, "especially since they could never find a way into the cache. I wonder if those boys will make a fort in it? I always wanted to do that."

"They might enjoy hearing about some of your adventures on the homestead," Mom said. "You could show them all your favorite places. It might give them some happy memories they can take with them when they leave."

"Yeah, we could show them the big birch tree we climbed and spent time pretending we were spies hidden away among the leaves," I said.

"And we can tell them about Moe and Queenie," Nancy added, "and they'll really like the swings. We could fly so high on them."

"Are we still on the homestead, Mama, since we don't live in the cabin anymore?" I asked, looking up into her eyes for the answer.

"Oh, yes. There are forty acres that belong to us, and our new home is on just a couple of those acres."

"I'm glad," I told her, squeezing her hand.

"So am I," Mom said, smiling.

The day finally came when Mom and Dad felt they could sell the five-acre parcel of land with the cabin, knowing it would always be there to remind them of their first home in Alaska. One thing we didn't take into consideration was that the cabin might not always be there for us to visit year after year. We just assumed it would be.

The cabin burned in the early 1960s. No one knew how the fire started. We walked up and gazed from the hill to where our cabin of memories once stood. It was painful to walk up close, staring at the remains of our home. The smell of charred logs flooded the air.

Our hearts break a little each year, watching the bushes grow over the wreckage of our home and noticing the small trees overtaking the rich soil of our garden. We will always mourn the passing of a homesteader's dreams of a simple life in the wilderness country of Alaska. I'm not sure if the day will ever come when we can let go.

Our family moved from the cabin in the early fall of 1952. We took with us all the memories of hard work and happiness we gathered over the five years we spent there.

Remains of a Dream

Cabin of soft, light wood now a charred black skeleton
rests among the sprawling branches of birch trees
guarded by a time-worn cache, keeping watch
like a settler claiming unpopulated land.

Fireweed awash in vibrant pink,
hugging the remains as a gentle
breeze strains their stretched necks
in a downward bow of respect.

A homesteader finds gray shade
against the burned frame of his cabin,
mourning his chosen dream of a simple life,
waiting for the day he can let go and walk away.

LETTING GO

*She silently walked
    the path that day,*

*Carrying my father in her arms,
    surrendering him to the earth.*

*Sprinkling adventure among the ferns,
    reviving stirring experiences.*

*Dusting the trees with energy,
    recalling how he endured.*

*Scattering fortitude among the flowers
    of a man who lived his dream.*

*Ashes showering the forest with memories
    traveling to places unknown.*

*The life of a man dancing with the breeze
    She let him go with love.*

JOHN STOCKHAUSEN, SR.

1917–1998

Epilogue

Growing up in Chugiak gave me a sense of belonging. The life my parents provided shaped me into the adult I have become. While working on and finishing the book of our homesteading years, I realized I'm achieving what I set out to do. I found that I could walk in my parents' footsteps, moving forward with the building of a community in a more modern age.

I had the opportunity to see firsthand the changes that took place as time went by. While the community took shape, it was also defining me. I was there to catch a glimpse of the early residents' fortitude and to their dedication to family and community. They passed that determination to me, showing how active participation brings a community together and projects get done.

Shortly after arriving in the area, twenty-two miles from Anchorage, Mom and Dad joined the newly formed community club and became active members in 1947. They gathered with other families to work toward getting electricity, telephone service, and a school for our area. The club had already named the area Chugiak, which means "place of many places."

I watched Chugiak grow from about twenty families in 1947 to a population of approximately 35,000 today. The community divided into three separate areas as the years passed. To the north of Chugiak it became Peters Creek, and to the south it became Eagle River.

Chugiak-Eagle River is no longer a frontier settlement. It's a busy community where I take an active role. I'm on the board of the Chugiak-Eagle River Historical Society, and I'm doing my part to carry on the vision my parents had for the community. The society's work is to remember those who came before us. They have a collection of pictures and artifacts dating back to 1946. With an eye on both the past and the future, I treasure each find as the early homesteaders open their photograph albums, sharing the rich history I was so fortunate to be a part of.

The historical society has given me the opportunity to volunteer at our local senior center, facilitating a group of seniors interested in writing their family histories. They receive a great sense of achievement and satisfaction as they complete chapters of their lives. Their autobiographies become a unique gift to be passed on to loved ones.

Public meetings are still held at the old Chugiak Territorial School. The historical society has offices in the building. I'm there several times a month attending meetings and community gatherings. It feels comfortable walking through the double doors of memories. Entering the building, I feel the rich history and pioneering spirit, and I reflect on my family's contributions that helped to make Chugiak a thriving place to live, work, and raise families.

I want to continue in my parents' footsteps by being involved in the legacy they helped to build. My vision is to hand down to future generations the knowledge, stamina, and ingenuity it took to raise a family and build a community. The spirit of the homesteaders made Chugiak and Eagle River thriving communities that have earned their place in the history books of Alaska.

Mom and Dad spent their lives soaking up all the new experiences they encountered. They lived their adventure in the Great Land and never regretted making the move to Alaska. I still reside in Chugiak. It has always been my chosen place to live and raise my family. Thank you, Mom and Dad, for the cherished memories of my childhood.

APPENDIX I

Mary Pilgrim's Diary

OUR TRIP TO ALASKA

FROM JUNE 9TH TO JULY 31, 1947

After 3 months of preparation, John Stockhausen and family and Kenny and I were ready to leave in our Army trucks with little houses built on them.

The Milwaukee Journal came out to 68th and North Ave. to take our pictures. That is the place we left from Monday, June 9th, 1947 at 10:00 a.m. (mileage 33284)

John had a very nice little house with sleeping and cooking facilities. Ours was quite a bit smaller with only sleeping facilities and, of course, we both had everything we owned stored in our little houses. As we went out through Hartland, I waved to Gary (then two years) who was in the yard. Kenny and John stopped at Bill's to say goodbye. John's oil line broke in Oconomowoc, had lunch there. And continued on to Columbia where we stopped for sodas. Arrived in Portage at John's sister, Bernie's, at 3:00 p.m. Made 100 miles and the mileage was (33384), and spent $5.54. They (Bernie, her husband and 5 children) had a very nice farm on the Baraboo River. Nice People. This completed our first day.

JUNE 10

Packed a lunch and took pictures 2-3-4-5 & 6 and left John's sister at 9:25 a.m. John's timing gear broke in Wisconsin Dells. They worked on it from 10:05 a.m. to 5:30 p.m. We ate lunch there. Bernie, the girls, and I wandered over town looking at all the Indian made items. Gas, 11.3 gals., $2.73, groceries, $1.28

and bought an extra timing gear for our truck for $2.25. We took Highway 12 out of Tomah and stopped for the night a little past Camp McCoy. Made 80 miles the second day, (33464).

JUNE 11

Had breakfast and left at 8:30 a.m. Got gas in Black River Falls, 6.9 gals., $1.60, 1 quart of oil, $0.35 and put liquid solder in John's radiator. There was a stop for lunch in Menominee, food, $0.55. Left Wisconsin and entered Minnesota over St. Croix River, (paid 5 cent toll). John's truck just quit after crossing the bridge. Arrived at my brother Meredith's about 3:00 p.m. We had supper with a cousin of Meredith and Kenneth's. His friend also came to see us. Played cards and stayed overnight but slept in our trucks in the back yard in Mpls., (33639) 175 miles.

JUNE 12

Had breakfast and left at 8:10 a.m. Got gas at 38th and Chicago, 15.4 gals., $3.56. Cashed our first travelers check (had over one thousand in travelers checks). Bernie and I had coffee in Waverly, $0.15. We had drinks in Kerkhoven, $0.80. Lunch was at Murdock. Entered South Dakota at 3:15 p.m. Stopped at school house overnight, (33818) 179 miles. Everyone was very tired. Stayed up late the night before at Meredith's.

JUNE 13

Started at 8:30 a.m. after breakfast. Towns are farther apart, climate is drier and fewer trees. Stopped in Milbank for gas, 11.9 gals., $2.84 and 1 quart of oil, $0.40. Lots of wild ducks and sea gulls. Got food at Andover, $1.15, very dirty town. Got coil for John's truck in Aberdeen and food and Cokes, $1.44. Got gas in Ipswich, 12.2 gals., $2.90. Stopped for overnight at a lake, (34003) 185 miles.

JUNE 14

Breakfasted and left at 8:45 a.m. Gas at Mobridge, 6.2 gals., $1.52, oil, $0.37. Crossed Missouri River, gained an hour and still no trees and hilly. White faced steer. Beginning to go up. Went five miles out of the way on wrong road. Stopped in McLaughlin, no toilets, very dirty and rough western town. Drinks were $1.05. Had hamburgers in McIntosh, $0.92, flashlight batteries, $1.40 - candy, $0.85. Stopped in Lemon, South Dakota for weekend at Petrified Wood Park, (34138) 135 miles.

Bernie and I washed clothes and hung them to dry in among the petrified wood of the park. Kenny got a haircut, $0.60. Got battery cable for our truck, $2.10 - mirror, $0.40 - stamps, $0.06 - drinks and groceries, $5.94.

JUNE 15

Sunday - did our ironing - got baths and wrote cards to everyone. Took girls to a movie. Got mad at Kenny because he, John and Bernie did the town. Took picture 7. The mileage for the week was 854 minus 5 out of the way.

JUNE 16

Had breakfast and left at 8:30 a.m. Entered North Dakota and stopped for gas in Hettinger, 10.7 gals., $2.63. Roads were under repair, terrible. Tumble weeds. Stopped in Marmarth for gas, 6.5 gals., $1.70 and food, $0.30. Entered Montana - had lunch - country prettier - more trees and higher hills. Stopped at Miles City for gas, 7.4 gals., $1.95 - food, $1.52 and John got his radiator flushed out. Saw Big Sheep Mountains. Lots of bearded men. John almost lost a wheel at the top of a hill headed down, five of the 6 bolts sheared off the back wheel. Was late so we pulled into a farmers field for overnight, (34345) 207 miles. Kenny changed oil.

JUNE 17

John and Kenny drove back to Miles City and had five bolts made for the wheel. They spent all day waiting for the bolts and had fun gambling on $2.45. When they got back, they told us to be careful of rattle snakes and the girls had been playing out in the high grass all day. (We had a terrible storm the night before). Finally got started at 4:00 p.m. Stopped at Forsyth, food, $2.33 - film, $0.88 - sunglasses, $2.00 (which they forgot to collect for) and gambling, $0.80. Stopped for overnight, (34442) 97 miles - 30 miles out of way.

JUNE 18

Left after breakfast 8:45 a.m. Stopped in Custer for gas, 11.0 gals., $2.80. Bypassed Billings, took Highway 87, saw Bull Mountains. Coal mines - beautiful homes and cabins. Stopped in Klien for food, $1.00. Had lunch in Roundup. Stopped in Lewistown for gas, 13.6 gals., $3.75 - oil, $0.35 - 3 pounds of grease, $0.90 and drinks, $0.95. Very good water for a change. Stopped for overnight outside of Stanford - record day of 343 miles. Mileage was (34685). Had a beautiful place on a hill with a river running down in the valley - So the boys shot a skunk and we all suffered all night from the odor.

JUNE 19

Started 8:15 a.m. - Little Belt Mountains are snow capped - Louis and Clark National Forest - stopped in Great Falls. We received letters from Augusta and Mom at the post office - Darlene and Nancy got haircuts, $1.00 each - groceries, $9.90, Caps and Nets, $2.60 - hamburgers, $1.30 - 4 cartons of cigarettes, $6.00 - ice cream and post cards, $0.14 - parts for the truck, $1.45 - (grease retainer) - rear axle, $15.95, never used. Left at 3:15 p.m. on Highway 91 out of Vaughn. Took picture of Rockies out of Dutton, snowcapped 60 miles away. Stopped in Conrad, 15.0 gals. gas, $3.88, oil, $0.35 and gas cap, $0.45. Stopped for overnight, (34812) 127 miles.

JUNE 20

Left at 9:00 a.m. Stopped in Sunburst for gas, 52 gals., $15.25 - Cokes, $1.50 - stopped in Sweetgrass - took 20 minutes to get through Canadian Customs at Coutts, Alberta - took Highway

4 - had lunch - Milk River - terrible detour, slid all over. Lots of gophers. Stopped in Lethbridge for food, $0.44, cigarettes, $0.33 - all American cars - took Highway 3 - stopped for overnight on a beautiful river bank, (34962) 150 miles.

JUNE 21

Started 9:20 a.m. Took Highway 2 out of Macleod - got gas in Nanton, 10.7 imp. gals., $3.90 - food, $1.37 - slacks, $2.39 - and had lunch. Stopped at Fox Creek on this side of Calgary for weekend. Beautiful Tamerak Forest - visited an artist who painted - beautiful copper kettles hung on his log cabin walls. One dollar for camping, groceries, $4.47. Bad night, (35072) 110 miles - lost 20 miles.

JUNE 22, SUNDAY

Bought two live chickens for one dollar. They got loose. I caught one. Poor Kenny was washing his hair and didn't have his glasses on and tripped chasing a chicken. Kenny and John worked on trucks - wonderful spring water - got water from creek for washing. The mileage for the second week was 954 - 50 miles out of way.

JUNE 23

Left at 10:00 a.m. - got gas at Calgary, 5 imp gals., $1.90 - 1 pint oil, $0.15, gum and candy, $0.15 and bowls, $0.69. Took highway 2 out of Carstairs - saw English army trucks with right hand drives. Had Lunch outside Olds. Stopped for gas in Minot, 10.5 imp. gals., $3.99 - food, $2.87 - stopped for overnight, (35270) 178 miles.

JUNE 24

Started 9:30 a.m. - got letters from Augusta, Mom, and Ethel at Edmonton Post Office. Stationery, cards, stamps and peanuts, $1.45 - lunch, $1.40. Went to Royal Canadian Mounted Police Dept. to get permits to use Alcan Highway through Canada and instructions. Got 32 imp. gals. gas, $11.65 - grease job, $2.50 -

groceries, $0.69 - Coke, toothbrush and lead, $0.51. Stopped for overnight, (35350) 80 miles.

JUNE 25

Started at 9:30 a.m. after changing oil - stopped in Tawatinaw for stamps and cards, $0.50 - food, $0.60 - stove gas, $1.30 and pick ax, $2.30. Had lunch through Smith - got gas in Slave, 13.8 imp. gals. $5.80. Beginning of Slave Lake which ran 70 miles to Enilda. Lots of Indians - High Prairie bought grease gun paid half, $2.62 - stopped near Triangle for overnight - food, $0.78, Citronella, $1.00, (35571) 221 miles.

JUNE 26

Left 8:40 a.m. on shortcut 34 - stopped in Valleyview for drinking water. Went across Smoky River on ferryboat - Kenny took picture - saw dead horse and dog and wrecked car. Stopped in Grand Prairie - food, $6.73 - drinks, $0.55 and mirror repairs, $0.35. I was interviewed by reporter and met the founder of the town. Back on Highway 2 - got stuck in mud - John pulled himself and us out. Stopped for overnight, (35730) 159 miles.

JUNE 27

Left 8:00 a.m. Crossed into British Columbia at Brainard - stopped in Pouce Coupe - got fire permit - food, $1.98 - 20.5 imp. gals. gas, $8.20 and half on grease, $1.87. Had guns sealed at Dawson Creek Police Dept. Began 0 mile of Alcan Highway. Took picture from high hill of beautiful Peace River bridge and had lunch. Fort St. John - flat tire - got water at Beatton River - John's oil line broke - Rockies at left. Stopped, (35939) 209 miles.

JUNE 28

Got started at 10:15 a.m. after pulling John. Sikanni River, had trouble with John's generator - had lunch up in Pink Mountains - took pictures - stopped for weekend at Beaver Creek, (35987) 48 miles. Kenny took more pictures of our washing clothes and hair.

JUNE 29, SUNDAY

Ironed - cleaned - Bernie washed - rained real heavy off and on, men worked on trucks - heated all wash water on open fire - mending. Made 895 miles the third week.

JUNE 30

Started 9:50 a.m. after pulling John. License runs out today. Lum & Abner - food, $2.43 - stamps and candy, $1.00. At Fort Nelson, got a battery for John's truck. Had lunch and fixed Kenny's flat. Saw a mother and baby moose ahead in road and waited until they took their good time leaving. Steep foot hills - more driving thrills - John slid back on hill. Stopped for overnight at Mill Creek, (36145) 158 miles.

JULY 1

Started at 10:00 a.m. Saw very clear, cold, beautiful creeks and rivers. Took pictures of Summit Lake and mountains - snowed some - had lunch on Racing River - took pictures. Stopped for overnight, (36330) 186 miles. Changed the oil.

JULY 2

Today is my birthday. Started 9:30 a.m. winding through a stretch of Yukon Territory and back into B.C. Lower Post - food, $8.72 - John's fuel pump broke - had supper - men fixed pump and we drove after supper, (36516) 186 miles - 5 extra miles.

JULY 3

The day started at 8:45 a.m. We got letters from Mom, Kenny's Dad and Statz's family at Whitehorse Post Office - food, $2.10 - drinks, $1.00 - book and ice cream, $0.35 - 40 imp. gals. of gas, $17.00 - milk, $0.50 and 2 films, $2.60. Stopped for overnight, (36719) 203 miles - 5 extra miles.

JULY 4

We began the day at 8:30 a.m. At MacIntosh Trading Post, got candy and popcorn, $1.20. John got the generator fixed in Burwash Landing. The time was set back two hours. I took a bath and washed my hair, in a public bath, for the first time since Minneapolis. Enjoyed seeing the Golden Mountains – It never gets dark – Decided to stop by Glacier Creek for the night – The water so cold and good, (36916) 197 miles - 8 extra.

JULY 5

Started at 8:00 a.m. Reached Canadian Customs (37011) - passed into Alaska (37028). Flat tire - candy and Coke, $1.00 - stopped at Gardiner Creek for weekend - did our washing - (37053) 137 miles.

JULY 6, SUNDAY

Cleaned house - Bernie washed - Kenny and John worked on trucks. Traveled 1066 miles during 4th week - 13 extra.

JULY 7

We began at 8:00 a.m. Went 12 miles off highway to Northway Army Base to get generator for John, but no luck. We went back another hour. U.S. Customs at Tok Junction, got map, $1.52 - food, $5.15 - apron and ash tray for Mom & Dad, $1.75. Took Tok cut off - saw 2 black bears and a mountain lion. We stopped for the night. (37239) 186 miles - 12 extra.

JULY 8

Started 8:00 a.m. Got candy, $0.25 and bread, $0.13 in Gakona. Took Glenn Highway - stopped for lunch at Caribou Creek bridge at mile 106 and were ready to leave when four Minnesota boys in a Model A Ford lost their brakes coming down the mountain and couldn't make the sharp curve and hit the bridge railing of the steel bridge and fell 25 ft. into the shallow part of the creek. One boy was seriously hurt, the other three fared better. Helicopter brought doctor, but air pocket kept them from taking patients out.

An ambulance arrived 4 hours later from Anchorage. We did our best to help care for them in the meantime. We loaded the litters on top of our truck to return to Ft. Richardson. The doctor had to ride back in the ambulance. We stopped for overnight, (37883) 144 miles - 2 extra.

JULY 9

Left 8:00 a.m., one month on road. Palmer, 12 gals. gas, $3.78, 2 quarts oil, $0.80 - dinner, $2.73 - spare fixed, $2.50 - Coke, $0.40. John had a charge put in battery. We drove through Ft. Richardson, dropped off the litters, and arrived in Anchorage at 3:00 p.m., mileage (37484). No mail at post office for us. Land office - hospital to see boys - food, $1.92 - saw John's brother-in-law, then drove all over to find a place to stay overnight.

The total mileage 4200 - 82 miles extra.

BETWEEN JULY 10 AND JULY 31

Kenny filed on 160 acres for $16.00. Brought wood in that we cut from property and started cabin. Saw Gen. Eisenhower —went to Army hospital to see injured boys. Saw nephew of fellow working at Kearny & Trecker. Moe, a pet bear cub, stayed around for a long time. We picked currants. Got water at Peters Creek where John and Kenny got a 32-pound salmon with their bare hands and a baseball bat, very tasty.

There were mountains in front of our property which was Township 15, Range 1W, Sec. 3, SE¼ SW ¼.

APPENDIX II

Anchorage 011576

4—1043

VOL 77 299

The United States of America,
To all to whom these presents shall come, Greeting:

JUN 12 1950

WHEREAS, a Certificate of the Land Office at Anchorage, Alaska, is now deposited in the Bureau of Land Management, whereby it appears that full payment has been made by John J. Stockhausen, according to the provisions of the Act of Congress of April 24, 1820, entitled "An Act making further provision for the sale of the Public Lands," and the acts supplemental thereto, for the following described land:

Seward Meridian, Alaska.

T. 15 N., R. 1 W.,

sec. 3, $SE\frac{1}{4}SW\frac{1}{4}$.

The area described contains 40 acres, according to the Official Plat of the Survey of the said Land, on file in the Bureau of Land Management: NOW KNOW YE, That the UNITED STATES OF AMERICA, in consideration of the premises, and in conformity with the several Acts of Congress in such case made and provided, HAS GIVEN AND GRANTED, and by these presents DOES GIVE AND GRANT unto the said John J. Stockhausen and to his heirs the tract above described; TO HAVE AND TO HOLD the same, together with all the rights, privileges, immunities, and appurtenances, of whatsoever nature, thereunto belonging, unto the said John J. Stockhausen and to his heirs and assigns forever; subject to any vested and accrued water rights for mining, agricultural, manufacturing, or other purposes, and rights to ditches and reservoirs used in connection with such water rights, as may be recognized and acknowledged by the local customs, laws, and decisions of courts; and there is reserved from the lands hereby granted, a right of way thereon for ditches or canals constructed by the authority of the United States.

Anchorage –011576

VOL 77 PAGE 300

And there is, also, res[erved] to the United States a right of way for the construction of railroad[, tel]egraph and telephone lines in accordance with the Act of March 12, 1[914 (3]8 Stat., 305).

Excepting and reser[ving a]lso, to the United States pursuant to the provisions of the Act of Aug[ust 1,] 1946 (60 Stat., 755), all uranium, thorium or any other material which [ ] may be determined to be peculiarly essential to the production of f[issiona]ble materials, whether or not of commercial value, together with the rig[ht of t]he United States through its authorized agents, or representatives a[t any t]ime to enter upon the land and prospect for, mine, and remove the same[.]

And there i[s reserv]ed from the lands hereby granted, a right of way thereon for road[s, railw]ays, highways, tramways, trails, bridges, and appurtenant structures [constru]cted or to be constructed by or under authority of the United States [or an]y State created out of the Territory of Alaska, in accordance w[ith the A]ct of July 24, 1947 (61 Stat., 418).

Anchorage Precinct, Anchorage, Alaska.
Filed for record AUG 21 1952 o'clock 2:50 P. M
F _____
At Palmer, Alaska

ROSE WALSH
District Recorder

IN TESTIMONY WHEREOF, the undersigned authorized officer of the Bureau of Land Management, in accordance with the provisions of the Act of June 17, 1948 (62 Stat., 476), has, in the name of the United States, caused these letters to be made Patent, and the Seal of the Bureau to be hereunto affixed.

GIVEN under my hand, in the District of Columbia, the **SIXTH** day of **JUNE** in the year of our Lord one thousand nine hundred and **FIFTY** and of the Independence of the United States the one hundred and **SEVENTY-FOURTH**.

For the Director, Bureau of Land Management.

By Bellis B. Jeffery
Acting Chief, Patents Section

Patent No. 1129221

Sources

Hayden, George. "Alaska Road Log." Anchorage, AK: n.p., 1946.

Hunt, William. *Passage to the North*. Harrisburg, PA: Stackpole Books, 1992.

Johnston, Austin Lefurge. *The Alaska Highway Guide, 1948*. Victoria, B.C., 1948.

The Milepost. 28th ed. Anchorage, AK: Alaska Northwest Publishing Company, 1976.

Pilgrim, Mary. "Our Trip to Alaska." Unpublished diary, 1947.

Stewart, George. N.A. 1: *The North-South Continental Highway Looking North*. Boston: Houghton Mifflin, 1957.

Stockhausen, Bernice, interview by author. Finland, MN, July 1995.

Stockhausen, John, interview by author. Finland, MN, July 1995.

United States Department of the Interior. *Code of Federal Regulations, Title 43–Public Lands: Interior, Part 181, Public Land Rights of Soldiers and Sailors* (Circular No. 1588). General Land Office. Washington, DC: U.S. Government Printing Office, 1944.

ORDER FORM

I would like to order my own or another copy of the book *The Chosen Place* by Darlene Halverson. Please send me:

\# books x $18.95 per copy = $ _____

+ Postage (first class) & handling @ $5.50/book: _____

TOTAL ENCLOSED $ _____

We accept cash, check, or money order made out to Northbooks, or VISA, Mastercard. Prices subject to change without notice.

(You may phone your VISA/MC order to Northbooks at 907-696-8973)

VISA/MC card # ☐☐☐☐ ☐☐☐☐ ☐☐☐☐ ☐☐☐☐

Exp. date: _____ / _____   Amount charged: $ _____

Signature: _____

Phone number: _____

<u>Please send my book (s) to:</u>

Name: _____

Address: _____

City: _____ State: _____ Zip: _____

Fill out this order form and send to:

Northbooks

17050 N. Eagle River Loop Rd, #3

Eagle River, AK 99577-7804

(907) 696-8973

www.northbooks.com

Breinigsville, PA USA
03 January 2011
252575BV00005B/3/P